East End Girl

Sally Worboyes

East End Girl

Growing Up the Hard Way

HODDER

Copyright © 2006 by Sally Worboyes

First published in Great Britain in 2006 by Hodder & Stoughton
A division of Hodder Headline

This edition first published in 2007

A Hodder paperback

1

A CIP catalogue record for this title is
available from the British Library

ISBN 978-1-444-71074-8

Typeset in Sabon MT by Palimpsest Book Production Limited,
Grangemouth, Stirlingshire

Printed and bound by
Clays Ltd, St Ives plc

Hodder Headline's policy is to use papers that are natural, renewable and
recyclable products and made from wood grown in sustainable forests. The
logging and manufacturing processes are expected to conform to the
environmental regulations of the country of origin.

Hodder & Stoughton Ltd
A division of Hodder Headline
338 Euston Road
London NW1 3BH

Photographs from the authors collection

Dedication

This book is dedicated to my dad, Bill Lipka, my mum Laura, my sister Laura and my four brothers Gary, Albert, Johnny and Billy and all of their children, Lorraine, Craig, Jackie, Karen, Terry, Garry, Max, Jac, John, Jo' and Emily.

Also: my grandfather Bill Lisbon and my nan, Lizzie. My aunts Sarah, Nelly, Mary, Sheila, Mary Reed, Lola, Christine and Lyn married to my uncle Siddy who let me hide in her kitchen when playing hooky from school. My uncles Jimmy, Harry, Albert, Johnny Hill, Sailor (Larry) and Billy Collier. All of my many first cousins and in particular Linda in Bethnal Green and Barry on Canvey Island. And especially to my great aunt Polly. To my uncle Bill Wood and all of my other great aunts and uncles and second cousins Billy, Mary, Brian and Richard, Johnny Collins and Helen and all of the others, too many to list. And also of course to my grandparents Ambrose and my aunts and uncles and cousins from the country.

East End Girl is also dedicated to my hop picking friends, Bobby and Viv and my school teachers from when I was four years old in 1950 until I left school, aged fifteen, in 1961. Miss Black at John Scurr School and Mrs Kate Flenner at Cephas Secondary Modern and her husband Ben and daughter Dawn. All of the dinner ladies at both schools as well as some of my special friends, some of whom lived close by to Bethnal Green Gardens and on the Bancroft Estate: Kenny Argent, Marion and her sister Doreen, Mavis Loaring, the Plummer family, Mr & Mrs Sainty, Leslie Marcovitch, Pamela Zeid, Lin Redmond, John and Charley Dormer and their parents. Michael and Max Walker, Milly and Arthur Cranfield and their three daughters. Also Irenie and Dennis Galsworthy, Pat and John Mackintosh, the very special Lakenby family, Jessie, Jo, John and Joan. Doreen Gotelph, her sister and three brothers and especially her hard working mother, Leah. The lovely Roberts family who are mentioned in this book, Jacqueline Simons, her sister Shirley and their parents. Mr and Mrs Lamb, Pat, John and Dennis. Ada and George Margrie, Alice Wiseman, Freda Cohen, Mrs Squibb, Mr and Mrs Fraser and the lovely old couple who took me under their wing, Mr and Mrs Weeks. Margaret's family: Julie and George McGregor, her two elder sisters Helen and Julie and her brother George. Mr and Mrs Hunt and their daughters Pauline and Brenda, Doreen Jackson, the Cunninghams and the Davenports, Johnny Sharp and the Clark family, Marian and Vivian Oakley. My close school friends: Jacqueline Birch, Carol Cross and the netball team: Val Skinner, Marian Aiken, Barbara Witchel, Ruth Miles, Kathy James, Irene Harris and Rene Middleton, whose lovely family welcomed me into their home. Also my old buddy Pat Tranter and Carol Smith née Hurst.

Last but by no means least of course is Margaret McGregor now Kent. Love and thanks for being there Margaret. It would have been a different and less vibrant story had you not been part of it.

Acknowledgements

I am indebted to my editor Helen Coyle at Hodder & Stoughton who gave her valuable time to me when I first began to write this story of my life. Relaxed and curled in armchairs by a glowing fire, Helen cleverly induced locked up memories of long ago to gradually drift out to the here and now. Times long since forgotten and others tucked away, too painful to air in everyday life: the loss of loved ones, the fear of strangers and the ending of childhood, mine, my sister's and my brothers'. We all seemed to have been grown-ups for ever with the children in us forgotten until that special little door was opened. Thank you so much, Helen.

My thanks also to my older brothers Johnny and Billy for helping with details of certain antics and mishaps when I was very young that I could only just remember. They helped bring it all flooding back, as did my second cousin Richard Wood, who not only supplied photos for this book but spent an afternoon with me talking about when we were kids on the street and in Kent, picking the hops and swimming in the river.

Contents

Foreword

This is my story, the story of my life in the East End, from the time I was born in the mid-1940s until the mid-sixties when I left to get married. I know the old East End as a wealthy man knows his estate. Every nook and cranny, the tramps, the trees and the tarts. The good, the bad, the sad and those others . . . who dare to hurt our children. This is my account of the old East End, full of real East Enders. Mostly it's a story about ordinary people living their everyday lives full of joy and sadness, drama or routine.

But the East End has become famous and infamous, of course, partly because of the abundance of characters that lived there. Some are even notorious, in particular the Kray twins. I think I can vouch for those living in and around Stepney, Whitechapel and Bethnal Green when I say that during my time there none of us had reason to fear them and took no more notice of the Krays than we did of the hundreds of other Jack the Lads. My elders knew them as just a couple of kids they had played street games with; at least, they did before their descent into the world of crime.

So really, this is about the East End as it actually existed, rather than the almost fantasy land it's been turned into. And its characters are the real people I knew. This is my story.

I

A Waste of Five Shillings

In December 1945 in the small hours of the morning, with the pealing of the Bow Bells resonating in the streets and after a party in a local pub, a young husband and wife were celebrating the Yuletide season in their small, damp and dreary bedroom, too drunk to think of any consequences. The footprints left by my parents in the thick carpet of fluffy snow would not have been the only ones to be irregular and curving, almost as if their owners had been dancing their way home. It was Christmas Eve and customary for beer and spirits to be plentiful and flowing in every pub in the East End of London. There might have been a full moon that night, or a fairy-tale, star-studded navy blue sky, but I wouldn't know because I had only just arrived into a small dark place where mystery knows no bounds. A place which, though my arrival was unplanned, was to be my home for nine months.

I was clearly not meant to be evicted from my mother's womb until I was good and ready, and I showed my characteristic stubborn streak at an early age, because the hot baths and gin hadn't worked. Neither had running up and down the rickety staircase of the two-up, two-down slum dwelling in Whitehead Street, E1. And though her name was never uttered out loud, only in a whisper, as if she possessed some unearthly magical powers, Fanny Five Shillings along the turning must have been considered a waste of time and good money. My strong will and desire for self-preservation formed very early in life, which was just as well, because I was going to need every bit of it.

With three striplings in the fold, the last thing Dad wanted or my mother needed was another baby to take care of, so I can hardly blame them for thinking that they had to try and flush me out of existence. Even though the Second World War was over, it left a deep emotional strain and scars on Mum and she already had to feed and clothe, on next to no income, two sons and a daughter, my brothers Billy and Johnny and my sister Laura. Dad having been on the run from the army at one time or another during the war meant that the army police sometimes knocked on Mum's door while he was hiding upstairs in the bedroom. Fortunately my godmother, Aunt Sarah, who at that time was unmarried and still living at Nan and Grandfather's house at the top of our turning, was a good friend to Mum and, from what she told me, had always been there for her in her hour of need.

I loved my godmother, my Aunt Sarah and I knew that she loved me. Even though I was proud that I had been given her name when christened, I much preferred Sally which I was commonly known as. By the time I was old enough to have met people outside the family I'd decided that Sarah was an old lady's name as far as I was concerned and the only time it was used was when I visited the doctor or the welfare clinic with Mum, when I would blush and want to curl into a ball. When I was saying my prayers before going to sleep at night I would always finish by saying, 'Pleasthe, God, don't let the children I play with find out that I'm a Sarah and pleasthe make the listhp go away. Amen.'

Teasing should have been the least of my worries because times were hard for most of us back-street children. We were undernourished and at risk from illness and malnutrition as it was, never mind the fact that we ran wild during those early post-war years living in bomb-damaged areas – especially in and around Stepney and Bethnal Green. Even when I was a tiny child, just a toddler, I played on the streets in broken houses. It was a depressed and confused time when scrawny girls wore faded frocks and spindly boys lived in patched trousers, old jerseys and hand-me-down boots. Most houses were damp inside and the doctors' small surgeries were crammed with patients – sickly people hoping for a miracle cure during harsh winters, when icy gusts of wind blew through inadequate clothing from November to March.

Dad worked in the docks and even though his height and build were in his favour, in that he stood out amidst hundreds of men, he, like many others, wasn't always picked out for a day's work, so a guaranteed wage was not always on the cards. Every day was a lottery. Even for good workers the stability of a regular job was foreign to all the dockers. But that part of London being such a close-knit community did help. People took the view that they were stronger in numbers than if they stood alone when striking for fairer pay and better conditions in the workplace.

Everyone was in the same boat and I suppose were bound together like shipmates at sea. In the main, neighbours were friends and there was always someone forming a club of one sort or another, whether it was getting together on one evening a week to play cards or arranging for a charabanc to take us all to Southend for a day out.

There was another club that Dad had belonged to, before the Second World War, which was spoken about only in whispers since all its members had followed the word of Oswald Mosley, who had given public speeches locally and sometimes marched with Blackshirts through the East End. This was in the second half of the 1930s when Fascist social clubs were dotted around London and further afield in England. This, Mum had told me, had given her reason to worry because she had good friends who were Jewish with husbands who had ganged up to fight the Blackshirts. And really, all that the people in our area wanted once peacetime came, from what I gathered, was to live in peace side by side and let bygones be bygones with no stigma attached.

Mum had answered me honestly when as a child I asked her about the Battle of Cable Street after a Jewish girl of my age had given me a mouthful, saying that my dad had been a Blackshirt. This is when the family secret came out. Mum told me how the Blackshirts marched through the streets and Dad, being over six foot tall with broad shoulders, had carried a banner or beat the drums as he followed in Mosley's footsteps on parade.

I asked her if my grandfather knew that his son had

4

taken part in all that and she shrugged if off, saying, 'I've no idea.' She then went on to tell me that it was no more than local gang warfare, with Mosley bringing a bit of fame to our streets, and that it was all over and done with and the ghost buried. She had gone with Dad to the Blackshirt club, though, when a dance or social evening had been arranged. I suppose in a way it was similar to when the Krays were at the top of the tree and frequented the Kentucky Club in the Mile End Road in the 1960s, rubbing shoulders with celebrities for a bit of kudos to add to their almighty reputation.

Our house was huddled in a narrow cobbled turning, with only dimly lit gaslights to see by, and halfway along the cul-de-sac and leading off it was a courtyard with older, run-down, shack-like buildings on either side. Here there was a rat-infested corner, where broken orange and apple boxes with bits of rotting fruit clinging to them were dumped. Scavenged from market stalls by children at the end of a day, the crates were piled high and used as fuel in the tiny fireplaces of our homes in the all too likely event that there was no money for coal or coke. The house lacked all modern comforts, there was no bathroom and the lavatory in the back yard often froze in the winter and we had news clippings, cut into neat squares and hanging from a string, to use as toilet paper.

Our kitchen was also a scullery with a copper boiler in the corner of the room, which was the only means of heating water. A smooth block of Sunlight soap sat on a cracked saucer on the surface of a small, chipped, white enamel-topped table and shirt collars and cuffs were scrubbed with it on a wooden block before going in with the rest of the whites for a good boil. We had a clothes line in the back yard for use on dry days as well as a brass fender around the fire for when it was raining. There was only one coal fire to keep us warm and dry during foggy, cold winter months and our linen flowery curtains were not much help because they were unlined. But then, it was the same for most of our neighbours and those living in similar turnings.

People longed for respite from the battle against damp conditions but when the much wished-for summer came it brought other problems – bluebottles buzzing with intent that went from one overflowing dustbin to another then landed on kitchen tables and un-refrigerated food. I don't know how my mother coped without central heating on cold wet days or cool air conditioning during stifling hot summers, when flies and bees used our passage en route to the back yard. Occasionally the rat-catcher would visit our street, leaving a gluey horrid substance which rodents and their babies would stick to and then lie in unseen for days. Dead or dying, their rotting bodies released foetid smells of decay and disease, tainting the air, which already reeked of drains and was the main reason why a corner of most back yards was devoted to the growing of a sweet-smelling climbing rose.

Honeysuckle was another favourite climber to plant since it took up little root space and perfumed the air. Other than the rose and honeysuckle, every bit of space where there was earth was given a good spread of horse dung before potatoes, cabbages, carrots, parsnips and sprouts were planted to supplement the meagre ration of food that had to go round. Our staple diet when it came to an occasional hot meal in the evenings was stew with little meat and plenty of barley, carrots and onions, and dry bread to scrape the bowl clean. I can still see my brother Johnny with a metal bucket and shovel furtively waiting for the rag-and-bone man to arrive in our turning, to beat everyone else to it and be first when the old mare obliged with a pile of steaming manure.

In Whitehead Street, the heart of a working-class area, most houses were cramped, with uncarpeted wooden staircases and no space inside for children to play. In the hearth of the tiny living rooms, tinder collected from the yard and broken into small pieces was often piled quite high. Our fireplace was small and not always alight when coal was scarce and the broken orange boxes in the courtyard had been scavenged, leaving nothing but a few small damp bits and pieces. Sometimes, the day before Dad brought home his wages there wasn't even a sixpence to spare for the gas meter so we lit candles as well as our small tin oil lamp and simply got on with it.

One vivid memory that has stayed with me is of a time when I must have been somewhere between two and three years old and too big to sleep in the family cot. I was put to bed with my sister, to share her single bed. We slept nose to toes in the front bedroom with Mum and Dad whose double bed was pushed into the furthest corner in some small hushed attempt at privacy. My brothers, Billy and Johnny, shared in the second bedroom, to the rear of the house. Although it was fun sleeping in a proper bed there was a downside to sharing because I wet myself and my unfortunate sister nearly always woke up when this happened. She would then whisper for me not to fidget and let in the cold air and sometimes Mum heard her and groaned, all-knowing, as she turned over. My wetting the bed was the last thing she needed. Dad would sometimes pick up the torch at the side of their bed and shine it across the room and on to my face for a few seconds.

I suppose this was his way of trying to get me to stop wetting the bed, not realising the fear that torchlight struck through me. I couldn't blame my sister for whispering loudly and waking them up because during the winter months it was vital we kept the warmth our squashed bodies generated under the sheets. There was no heating in the house once the small fire in the living room dwindled to the last embers and there was often ice on the inside of the windows. Laura knew, as I did, that a cold, wet part of the bedding made things so much worse when lying in the dark, trying to keep in the heat, until daylight or the sound of a neighbour's cockerel marked the hour.

The early morning echoing clip-clop of the rag-and-bone man's carthorse could easily be heard on the cobblestones as he went out on his daily rounds, as could the familiar clamour in the surrounding streets and courts as early workers began their day. The sound of pedlars pushing their wheelbarrows out of our turning and the rumbling noise of the wheels was welcoming and reassuring. Even though I was tired, I liked to hear that noise, because it told me the day was beginning as it should and I could finally slip out of my damp side of the bed and slide in with Mum once Dad was up and away to work. Failing this, I could glide in beside my brothers, Billy or Johnny, without them knowing until they woke up to find me fast asleep. By the time I got back into the bed at the end of the day, a clean dry sheet would have replaced the soiled one, rinsed out and dried by the fire. Without washing machines and with only our copper boiler and the public baths to do her laundry, Mum could hardly keep up.

Of course life was easier in the summertime when the sun streamed through the gap between our faded floral curtains and brought a cheering warm glow to my cheeks whether my bed was dry or not. The saving grace for me, even at the age of three, was that the world outside our home was a vast and wonderful playground full of adventures, imaginary or very real, like the mysterious old derelict and war-damaged buildings we kids loved to explore. We were at risk and courting danger and I heard of more than one child who fell from an unstable rooftop to cellar, but I suppose that was the furthest thought from any of our minds when we were running wild and free. We needed an escape from hardships at home and we found it in the streets outside.

A pastime and escape from reality for our parents came in the form of borrowed paperbacks. Doing the rounds would be romantic novels for the women and gun-slinging westerns for the men, the pages worn and corners curling. When Dad was in his armchair reading he commanded silence with a certain look and no words needed. My parents also enjoyed their sacred Saturday night and Sunday lunchtime at the pub, something that could not be forsaken at any price. Their other treat, apart from a couple of pints, was to often enjoy fish and chips on Friday evenings. For us children it was a mouth-watering portion of piping-hot chips, and as soon as I was old enough and could walk without reins I was allowed to go with my brothers to that heavenly shop. It was warm, steamy and brightly lit, and people queued eagerly and watched with longing as the fryer shovelled up perfect long golden chips into paper bags, then sprinkled on salt and aromatic vinegar.

The next morning being Saturday was a double treat because I loved to sit outside on our windowsill and watch the children who were normally at school playing in our turning. I hardly ever joined in because I was horribly shy and blushed red at the least thing. I was content enough to be an observer, especially when our street became a busy playground resounding with shrieks and laughter while games such as Tin Tan Tommy or kiss chase were going on. The older boys of course played cricket using a piece of old fencing for a bat.

Ours being a dead-end street meant that the boys could have a kick around and play football without having to worry about passing traffic and the girls could play ball games or hopscotch in safety. The only thing to cast a shadow over this carefree playground were the sinister-looking black iron gates, topped with sharp spikes, to keep thieves and vandals out of the Toby Club, owned by Charrington's brewery, that stood at the end of the turning. The spikes were a deterrent for sure and for the most part we had no wish to break in, as there was always enough to amuse ourselves with, outside of courting danger. Mind you, looking back it seems inevitable that an accident was just waiting to happen.

One day, while playing football with the other boys, my eldest brother Billy, who was ten at the time, got over-enthusiastic and kicked the old worn leather ball over these iron gates on a Sunday lunchtime. His commitment then of course was not to lose face and do the job no one else relished – get back the football. I was only three and frightened that he would get into serious trouble for trespassing and of the possibility of him falling and breaking his neck.

I sat cross-legged, biting my nails, as was my habit, my stomach knotted with dread as I watched Billy climb over the gates to drop down into the yard of the Toby Club and throw the ball back to the boys. Even though he gave me a reassuring wink as he smiled and climbed out again it looked to me as if he were trapped, in prison behind bars, and my heart felt as if it were in my boots watching him. But he did manage to clamber to the top. I looked away, breathing a sigh of relief, only to hear his piercing screams of agony echoing through the turning. He must have lost his footing, as a spike from the railing pierced his knee and wedged him there, trapped. All hell broke loose as my other brother Johnny ran shouting for help and a ladder to try and rescue him.

It being a Sunday, Mum and Dad were enjoying their usual drink with our aunts, uncles and friends in the local pub while Sunday lunch slowly cooked in the oven at home. Nobody in our street had a telephone of course and the nearest public phone booth was in the Mile End Road outside the ABC picture palace – a good ten- to fifteen-minute walk away.

Having no choice and in dire pain, but with a strange calm that shock can bring, trembling and white with fear, my brother slowly freed himself by putting pressure on both palms of his hands on the railings either side of him to ease his knee off the sharp point and then slowly climb down the gates with blood pouring from his leg. The other children following behind in a scared hush, my brother half walked and was half carried by Johnny and another lad to our grandfather's house, where Aunt Sarah bathed Billy's wound and put on a clean bandage – a strip of threadbare white sheeting.

My brother was then considered 'seen to' and that bandage remained on his leg without further thought as to how serious the wound might be or what was going on beneath the grubby dressing. Our father, who was sometimes a touch dictatorial, didn't like the boys to cry or complain so tears of pain were saved for bedtime and weeping into a pillow to muffle the sound.

A couple of weeks after his accident, on a Saturday when Mum and Dad were in the local as usual and I was sitting on the step outside, next to Billy, who was in charge of me at the time, a work colleague of Dad's arrived, friendly and all smiles, until he saw my brother's face and the pain showing in his eyes. When he asked what was wrong Billy broke down and confessed that his leg was giving him a lot of trouble and that he was in great pain. With mounting concern, Dad's chum asked him to pull up his trouser leg and was clearly shocked when he saw the injury and the swelling around it.

Worried for my brother in case he was going to get into trouble, I tugged at the man's sleeve as I peered up at him and said, 'It wasthn't my bruvver'sth fault. He couldn't help it.'

'Don't you worry, sweetheart,' he said, winking at me. 'Nobody ain't gonna tell off a brave boy like your Billy.'

Still worried, I wouldn't take my eyes off the man's face and as I searched his expression I could tell he was angry but also felt he could be trusted. 'Dad might 'ave a go,' I said, which made the man chuckle.

'No he won't, love. Stop biting your nails over it.'

I hadn't been biting my nails but, still, I knew what he meant. He pushed his shoulders back and went into the public bar and gave my father the sharp end of his tongue, telling him that his son needed to go to hospital straight away, and should have gone weeks ago. Once things cooled down, they had a quiet chat and decided to take him to the London Hospital in Whitechapel and I was allowed to go with them, enjoying a piggyback from Dad's tall and broad friend, who was back to smiles and jokes to lift us children from the gloom. Billy's leg was duly X-rayed, cleaned and bandaged before he was wheeled into a ward and put to bed, where he was to stay until the swelling went down and a plaster-of-Paris cast could be set from his ankle to his thigh.

A week later he came out of hospital on crutches with strict orders to rest and not to go out in the streets to play. His kneecap and part of the shin bone was shattered and we didn't know if he would ever walk properly again. Eventually he did, but with a slight limp.

My brother spent his recovery reading borrowed paper-back books on the sofa at home and was not allowed to have friends or cousins to visit unless he promised not to discuss what had happened. But one day a second cousin from Wapping dropped in on passing and asked what had happened to his knee. Billy told the story and I, then the baby of the family, listened while curled up on an armchair.

'I was climbing the big gates at the end of the turning and got wedged when one of the spikes went through my knee,' said Billy, a touch on the casual side.

'Fucking hell,' said our cousin, 'I 'ope they called an ambulance.'

'Nar,' said Billy, 'Aunt Sarah wrapped a strip of old sheet round it till it turned septic. Then Dad's mate got 'im to take me up the London. Two weeks after the accident.'

'Sod that for a lark,' said the cousin. 'Why the fuck didn't you go before that?' Before Billy could draw breath and answer, Dad, on passing through from the scullery, gave my brother a clout to the shoulder as a warning to not blag like a girl. Guilt for not seeing to his eldest son's welfare was the underlying cause of him feeling defensive and belligerent. He wanted no discussion of it and no one could argue with that.

My other brother Johnny, a couple of years younger than Billy and almost eight years old at the time, brought home a present to help cheer up the invalid. Playing around in the debris of a derelict house he found in a corner of the yard four tiny and starving new kittens abandoned by their mother, who herself was probably a stray cat that nobody fed so was living wild and feeding on mice. Her babies could only have been a week or two old when Johnny rescued the adorable, tiny mewing bundles of fluff. The big wide smile on his face as he tenderly placed them in Billy's lap was soon to fade. After the initial fussing over the new arrivals in our sitting room, Mum arrived back from the corner shop with my sister and her few items of basic groceries, took one disdainful look at the kittens and then at Johnny, her face severe.

'You can take them straight back to where you found them!'

Feebly arguing his case Johnnie said, 'They were starving hungry, Mum. Their mother was dead not far away from the nest.' This little white lie was to try and win her over. He hadn't been able to find the mother. 'I had to bring 'em back and give 'em some water and keep 'em warm.'

'Either take them back now, to where you found them, or carry them out into the back yard, fill our tin bucket with water and drown them.'

I know this heartbreaking order never left my brother's mind. I followed him out into the yard but because he was crying and pleading to keep them, saying, 'Please, Mum. I'll find an 'ome for 'em. Don't make me drown 'em. I'll take 'em up to Nan; she'll know where to take 'em. She'll know of a cats' 'ome.'

'Don't talk so daft,' said Mum. 'Cats' home. There's not enough room in children's homes to take in unwanted kids never mind cats. Where's your sense?'

I kept well back and could see that Mum was sad but unyielding as she stood over Johnny, arms folded and lips pursed, while he pushed the tiny bundles under the water and held them there, sobbing his heart out and looking away so as not to witness the desperation and shock in their eyes.

Mum's reasons were sound enough. She was being cruel to be kind because the kittens would have died slowly without their mother to feed them. I knew then that I had to protect my secret pet mouse that lived under the floorboards more than ever. If anyone ever got wind of that, the consequences would be unbearable for me and my little friend.

It took a while for Johnny to get over that tragic event and it took a painfully long while for Billy's leg to heal, but at least he could enjoy a bit of time off school. Once he could sit outside in the sunshine, he made friends with a foreign gentleman who lived in the courtyard off our turning who had given him a glass of water after he climbed down from the gates on the day of his accident. This quiet, kindly gentleman continued to pass by our house once my brother was back at school and smiled amiably at me should I be outside sitting on our front doorstep. I was fairly intrigued by him because he was a black man and I wanted to know where he came from – but was also too frightened to say hello. He looked so different from the rest of us. He was very handsome and sometimes wore a spotless white turban or a brightly coloured one but his clothes were ordinary: a smart gabardine belted mac over a lightweight suit.

Later on, Johnny told me that the man was one of the Three Kings of Orient who followed the star of wonder all the way to Stepney, looking for Mary's boy child Jesus, and I believed him. A week or so after he told me this I intrepidly ventured into the courtyard where the king who wore the turban lived, to find that more of his family had moved in. The girls of the family were dressed in their beautifully coloured traditional flowing clothes and looked like magical princesses, serene and quiet. I was in absolute awe of this family, until I was old enough to rake around the streets in Stepney, Bethnal Green and Aldgate, to find that there were many such families. Most were poorer and less famous than our King of Orient, though, and living in worse back-street conditions than ours.

Our way of life was basic, with women helping out the family finances by earning money too. Mothers, young and old, sat outside on kitchen chairs tending to piecework – hand-stitching hems, sewing on buttons, threading and knotting crochet lace collars and cuffs or whatever else would earn a few shillings. They gossiped or cracked jokes or sang old familiar songs while they worked to help the time go by. One of our neighbours, who took in washing, often stood outside her downstairs window on warm days, listening to an old-fashioned wireless from within as she ironed sheets. She always had two irons on the go: one warming on the stove and the one she was using to do the pressing.

The hope and dream that kept everyone going was that one day they would receive a letter to say that they were going to be rehoused in one of the modern flats or maisonettes under construction at that time. With six of us living in a two-up, two-down terraced house we were a priority case and so were one of the first to receive our letter. Even though I was only just over three years old when it arrived, I can still remember how ecstatic Mum was. She threw open the front door of our house and charged gleefully outside into the street to announce her good news with loud whoops of delight to anyone who was around. Neighbours gathered excitedly and expectantly because now they knew for sure that our small decrepit corner of London was not forgotten and the hope that they too would soon be rehoused was rekindled.

2

Goodbye, My Pets

Packing everything up during those few days before we left our house to start afresh was quite emotional. Mum, Dad and my brothers had been busy packing enormous cardboard boxes and tea chests and stacking grimy, worm-eaten, unsound furniture into the yard for a bonfire. Normally, of course, this would have been piled up with the orange crates for our neighbours to use as firewood but everyone believed that they would also be rehoused soon and wouldn't need it. Some were, but others had to wait a year or two, as it turned out.

All that I was able to think about while all this was going on was having to leave behind Peggy, my dog, who we couldn't take with us. There were signs on the new estate saying, NO DOGS. NO CATS. NO SPITTING. I knew that my Great-Aunt Rose and second cousins would be moving into our house the following month for a year or so and a neighbour had agreed to look after our dog until then, when my aunt would take care of her, but this felt like small comfort. My grandfather, who lived in Cleveland Way, a narrow road at the top of our turning, tried to make me feel better by saying that he would look out for Peggy. My nan said that my pet would probably follow me to the new flat in any case and sneak in when the caretaker wasn't looking.

I was three and a half by then and my most vivid memory of moving day is of sitting on a favourite low windowsill of mine watching and swinging my legs as our belongings were lifted on to an open-backed truck. I was nervous in case things fell off during the journey to our new home and my main concern was that I would lose my only real toy, a beautiful shiny doll's pram, stolen from the posh store, Wickhams, by Uncle Harry and Dad after a beer too many when they felt bold and ready for a lark. The department store was only a stone's throw from where we lived so Mum didn't want to take the risk of an arse-licking employee seeing it in the street and reporting us to the police. There was a lot of nicking going on in our area, but there was always a telltale grass around somewhere who liked to be mates with the bobbies on the beat. So I hadn't been allowed to wheel it outside into the street or play with it in our back yard, and of course I held my parents to their promise that I could push it about in the grounds of the new estate once we moved there.

There was a rare sparkle and carefree look in Mum's eyes on moving day. Once everything that was going to be taken from our old house was loaded carefully on to the truck, she left Dad with a couple of his friends from work who were helping him and eagerly took me and my sister to our new home. Carrying shopping bags with the remains of our groceries and cleaning equipment from the cupboards, Mum led us through the quiet streets to the new council estate, a fifteen-minute walk away. With a permanent smile on her face, she patiently allowed Laura to bombard her with questions about the estate and other children who might be living there. And through it all I managed to hold back tears and not be a misery. Everyone else was happy and excited so if I started to cry I would have ruined it all and been seen as a wet blanket. I knew I could always go back to see my dog Peggy whenever I wanted and yet I was still scared of what lay ahead of us and of leaving the comfort of the familiar behind. In some ways I didn't want to leave our street, or the house that, from now on, our relatives would be living in. I already missed our house and our back yard and my furry friendly mouse who lived beneath the floorboards and came out through a tiny hole in the skirting board next to the fireplace. I felt sure he would be looking for me.

On the cracked red tiles, inside the black iron fender, I had sometimes placed a few breadcrumbs and then waited patiently in the quiet until the tiny creature came cautiously out to investigate. Trying not to move a muscle, I watched while he sniffed around and then ate the meal before scampering back to his nest. I don't suppose it was the same mouse; there were probably several of them running around beneath the floorboards, but to me he was the only one that I was protecting from the wooden rolling pin. To hide evidence of him having been there, I crushed any droppings left in the fender with the sole of my black ankle boot. Once I knew for sure that we were moving out, I had worried about my untamed pet for several nights in bed in the dark. I imagined him slowly dying from starvation. But weeping into a pillow wasn't that unusual and was something I liked to do, because it made me feel warm inside once I stopped and was ready to drift off to sleep.

Despite the worry of it all I vividly remember the thrill of that first day when my sister and I ran from one freshly decorated room to another in our new flat, flicking light switches on and off with delight at the novelty as we followed Mum, who had tears in her eyes and a radiant smile on her face. Since her marriage, Mum had had to cope with squalor and shortage of space which she was not used to. Her family were a class above us. On her father's side the men were in the police force, except for her father himself, who chose to work in the docks, and her mother's family were from Essex and I believe they ran their own small chain of hardware stores and owned their own modest homes. My grandmother Ambrose, I later learned, was not best pleased about her daughter marrying down but said, once she discovered Mum was pregnant with my brother Billy out of wedlock, 'You've made your bed, my girl – now lie on it.'

Mum being pregnant wasn't the only thing that Grandma wasn't too impressed with – apparently she didn't like the sound of Dad's surname either, Lipka. It sounded foreign and too much like an immigrant's as far as she was concerned, which is perhaps why we hardly saw anything of her or Mum's brothers and sister. They weren't too keen to visit the East End, it seemed. They lived in lovely houses and were proud of their unchipped dinner services and silver cutlery. The trouble of course was *where* they lived – a somewhat dull area in the suburbs of Essex. We might have been in the East End but we were in London and only a ten-minute train ride from the city.

So, yes, from a different background to Dad's family, Mum had a certain majestic aura when she walked through our estate. We may sometimes have gone without a hot meal in the evenings but she was hardly ever without a new coat each winter, keeping up with the latest fashion. She had been used to this as a child and I suppose Dad wanted to thank her, in his own way, for putting up with drudgery. Mum always wore rose-red lipstick and a little face powder, needing no eye make-up. She always looked beautiful no matter what she wore because she had a slim and shapely figure, and we children were proud of the way she dressed. People often said she looked like a Hollywood movie star.

Most families in and around Stepney had someone in the fold who worked at Charrington's brewery – name and place went hand in hand – and those who did were proud to be part of a wealthy, flourishing and famous firm. We were no exception. My mother wore a green uniform with little hat to match that complemented her short, dark chestnut, wavy curls showing beneath.

Life was still hard for Mum even though she was in her palatial flat now. She was working five days a week at Charrington's brewery, a stone's throw away, as well as having to look after four children. So looking back I can understand why she once lost her temper with me one morning and hurled our wooden hairbrush across the room to hit my forehead with a crack. I was four and a half and had just started infant school. I remember it well because I was upset that I had to eat my porridge off a chipped enamel plate while Laura ate hers from a china one. Mum was brushing Laura's long brown hair, which she was to have in a ponytail, and I was sitting on a chair eating my porridge oats. I was grumbling a little too much, I suppose, having harboured my grievances for too long. I remember saying over and over, 'I want to eat from a china plate.' Not that ours were bone china but at that age I didn't know the difference.

Mum gave me that certain look of warning and said, 'Be quiet or go and sit in the kitchen.'

I had seen that anger in her big brown eyes a few times before so should have known better. She continued to brush Laura's hair, probably getting firmer with every stroke, and I continued to moan about unfairness and favouritism until her patience cracked and that's when the wooden hairbrush came hurtling through the air and caused me quite literally to see stars.

Rushing to my aid, Mum licked the bump, which was swelling by the second, and gave me a threepenny bit, saying that I wasn't to tell my teacher what had happened in case I got her into trouble. She was my mum so of course I wasn't going to tell tales. She could have beaten me black and blue and I would never have told a soul. I had been thrown off balance by that crack to my forehead but at least Mum and I shared a secret that I was to keep and I experienced a special kind of bond between us that I hadn't felt before. I went to school with a loved feeling even though my forehead was throbbing and the bump looked like a bird's small shiny egg.

My teacher looked at me disdainfully when I walked into the classroom as if I were harbouring some kind of disease. But then she broke into a sympathetic smile and told me to go and stand by her desk, while she attended to another child, a new boy with dark skin. Once the new boy was settled in she sat in her teacher's chair and raised an eyebrow as she gently brushed away strands of my hair from the bump on my forehead. She asked if I had fallen over or knocked myself.

I could feel the blood rush to my face because I was about to tell a lie. 'I fell down a sthtep, misth,' I said.

She asked if I had any other bruises. I said no. 'Not even a grazed knee, Sally?' she asked.

'No, misth,' said I.

She made me promise to let her know if I felt unusually tired or if my head ached during lessons. I said I would. Later on when I lined up to go into the dinner hall she asked me again if I felt all right and laid a hand on my forehead. I said I was all right as I smiled up at her.

She said, 'Are you hungry?' I said I was. She thought this was a good sign.

It was never mentioned again but a letter did go home to Mum and was spoken about in angry, hushed whispers before she questioned me as to what I had said to my teacher. I explained and she brushed it off as the teacher taking her role a bit too seriously. But at least it ended there.

With the bump to the forehead I was a bit of a star when lining up for school dinners that week. The multicoloured bruise stood out against my pale face and the other children were intrigued. I felt like a child film star basking in the limelight. School dinners were always tasty and filling and the puddings wonderful. Sometimes we were allowed seconds of the first course as well as the afters and all for a sixpenny bit. The dinner ladies knew that for the majority of us this was the main meal of the day. No evening meal for children of families living on the breadline. All that might have been available once home from school was bread and dripping or bread and jam although I did have Quaker oats each morning until the porridge packet was empty – which it usually was by midweek. Then a cup of sweet tea was all that lined my rumbling belly in the mornings. Most of the children around our way were hungry for most of the time, but we were never ashamed of this or of our second-hand clothes and there was always something to be proud of, somehow.

Grandma Ambrose, even though from a comparatively wealthy background, might have changed her mind about the East End had she known that in the mid-nineteenth century Stepney and Bethnal Green looked very different, with oats and wheat growing in the Globe fields, hawthorn hedges, stiles, field paths and large clean ditches fished by boys from the Bancroft School. A much changed picture from when we were there in the twentieth century, living on the brand-new Bancroft council estate.

Had we known our local history when Grandma Ambrose paid us a royal visit, we might have been able to persuade her that we East Enders weren't to be sniffed at. Our mother did take us to tea at Grandma's posh house in Essex once or twice but I'm afraid I found the atmosphere stifled and uncomfortable, with the motto clearly being: Children should be seen and not heard. Afternoon tea in the beautiful dining room, however, was not quite as grand as we expected. It consisted of hard-boiled eggs sliced neatly and arranged on an oval china plate and cleanly cut fish paste sandwiches on another, with a little lettuce and cress in each. We had to eat some of everything if we were to have a slice of home-made fruitcake afterwards. By the end of those visits I was always still hungry, with no desire to visit again, large house and lovely garden or not. I felt under scrutiny and scorned for any wrong movement and the memory of those Sunday afternoons is still etched in my mind.

3
Margaret the Catholic

Mum, just like the rest of us, was so happy in her sparkling new flat and it didn't take any time at all for us to settle into our new routine and get used to having no upstairs bedrooms and no back yard. The stone floors were almost covered in dark red lino which had fallen off the back of a lorry. In each of the three bedrooms there were built-in cupboards with rails for coat hangers, and in the kitchen, floor-to-ceiling units with more cupboards. In the bathroom sparkling chrome taps shone beneath the light bulb and the walls were tiled in white with spacious, purpose-built, red tiled shelves fitted under the window for shampoos, soaps and shaving gear. The dream of all dreams was fulfilled for all of us now we could have constant hot water (providing there was a shilling in the meter) which came from an immersion heater and through pipes into our gleaming white bath magically, at the mere turn of a tap.

We even had our own private back balcony with window boxes for growing flowers, where we could sit in the sunshine and be much closer to the sky than we had been in our old back yard. Mum loved this and the joy of it all showed in her face. Before she had had to look after us four children in cramped conditions and suddenly her dream had come true and on a nice day sunshine flooded through windows into every room, where a faint smell of freshly cut timber and newly dried paint still hung.

When Mum first received the letter in 1949 telling her where she could pick up the keys to our new home, she had said over and over that she was on the brink of a new beginning, which worried me a little at the time. My hard-working mother hadn't had much time to spare for me, being the fourth child, and what with everything else going on, I wasn't sure if I was going to be part of this 'new beginning' that was much talked about. I was a bit of an inquisitive child by nature and always asking questions so whenever I caught Mum in a cross mood or too impatient to be bothered to answer me properly, she would tell me to shut up for five minutes or say, 'If you don't stop talking and give me some peace I'll put you in a children's home.' Of course she was joking but this played on my mind because she was always straight-faced when she said it. I eventually asked my brother Johnny if they were going to send me away and he joshed and teased me over it until he finally told me that Mum had only been kidding and so managed to put me at ease.

There seemed to be people everywhere on our bustling council estate and some poorer than we were but there was a warm neighbourly atmosphere and many new things for me to be excited about – such as being able to use our lift which would take me up and bring me down as many times as I wanted. I could only just reach the button marked 2 for the second floor where our flat was. Not quite brave enough to use the lift during the first week of moving in,

I bumped my stolen pram up and down the flights of stairs by myself unless a neighbour was around to carry it for me. The pram, which my sister thankfully showed little interest in, meant everything to me. With it I could go quietly into fantasy worlds and be whoever I wanted: a private nurse to a baby prince; a poor ragged woman begging for food for her infant; or a proud young mother rocking her child to sleep. To anyone else, of course, my bundle of joy in the pram was no more than a paper bag stuffed with bits of rags and tied with string here and there to resemble the shape of a newborn. But this was my very own doll. My baby.

I suppose I did live in a world of make-believe for most of my childhood and I think this might have been because I spent hours and hours in my bedroom, alone, having been sent there by Dad for talking too much when he was trying to listen to the wireless. When a boxing match was on, it wasn't enough to be silent when in the sitting room: I wasn't allowed to move and certainly not walk in front of the radio set. None of us were. Dad claimed that we blocked his view. By the time I was five years old I was already answering him back and not because I wanted to be cheeky – I just had to say what I felt if and when I felt strongly about something. And I often did where Dad was concerned.

When Mum left Charrington's to work in our local picture palace I was going on six. She opted for this because it meant that she could be at home all day and work in the evenings selling ice creams which I think was a bit of an outing for her. She loved being in that spotlight during the intervals. This meant that Dad then had the responsibility of looking after my sister and me while Mum was on those evening shifts, Monday to Friday. Being the youngest of the flock I was, of course, the first to bed and one less responsibility for Dad to have to think about, but this apart we did seem to rub each other up the wrong way. He would sometimes give me a look to kill if I answered him back and I learned how to imitate him and glare back defiantly, especially on those times when I had been sent to my room for no other reason than to be out of his way. This didn't bother me much at that young age because I had my pretend doll and I also had my beautiful Cinderella tea set which had come my way.

The very first Christmas at our flat a children's party had been put on by Charrington's as a goodwill gesture for their employees. I was quite poorly at the time with flushed cheeks and painful, swollen neck glands, but this wasn't going to stop me from enjoying the charity party, even though Mum told me on the way there that I was going to have to give up whatever present I received from Father Christmas to my sister. Laura, being the eldest, was the one meant to go to the party but she was tucked up in bed with a hot-water bottle not too well either. As with many families, there were undercurrents of tension and rivalry. Laura and I are best friends now but we weren't close to each other as children and had a different set of friends. One of the reasons we didn't play together was to do with the two-year age difference of course, but also I think because of the unspoken feeling I had picked up that in some way Mum and Dad preferred her to me. I felt she was dressed in nicer clothes and unlike me she wore ribbon in her hair and not strips of rag, her reward for being a good, helpful girl and rightly so. Laura was obedient and I wasn't.

The pretend Father Christmas on duty at the party offered the gift to me and couldn't know how happy he had made one small child. It was the best tea set of the selection. A fabulous one with each small plate, cup and saucer having a different picture of Cinderella and Prince Charming. And even though I saw that Santa Claus's long white beard was hooked behind his ears it mattered not one iota. He smelled of pipe tobacco too but had a lovely smile and that wonderful old man, my Uncle Christmas, had given me the best present in the world. I hadn't been able to enjoy much else of the party, though, since even a spoonful of ice cream drew sharp needle-like pains to my neck, glands and ears, as if a thin, icy-cold wind was whistling through them. But still it had been worth going because in my mind that tea set was mine and in the quiet of my bedroom I played with it for hours, then put it neatly back into its box as if it hadn't been touched. When Laura took it out of the box, and she hardly ever did, I told myself that I was allowing her to borrow it.

My doll's pram was still my most favourite thing in the world though. I hadn't been able to wheel it about in our old street because it had been stolen locally, but I had been allowed to play with it upstairs in the bedroom, living out dreams of being someone else and somewhere else. Once on the new estate I could push it proudly around the play-ground because we were further away from the department store. Dad and Uncle Harry hadn't been able to smuggle out a doll to go with my pram but a promise had been made by my uncle and I felt certain that I would get one if my brother Johnny wrote out a neat note to Santa Claus for me. He did and my wish was granted. On the first Christmas morning after we moved into the flat I found a small black doll in my pillowcase, one of many that I had seen on Charlie's Cheap Stall in the market and fallen in love with. I was also given an orange, an apple, a few wrapped sweets and nuts and a colouring-in book.

The children living in and around our block of flats were different ages but there were quite a few four-year-olds for me to play with. It was like a new world, with boys kicking a football and girls skipping blithely around or walking on a low brick wall, which separated our playground from footpaths. There was one girl in particular that I took notice of who, even though she wasn't as shabbily dressed as I was, smiled at me when we were in the grounds playing. She was the same age and wore a proper ribbon in her jet-black, unruly, curly locks instead of a strip of rag like mine. A red ribbon. Her name was Margaret McGregor. Drawn towards her, I said a brave hello and she asked if I wanted to play in her front garden, which of course I did and might have been the reason why I hung around. Her family were Catholic and never missed going to church on Sundays and I was told sternly from the outset by Margaret that she wasn't allowed to swear the way I did or tell lies. I told her I never told lies in any case, even though I did swear. She thought that might be all right so long as I didn't expect her to curse. We agreed and shook hands on it.

Other girls that I gradually got to know and who lived in our part of the estate were of mixed religion but there was no difference between us when we were out playing together. Josephine, a Jewish girl who I struck up with, had short, dark curly hair and freckles; Irene, a Christian, wore neat clean clothes that her father made for her and was a snob. On the third floor was Linda, who was half Jewish and who became a good friend, and living next door to her was the lovely Jewish princess, Pamela, who wore perfect satin ribbons in her hair, was squeaky-clean and had a lovely friendly smile. Living in one of the cottages was Pauleen who I sometimes played with. She was a chubby and neat Catholic girl. Next door to her family lived the Jacksons who had a daughter called Doreen who had the best collection of beautiful coloured glass beads in a tin that I had ever seen. So really the only thing that I missed in this new world were the sounds of our old street, my pet mouse and of course Peggy our dog. But I had found a best friend in Margaret.

It wasn't all fun and games, though. I learned, for instance, just how mean boys could be when I was asked over and over what my name was and my answer, Sally of course, never Sarah, was drowned by laughter. Up until then I hadn't really thought much about my lisp. My brothers used to torment me fondly over it and I never minded but I hated being teased by strangers. So to try and overcome this speech inflection I began to stay in my bedroom even though I hadn't been sent there, to quietly repeat my name over and over, trying to lose the lisp by using my tongue differently. And it did work a little.

We had embarked on a new life in a new world and more important than anything was the fact that our family was no longer living in squalor. This showed in so many ways, not just the electricity and hot water, but the comforts we now had. Mum and Dad at last had the privacy of their own bedroom, and their second-hand blue iron bed, with beautiful coloured birds painted on to the headboard, had been brought from the house to the flat for me and my sister to sleep in. This was the bed we shared until we left home to be away and married. Billy and Johnny shared the third bedroom.

It was 1949 and I don't know where it came from, but we had a brand-new wireless, which sat on the windowsill in the living room next to the veranda door. The Lipkas were on the up and up. Everything felt so new, so luxurious and thrilling. The magic of light at the flick of a switch had yet to become commonplace in the older parts of the East End and magic was something we could all appreciate.

My temper, which could flare up at any time, did get me into trouble with Dad, so I found a way to burn energy when I felt fit to burst over some injustice or other which was brought on when my idea of right and wrong was challenged. Occasionally, when my indignation over something rose to the surface and neither my clenched fists nor my willpower could keep anger subdued I found a way to get round it. I charged out of our flat before I threw everything I could get my hands on in my bedroom and ran fast around our block of flats swearing as I went, using the same pair of words over and over. Words I heard the grown-ups using either in a kind of singsong tone or in anger. Two little words that would, by the simple change of a tone, express feelings and give vent to fury as no others could: '*Fucking bastard, fucking bastard, fucking bastard . . .*'

The first grown-ups to smile and say hello to me when I had ventured down into the playground had been a charming old married couple who stood outside their front door leaning on a wall, chatting and smiling. These nice old-fashioned people were retired schoolteachers from another part of London and any child's dream grandparents. Mr Weeks had lovely light blue eyes, a friendly smile, silver-grey hair and a shiny bald patch, and smelled of nice soap; he wore a white open-necked shirt, grey flannels and leather belt which came just over his slightly paunchy stomach. His wife had silvery hair too and smelled faintly of lavender and wore soft crepe dresses in natural shades or a black frock with tiny black dots.

From the first week of moving to our flat I warmed to them and they took to me. When not playing with Margaret, sitting on a stone step in the entrance to our block of flats, I chatted to them as they leaned on the brick wall outside their front door enjoying fresh air and sunshine. I must have said some strange things because I can see them now, looking from each other to me and quietly chuckling. Not long after this I was invited into their front room and made welcome in a gentle way and I remember the request rather than rule that Mrs Weeks once whispered: 'Don't come knocking on the door, dear, in case Mr Weeks is resting.' So I never did but was sometimes invited in, especially if I was wandering around outside by myself. I loved sitting on their small old-fashioned pale green and grey sofa in awe of the living room, which was draped with silky throws from another lifetime with old oil paintings on the walls and never minded one bit when Mrs Weeks would wipe my face with a warm, sparkling white, wet flannel.

Curled up in a high-backed, faded red velvet armchair, I was mesmerised by the children's stories either of them read aloud from old and worn books. Books without pictures but with characters I could fantasise coming into the room they seemed so real. And while Mr Weeks read these stories, Mrs Weeks sat in another armchair, embroidering the corner of a white handkerchief as she listened to her husband's warm voice and the gentle ticking of the black marble clock on the mantelshelf.

The devoted couple sometimes spoke of their rented Victorian cottage in Essex which they had had to give up on retirement because it had been part and parcel of the old man's position as head teacher of a local school. They also told me stories of the things their cats had got up to before they moved. They had had to pass the cats on to their married children to look after because of the council rule of no animals to be kept in our flats. They seemed happy and content in their new home in the East End and the old boy enjoyed going out a couple of afternoons a week to work in the nearby library.

The first time I was allowed into their sitting room the reason had been to look at Mrs Weeks's array of beaded material which she kept in a polished mahogany sewing box with a lovely old tapestry beneath the glass lid. It was crammed with all kinds of colourful iridescent glass beads as well as strips of delicate fabric covered with sequins, tiny pearls and what looked like diamonds. She gave me scraps of her beaded material to add to my collection that I kept in a flat, square sweet tin. The beads were beautiful and they were my jewels to be hidden away at the back of my drawer in the bedroom. I took them out every so often and spread them on to my pillow to examine each and every one.

Mr Weeks, having been a schoolteacher for so long before he retired, made me feel better about myself, telling me stories of other children he had known who were my age and much more shy than I was when in the company of strangers. This helped a great deal and even more so when I found that at the Cephas Infants there were other girls who weren't used to being spoken to at home either. So we chatted to each other as we sat on a wooden bench beneath a large old tree in the playground, and within no time at all fears and anxieties over the outside world were shared and halved.

Even though I had the comfort of knowing that my grandfather's back garden backed on to the school play-ground and that we were only separated by a brick wall, the build-up of nerves and excitement at the prospect of that very first day at school had been too much for me to cope with. By the time I had settled into my classroom and sat at my desk next to a boy I never knew, I wet my knickers and cried, shamefaced, as the puddle on the floor spread outwards. Nervous in new surroundings amongst strangers,

I had been too intimidated by the atmosphere of the classroom to raise a hand and ask to be excused. I had tried desperately to hold on until playtime when I could go to the lavatory and it hadn't worked. Believing that I was to be given a whack across the palm of my hand with a ruler, I had to stop myself from running out of the school building as fast as I could. But I was wrong. Instead of being punished my teacher came quietly to the rescue with an expression of warning to the rest of the children, challenging them to laugh or utter a sound. I was then led by the hand to the secretary's office where a clean pair of knickers was supplied. I was relieved when walking along the corridor with her when she said, 'It's all right, Sally, and you won't be the only one to have wet your knickers on the first day at school.'

'I've never done it in my life before, misth,' had been my feeble reply.

'And you probably won't ever again now that you know it's not the end of the world to put up your hand and ask to be excused.'

'I won't,' I said. 'Not now that I know.'

'And do you think you're going to like school?' she asked as she smiled down at me.

'I already do, misth. I love it.'

Later on that day, with the disgraceful accident behind me, I, like the rest of the children in class, was given a pen, which had to be dipped into a tiny white china inkwell set into a hole in my small wooden desk. To me that pen was nothing more than a long and awkward pencil, with a nib instead of a lead point and I could hardly hold it properly let alone copy the word written on the blackboard. Within seconds I had black ink on my hands and splodges on the clean sheet of paper in front of me. I kept trying to write but couldn't get the hang of it, while other children seemed to be going full steam ahead.

I tried to stop myself crying and hid my face in my arms and leaned in defeat on my desk to weep into my cardigan sleeve. When the teacher came up and placed a hand on my shoulder, I looked up at her and only just managed to speak. 'I haven't ever usthed a real pen before,' I said, 'or proper ink.' The teacher stroked my hair and spoke loudly enough for the others to hear, telling me that I had done well for a first try. This put me at ease and after a few attempts on a clean piece of paper, I managed to produce something that resembled the word CAT.

The other thing that I loved was the afternoon naps on the camp beds in the Quiet Room, where the other under-fives in my class were treated as if we were cherished babies. I was a bit tired by the early afternoon due to the onset of the problems I was to suffer with my neck glands throughout my childhood. There were, it seemed, all kinds of sympathetic people surrounding us children: teachers, dinner ladies and school cleaners. My two and a half years at the infants were the best any child could have hoped for. I can still smell the newness of fresh coloured Plasticine and paints in pots, the polished inlaid wooden floor in the corridor and assembly hall, and in my mind see the warm, friendly classroom and the long sash windows overlooking the playground and the old tall brick wall of Grandfather's back yard. I adored going to school.

I was made monitor after only a few weeks and put in charge of the cupboard that held the different coloured bean bags, hoops and sacks that we used in the assembly hall each afternoon for games and PE. During our lessons we were given coloured squares of sticky-backed paper to cut into shapes and to press on to a sheet of grey paper. I don't remember any of us being grumpy or unhappy and the teachers played their part by making sure that we were safe and secure. And I hadn't minded in the least when our music teacher, during a lesson in the weeks leading up to Christmas, took me aside to quietly tell me that I was getting part of 'Away in a Manger' wrong. That it wasn't 'the kettle is blowing' the baby awake, but the 'cattle are lowing'.

I simply stood further away from her in the school hall and quietly sang what I believed to be the right words. I thought it made sense that the kettle would have been blowing steam so that Mary, mother of Jesus could have a nice cup of tea. Some children thought that Jesus only existed in Bible stories but I didn't. To me he was always there, especially at bedtime, listening to my prayers and requests. I hadn't seen him of course, but felt his presence. A fantasy or not, he was my comforter who, although I suppose only part of my vivid imagination, filled me with warmth.

By the time I was six and used to school, I was thrilled to bits when the seven-week summer break came round. I was beginning to not be quite so shy in the company of adults and had grown a protective layer of sorts, but this didn't mean that I was less vulnerable when it came to certain men on the prowl. Of course I heard stories of girls and boys who escaped capture before being lured away or had run from someone who tried to drag them into a car, but, like everyone else, I didn't think it would, or could, happen to me. Experience, however, showed me that it certainly could. I had been in the picture palace, sitting in the second row from the front during an afternoon matinee. My sister had been on one side of me and a fat man with a leery smile on the other. Next to my sister was our cousin Mary Lisbon and, she and Laura being the same age, they were chatting nineteen to the dozen while snippets of the forthcoming attractions were showing on the screen during the interval.

Mum was in the staffroom at the time, donning her pristine uniform ready to serve ice creams, and by the time she appeared with her tray fixed in front of her the horrid man had already pushed his hand under my skirt. I was close to tears but too frightened to say anything and deeply embarrassed and I suppose shocked and too intimidated to tell my sister what was happening to me. Mum picked up on my expression of helplessness as she glanced across in the warm glow of the cinema lights and semi-darkness to stare at the man. She then called out to me in a tone to freeze, saying, 'Are you all right?' I was too terrified to say anything so I rapidly nodded my head, holding firmly on to the tears welling behind my eyes. What I really wanted to call back was, 'Mummy, *please* help me!'

She hadn't physically rescued me from the stranger but the look of warning she gave put paid to his antics. He rushed out of the cinema as soon as her back was turned while she was serving ice creams under the spotlight. Later on at home in the kitchen she wanted to know if the man touched me. With her eyes boring into mine and my cheeks hot, I burst into tears. She stared out of the window, slowly nodding as she murmured, 'I'll have him for it. He's been in before.' I still felt awful inside out and wanted her to take away the feeling but it was never mentioned again. My sister Laura came into the kitchen to see me crying and I knew from the pained expression on her face that she wanted to look as if everything was all right. She had blamed herself for not keeping an eye on the horrible man who had abused me.

While lying next to her in bed one night, we made a pact that should either of us ever be troubled by a strange man we would always tell one another about it. 'What I don't understhtand, Laura,' I said, 'is why Mum wasth crossth with me over it. It wasthn't my fault.'

'Course it wasn't your fault and she wasn't cross,' she said. 'And don't you worry, I'll look after you from now on. No one's gonna do that to you again.' Unfortunately she wasn't always around at those times when danger lurked in the dark.

That night in bed I asked Lord Jesus to make the man not be horrible to other little girls. My family weren't practising Christians so I had little idea about the differences between religions except that my new friend Margaret went to church every Sunday with a scarf on her head, clean socks and wearing her best frock. Very occasionally I did go to Sunday school at our local church and into the church hall to play afterwards, so that I could get a stamp to put on one of the pretty cards the vicar gave out until suspicions over him began to spread and mothers who gathered outside the hall to deliver or collect their small children began to speak in surreptitious whispers.

The preacher, I later learned, was also thought to be one of the dirty old men that we were being warned about. Whether he was or not I have no idea but we children thought it great fun when we stood in line for our turn of Wheelbarrow, when the vicar would hold on to our legs, our hands flat on the floor, to run maniacally around the church hall to our shrieks of laughter. I don't know if his demise came about because of the tale of the little magic cupboard next to the stage in the hall, which it was said he sometimes invited good children into, or because of the flying angels he gave us, when he would lift a girl on to his shoulders, her skirt over his face and then gallop around to whoops of laughter from the person along for the ride. We were always safe from falling because his hidden hands would be gripping the tops of our bare legs. The vicar departed one day without a by-your-leave and then it all came out, as parents and children whispered together. It seems that we had been placed in the care of a somewhat questionable preacher of the Bible.

I never did get to go into that magic cupboard where the good girls went but I did have a few of those flying angels, and it was quite frightening the way the vicar galloped around the hall at speed. Margaret didn't think that a Catholic priest would ever have behaved like that and Leslie Marcovitch in our flats said that a rabbi definitely wouldn't. It didn't matter any more in any case because the vicar left the area, probably on one of the fast trains that chuffed past our block of flats. A train that one or two of the lads might have spotted while on the roof of our four-storey block, having climbed from the bottom of a drainpipe to the top. Something that I wanted so badly to do but hadn't the courage at that point in my life.

It was good living by the railway and listening to the sound of the steam trains racing by. The best time of all was when I was warm and dry in bed in the early hours of the morning listening to cattle on a train which had stopped on a nearby track. Here it would rest until it was time to move onwards. During the weeks leading up to Christmas, my first one at school, I heard the cattle lowing nearby while in bed and I thought it had to have something to do with the birth of our Saviour. In class the day before we had begun to create a nativity scene complete with donkeys and cows.

I was in charge of spreading and peaking snow around the manger and then sprinkling it with silver glitter and was given a yellow star for good work, mainly because I made the snow from a family recipe, washing powder mixed with a little water, to form a sparkling white paste which hardened. I loved the build-up to Christmas during school time.

Whilst having my straggly hair plaited before school one morning I was humming the tune to 'Away in a Manger' to distract myself when long strands of loose fine hair from the neck were being tightly pulled in. I asked Mum about the cattle lowing in the trucks on the railway line and whether they had anything to do with the baby Jesus. She gave me a rude awakening but at least it was to the point and the truth: the cows were on their way to Smithfield market to be slaughtered before going to the butcher shops. I pushed that bit of information from my mind because I didn't want anything to spoil that magical time of the year when all the teachers and most parents were involved with the season of comfort and joy.

Even our reasonably strict music teacher joined into the spirit of things by allowing us to listen to carols from her own records, which she brought into school especially. Short and slim with a neat bun at the back of her head, she wore black plimsolls on the wrong feet because her toes turned outwards – which made her look like a penguin when walking along the corridor. Normally, during the school year, we would listen in silence while she played classical music on the piano and then talked about the composer. Really, it was all way above our heads but somehow she did manage to bring it down to a level that we could understand. She spoke about feelings and moods. At question time, when bold children put up their hands longing to be chosen to answer questions, she succeeded in drawing even the most bashful of us in. When her attention was on me I blushed and went hot and the lisp would worsen, but she disregarded this and made me feel that I was no less important than those who were bright and alert and eager to answer questions they knew the answers to. School for me was often better than home life.

Our class teacher, a square-set woman, showed a soft side to her nature when she was not in front teaching or keeping order. I can still hear her voice after she once called the register and then took me aside saying, 'Sarah, don't ever be ashamed of your name. It comes from the Bible, dear.'

'But I'm Sthally, misth,' I quietly said. The lisp inflection hadn't improved much and the blood still rushed to my cheeks when an adult spoke to me. 'Everyone elsthe callsth me Sthally.'

'That's as may be,' she said warmly, 'but on your birth certificate and medical card you are Sarah. Sarah Anne Lipka.' She then smiled and made it clear these would be her first and final words on the matter. She never mentioned it again so I thought it wasn't that important to her. But to me there was a huge difference in the sound of the names and I began to like the fact that even though I was Sally I could be Sarah if and when I wanted.

My middle name, Anne, I found out later on in life had been chosen by Mum to get in a dig at Dad who had strayed during wartime when he was home on sick leave and in a hospital out of London. This was after Britain's defeat on the beaches at Dunkirk where he had received a bullet to the knee. While in hospital he apparently had enjoyed a clandestine romance with one of his nurses. A love-child came from this and when Mum discovered it by reading a letter carelessly left in his pocket, towards the end of the war, she christened me, his next-born child, with Anne as my middle name. A constant reminder and a punishment for him having betrayed her.

Mind you, from what she told me once I was an adult, she had also had her fun during the war as did many women, married or single. She told me about the heavenly romancing that had gone on with wealthy American soldiers towards the end of the war when they gave lovely presents of nylons and lipsticks and how her mother-in-law, my nan, kept a close eye on her when evening fell. Apparently Mum still managed to slip out for a drink now and then and who could blame her or any woman coping alone at that time. She did once tell me that she had had a romance with a German who had come over to England as a child with his family and who lived in our turning, a tall, blond, blue-eyed hunk of a man similar to Dad. Mum had to look after two young sons and my sister as a baby in our old house while bombs were dropping around her. So to find out later on that this entire time Dad had been enjoying a love affair while she was struggling to keep herself and their children warm and fed must have been galling. Laura was born in 1944 and conceived while Dad was either on a deserter's run or on sick leave. I followed in 1946 when it was all over so it would seem that during Dad's time in hospital and afterwards, while convalescing, he had gone from one woman, his mistress, to the other, my mother, leaving each of them pregnant at one time or another with neither woman knowing about the other's predicament.

Obviously, since it was wartime, rules were bent a little more than usual. I don't think that Mum ever really forgave Dad for having a proper relationship, which ended with his other woman having his baby and resulted in me being given the name of the woman scorned. My nan hadn't known about the woman so had no problem with calling me Sally Anne – bread and jam.

4
A German Called Rose Lipka

I did eventually stop being so shy at infant school and stopped minding when the lads teased me over my lisp or took the rise because I was skinny and dressed in shabby second-hand clothes. Studying those around me, I began to realise that I wasn't the only one who didn't wear sparkling white socks and neatly ironed frocks and not everyone had the scent of shampoo on their hair. What I did have, though, was my treasure tin which held my beautiful beads and my bits of fabric and real lace from Mrs Weeks. Not long after she had given me those gifts I found something else to put in my sweet tin, a lovely necklace, a gold chain, with long engraved links marked 15 carat gold. This I found when I was six and had been at school for almost a year and was rummaging around in one of the bombed houses where I picked up a small wooden box, which had rusty tools and old ink bottles inside as well as the gold chain.

I ran home with my booty gripped in the palm of my hand, bursting with joy and telling no one, not even my sister or cousins who were there in the derelict house when I discovered real treasure, real gold! I knocked for Margaret and beckoned her out into the grounds where I discreetly and delightedly showed it to her. She thought it was valuable and we agreed not to say anything or to show it to anyone in case I was ordered to take it to the police station as lost property. We made plans to go back to the old bombed house the next day to search for more jewels – which of course we did. We found some interesting old things but no more valuables.

I had been so excited about my gold chain that later on that day after I had sat on the bed and looked at every single beautiful engraved link I had clutched it so tightly that by the time I went into the bathroom to wash it with soap and water it lay in the palm of my hand in a small pool of dirty sweat. But I watched joyfully as it slowly began to glisten as the black grime and dirt washed off. It was beautiful and in perfect condition. Old-fashioned, but not even one link was damaged and the clasp worked properly. This all being too exciting to keep to myself and wanting to please both Mum and Dad, I burst into the sitting room that Saturday and showed them my gold necklace, saying proudly, 'Look what I found!'

Clearly impressed, Dad raised an eyebrow and smiled at me. 'Well, I take it all back. You're not such a Silly Sally after all. Where'd you find this then?'

I watched as he took it from me and let it hang from two fingers to admire it. 'In an old box in a bombed ruin,' I said, unable to stop myself from grinning.

'I'm very impressed,' he said. 'Not many treasure hunters would find something like this. I reckon this deserves a silver sixpence.' He then pushed his hand deep into his trouser pocket and gave me the coin. I could hardly believe it. Not only was he smiling and pleased, he had given me a treat without my having to ask for it. 'That's for being a good treasure finder,' he said.

My suspicions clouded my joy a little because I wasn't sure whether he was going to give it back to me or not. 'Mum wouldn't wear it,' I said. 'It'sth too old-fashioned for her.'

A hidden sigh of relief escaped when Mum agreed with me. She wasn't in the least bit interested in it, possibly because she didn't believe it could be gold.

'Put it away somewhere safe,' Dad said. 'That's an antique that is.'

'I'm gonna keep it wiv my other fingsth in my bead box,' I murmured.

'Bead box? You've never shown me that.'

'I didn't fink you would wanna look at beadsth.' I was beside myself because he seemed proud of me and was talking to me and not at me the way he usually did. Not that he always shouted – this only came when I was being defiant about not wanting to go to bed early for no reason. 'I've been collecting 'em for agesth, Dad,' I said.

'Have you? I didn't know. Go and get your tin and let's have a look at what else you've found,' he said, giving me a fatherly wink.

'I haven't got anyfing elsthe that'sth real gold,' I said. I didn't want the bubble to burst and I felt that it might, once he had seen my less valuable collection. 'I collect material with beadsth on. Mrs Weeksth from the ground floor gives bitsth to me.'

'Well, I'll tell you what,' he said, handing my gold chain back to me. 'Put that in your tin and go out to see if you can find something to hang on it – in one of your old bombed houses.'

'There wasthn't anyfing elsthe in that filthy old drawer except old rusthty toolsth and that,' I said. Wild horses weren't going to drag me away from this warm family scene.

'Oh well, in that case you'd best look after that then,' he said, 'and don't take it out to show your friends. Someone might nick it. That's a one-off that is.'

I didn't know what a one-off was but neither did I care. My gold chain was back in my hand and my dad was pleased with me and talking in a nice friendly tone. But that sense of happiness was not to last very long. No more than a few days in fact. Since I was out in the streets far more than I was in, Dad had every opportunity to find my tin and help himself to whatever he wanted if the whim took him. I had been out playing in the Bethnal Green paddling pool with Margaret when my nan popped in to see Dad the following Saturday with smoked salmon wrapped in greaseproof paper from Baron's where she worked. This was not an unusual occurrence, Nan often did this. But this time Dad had given her something in exchange for the fish. He had gone in search of my treasure box and given her my gold chain which I only discovered missing once she had left. I burst into tears of sorrow and anger and confronted Dad, and no matter how nicely he spoke to me, saying that it was old-fashioned and not something I would ever wear, I couldn't forgive him. I wouldn't forgive him. I wouldn't listen to any excuses.

It was on that day that I realised Dad only spoke in a

kind voice when he wanted a favour of me – to run an errand, make a pot of tea, or run his bath. In this case it was to stop me from letting the cat out of the bag by telling Nan that it was *my* gold chain he had given to her and not one he had come by. I was robbed of something important to me and I was determined to get it back.

When the next Saturday afternoon came round and the family were gathered at Grandfather's I saw my chain glinting on Nan's neck. She was proudly showing it to my aunts, saying that Dad had bought it for her. I knew that I couldn't say it was mine and that I wanted it back because she had no idea of the fib that had been told. Worse than this, I couldn't tell them about my clever find. I left Grandfather's house and strode home, my lips pursed and angry. Dad was at the kitchen table studying the racing page of the newspaper and writing out his bet when I stormed in. Tears of anger burst forth as I demanded that he got my necklace back. He answered in his chummy voice at first, telling me not to be mean. But I stood my ground and decide to use the same persuasive tone back.

'Nan won't mind once she knowsth it'sth mine, though, will she?' I said, trying desperately to be angelic the way Margaret could if needs be.

'You can't take a present back once it's been given,' he sniffed. 'And anyway, it's too old for you.' His repartee at an end, he glanced down at his newspaper – but I was not done.

'It'sth old becausthe it'sth treasure,' I said, 'and that'sth why I want it. It'sth mine. I found it.'

'No, it's not,' he murmured, turning a page. 'It's your nan's now. I don't wanna hear any more about it.'

'I don't care,' I said, backing out of the room. 'I'm going round there now to asthk for it back.'

He gave me a sideways glance that spoke volumes and then, in a voice filled with warning said, 'That's enough. It's too good for a bead tin. Put the kettle on and make a pot of tea.' With that he stood up and the giant of a man slunk out and went into the sitting room to leave me fuming in the kitchen.

'I'm only sthix!' I yelled. 'That'sth too young to use sthcalding water! My teacher sthaid stho!'

Startling me, he came back and stood in the doorway and filled the space. He glared at me and then said, 'If I find out you've bin telling teachers at school things about home you'll get a good hiding.'

Once he had gone back into the sitting room I stood in the doorway as he settled into his armchair. 'I don't care if I do get a good hiding. Costh I'll show everyone the red marks you make where you sthmack me. I want my gold chain back!' My hands were clenched so tight that even my half-bitten nails were digging into my flesh. 'And I'm goin' round Nan's to get it.'

'No, you're not,' he said, 'you're going to your room. Get in there now, you saucy little mare!'

'If I go in there I'll only climb out the winda down the drainpipe! I can easthy do it. I've stheen the boysth going down drainpipes loadsth of times!' I was tempting providence. I knew this could easily lead to my receiving a slap from his leather belt.

He stood for a few moments looking at me and as we stared at each other the die was cast. Beneath my breath

I told him I hated him and I think he might possibly have been doing the same thing. I turned away and was out of the flat in a flash, slamming the street door loudly behind me. Once downstairs in the grounds I sat on the low brick wall and waited for Margaret to come home from her aunt's house where she'd gone with her mother and elder sisters. My best friend was the only other person I had shown my gold chain to. I felt sure that Margaret would understand and tell me what to do about it. My arms folded defiantly, I stared down at the tarmac playground until I glanced up at the balcony to see Dad staring down at me.

With a thumb jerk and fierce face he ordered me back up to the flat. But I didn't go because I didn't deserve a hard punishment, which I could tell I was in for. I ran away to Barmy Park instead and swung higher than ever on one of the ropes of the multicoloured umbrella roundabout, quietly swearing at Dad, repeating my favourite 'fucking basthtard'. Most of us East End kids had learned to swear before we had memorised the alphabet – I wasn't the only one.

I wept into my pillow for days after the theft even though this was causing my eyes to be red and puffy. I missed taking my gold chain out of my bead box to look at. I hope it's still around someone's neck in the family glinting in the sunshine and will find its way back to me one day.

It wasn't the only treasured possession of mine that Dad gave away without asking me. We didn't have many toys as children and certainly wouldn't have had as many as our cousins from the country, on Mum's side of the family. And yet the following Christmas time when I wasn't quite six and a half but told people I was, I had had to stand on our front balcony and watch, gutted to the core, as a cousin, who I hardly ever saw, walked across to my uncle's shiny car in the grounds below and climbed into it with my toy till and pretend money gripped in her chubby arms. Once again I had been robbed of a treasured possession and hours of playing shopkeeper with my imaginary customers in my bedroom. The till worked exactly the same as the one in Higgins corner shop. Once the relatives had driven away I just managed to hold back my tears to ask Dad why he had given it to my cousin.

'You're much too big to be playing with toys like that. You should have joined the library by now and be learning to read!'

'The cousthin from the country isth the sthame age asth me!' I said, stamping a foot.

'I know that. But she's backward.'

'No, she'sth not! She'sth ordinary! I want my till back!'

'She's a country bumpkin, silly,' he said, all sweetness and light. 'You're much cleverer than she is. You don't need a silly till.'

'I do! I play shopsth wiv it! And I'm gonna get it back. I'm gonna bunk on a train and go down to the country where they live and fetch it back!'

'You'll do no such thing,' he said, pointing a finger at me from where he sat in his favourite armchair. 'If I catch you bunking on the underground train with that Margaret you'll get the belt.'

'I don't care if I do!' I yelled, safe in the knowledge that Mum and my brothers were in the flat somewhere. 'I don't fucking care! I want my cash register back! It'sth all I've got to play wiv when you sthend me to bed before bedtime! When I'm not tired!'

'Enough,' said Dad, offering me a look I had seen before and one that was sometimes followed by a painful, stinging smack to the leg. Giving a final show of defiance I screwed up my nose and pointed my tongue out at him. Mum had heard it all and came into the room, not best pleased with his grand act of generosity. But she had been in an awkward position. Dad had been playing the big 'I am', probably because my mother's family, in their own innocent way, intimidated him. They were posh and we were poor and Dad was keeping up with the Joneses. I was angry and confused and hurt over the loss of my till so tried again to argue my case with Mum on my side. Dad was still giving me that sideways glance of warning but I was on safe ground right then.

'It'sth not fair,' I wailed, my spirit a touch broken by then. 'That wasth mine. You're not sthupposed to give uvver people'sth fingsth away! You're bad!' It was a brave and foolish protest which could so easily have seen me sent to bed early with a belting.

'You've had it for two years – since you was four!' was his retort. 'You're too old for it!'

'I don't care! I still played wiv it! I want it back! And if I don't get it back I'm telling Uncle Harry, Uncle Albert, Uncle Jimmy and Uncle Siddy what you did!' I thought this might have swayed him since I was a pet niece and they had come to my defence before, when Dad was about to mete out punishment when I had been cheeky.

It was Uncle Harry who once whispered something that I thought was the best ever advice in the world. Trying not to laugh, he had said, 'It might be better if you call him a bucking fastard instead of the proper swear words when you're trying to win an argument wiv your dad, Sally.'

This probably was the right time to try this out but Dad was glaring sideways at me with a look to kill which fuelled my temper again. On and on I went, showing my stubborn side, telling him he was mean and cruel, ignoring the expression of warning on his face. Then, backing off, my hand on the living room door handle, ready to make a quick exit out of the flat, I snarled at him, saying, 'I'm gonna fucking run away from home and it'sth *your* fault!'

'Good,' he said, 'one less mouth to feed! And don't slam the street door behind yer!'

'I fucking well will if I want!' was the answer once safely on my way and then, 'Bollocksth!' to end it. Another gutsy word I had learned from listening to him.

Slamming the street door shut behind me, I ran for my life, down the stairs, across the playground, round the block, across one quiet road making my way to our old turning. No sooner had I turned into Whitehead Street, out of breath and with a stitch in my side, than Peggy, my old dog, bound happily towards me, stopping just in time so as not to send me flying. It was lovely to see our old neighbours again too. They looked up at me as they tended to their piecework on kitchen chairs outside their front doors and their welcoming nods and hellos made me forget my worries and wish that I was still living in the turning.

Once I had got my breath back and calmed down, I

chatted with one of our neighbours and told her about my necklace and my till and running away from home. She chuckled quietly and shook her head, saying, 'Just as well that you learn now that it's not a particularly fair world, sweetheart.' I told her that I knew it fucking well wasn't and this made her smile. She then went inside her house to fetch out a glass of weak sherbet water for me to drink.

Since it was my Great-Aunt Rose, Uncle Tom and my second cousins who had moved into our old house, I felt easy and comfortable about going back to visit. I had found my way there on my own when I had first started school. The girls' gate was opposite Whitehead Street and since Mum had started working at the local cinema in the afternoons as well as some evenings, my Aunt Rose sometimes looked after me until my sister, who at eight was deemed old enough to be a child-minder, arrived to collect me. We then went home together and let ourselves in by pulling the key on a string through our letterbox.

I loved going to our old house because of Peggy for one thing, and I loved my cousin, Johnny Collins, and his baby sister, Helen. They were in the house where my mouse lived after all. I also liked the unlocked door which was set in the ivy-clad red-brick wall at the end of the turning next to the Toby Club where my brother hurt his knee. The small green door led through to Trinity Almshouses where any of us children or adults could go to visit family or friends or simply play on the green. It had a real country village atmosphere, even though it was tucked away in the heart of the East End.

That door led to a magical kingdom as far as we kids

were concerned. It was our secret garden. My Uncle Jimmy lived in one of the almshouses with Aunt Sheila and four cousins, Jimboy, David, Johnnie and Linda, and I often used to visit them after school. They were the first in our family to have a television set, and it was in their home that I first saw one in action. I had gone there in the afternoon straight from school to watch a children's programme in black and white on a nine-inch screen. It was the most wonderful thing in the world – even to a child who, by then, had seen several films on the big screen in a cinema, which of course I was able to do because I could go in for free when Mum was working her shift. I told the children in my infant class about this amazing new purchase in my aunt's house, and then turned up that day at her door with about a dozen local kids in tow. My aunt laughed at our cheek but turned us away because she couldn't get us all into her tiny sitting room so told us to play on the green. Of course one or two watched through the window while the remainder of the scruffy bunch, myself included, went off to climb trees or play chase.

From there I often slipped through a gap in a partly damaged brick wall where I could venture into another bit of paradise – the much grander Trinity Square, which led out to the Whitechapel Waste and was to become an important playground for Margaret and me. The grassy square, edged on either side by late seventeenth-century houses, butted up to an ancient war-damaged chapel, a beautiful building that stood majestically at one end and which our famous Captain Cook attended when living on the Mile End Road. Built in earlier times from a donation given by

Captain Henry Mudd to the Corporation of Trinity, the houses and garden were for the use of twenty-eight retired or wounded masters of ships or their widows. Badly damaged during the Second World War, the rooftops of the houses were stripped of lead by local lads, my brothers and cousins included, to sell on. Neither the houses nor the chapel were renovated until the mid-fifties.

This of course meant that we were able to enjoy a world of fantasy and treated Trinity Square as another playground until it was cut off altogether by the repaired old brick wall at one end and locked wrought-iron gates at the other. The square was rumoured to have a ghost roaming in and out of the chapel and the houses. Hearsay had it that during one particularly bad attack in the Blitz, a man had been sheltering in one of the houses and had been killed by flying debris and that his spirit returned at certain times of the year. On one occasion Margaret swore that she could hear a lovely tune from a penny whistle coming from a cellar. I was determined to investigate but having eased my way through a gap in a boarded-up doorway in the basement of the house I found it was darker than I imagined it would be, with only a shaft of light coming through a gap, which I squeezed into.

Once inside I turned around slowly in the small room, my eyes searching for another doorway that I might go through, when I saw a shadowy glow in the corner next to a filthy old cooking range. Shocked to the core, I could not move a muscle or call out to Margaret who was wandering about on the floor above me. When the strange glow dulled and merged into what appeared to be the figure of a man, my throat and mouth were so dry, I could hardly swallow. The ghostlike image bearing a puzzled expression was looking around the room and right through me – as if I were the ghost. He then glanced over my shoulder and began to walk towards the semi-boarded-up doorway where I had come in, but before he actually reached it he disappeared into thin air. Petrified, I made my way out and as I pushed through that gap I felt what seemed to be the tips of icy-cold fingers brush against the side of my face, as if someone were gently sweeping away strands of hair.

Outside in the daylight it all seemed unreal and as if it hadn't happened. My heartbeat gradually slowed and my throat was no longer dry. It was very strange. I told Margaret what I had seen and she lost no time in squeezing her way into the cellar to see what was there. But of course she was disappointed because nothing happened, the atmosphere was ordinary and it didn't even seem to her to be all that dark.

Close by was the Great Assembly Hall which Frederick Charrington of the Charrington brewery donated huge funds to in the late 1800s and encouraged other wealthy folk to give substantial amounts to help build the rather grand hall for the people of the East End of London. I had been in there with Mum and my sister several times between the ages of three and six, when charity events were held and when the atmosphere gave those of us who lived in the vicinity a sense of belonging. We sang hymns shoulder to shoulder with hundreds of other mothers and children and were given tea of sandwiches and cake afterwards as a treat. This was the company's way of bringing together those families employed at Charrington's, as well as those out of work or on low pay through no fault of their own. By then, of course, Frederick Charrington, the wealthy benefactor, had long since passed away but the legacy he left behind continued to sustain a close-knit community in an area that had been neglected for centuries. Apart from his charity work he also brought to light the fact that the East End was not only inhabited by vagabonds, thieves and pimps but intelligent, hard-working people too, who deserved a little respect.

Charrington was born in the East End close to the sound of the Bow Bells in February 1850, heir to the prosperous brewery although he rejected this role in order to pursue the causes of teetotalism and the eradication of vice. My gran told me that at seventeen the man was already leaning towards evangelism, having spent a brief spell as a voluntary Bible teacher in a hayloft in the East End where he managed to gain the attention and respect of tough young men from the area, my great-grandfather included.

Frederick's main vocation during the days of Jack the Ripper was to keep women off the streets of Whitechapel and out of prostitution, but he also helped hundreds of poor people. In his campaign against vice in 1888, Charrington helped sweep out of existence over two hundred brothels from the East End and saw the girls provided for at a converted mansion where they were trained for service. He also allowed the Mission hall to be used by Annie Besant, the leader of the Bryant and May match girls strike in the late 1890s. What a picture they must have made, hundreds of girls chatting and laughing as they made their way along the Waste, evoking a sense of camaraderie between women, which had been unheard of until then.

We revisited Trinity Square often and when I was six going on seven we were monkeying around in there again searching for evidence of a skeleton, but we found not one bone or any sense of a ghostly presence. When it was time for us to leave we squeezed through the railings to come out into the Whitechapel Waste and I remember smiling up at two women who had been watching us scrabble around. I said hello because it was the most natural thing to do in those days in that part of the world. 'Well, if you're not a little German,' said one of the women, with laughter in her voice, 'then I'm a Dutch Herring.' She then nodded a farewell to her friend and walked slowly away.

I asked the second woman what she had meant by it.

She just smiled and ruffled my hair, saying, 'Because of your white curly locks, silly.'

'But my 'air'sth sthtraight,' I said, squinting up at her, wondering if she was from the lunatic asylum.

'I'm only joking, Sally,' she replied, smiling. She told me that she knew who I was from visiting her old mother who lived in the same street as my grandfather and she knew that I was Bill and Laura's girl and had seen me coming and going along Cleveland Way on my visits to Grandfather's house.

'Who wasth that other lady?' I asked.

The woman drew breath and shrugged, saying, 'Why do you want to know?'

'I'm not that bothered,' I said, not wishing to get a telling off. 'I justht wondered, that'sth all. I wasthn't being nosthy.'

'Well, that's just as well then.' She smiled, a thoughtful expression on her face. 'And never you mind who she is.'

Margaret very politely intervened, saying, 'But it isn't right for people to talk to us if we don't know who they are or what their name is. Especially if they know ours.'

'I don't know what your name is though, do I?' the woman chuckled.

'No, but you knew my best friend's name. That woman did anyway. I heard her say it.'

'Well, I s'pose you'd better tell a policeman then, hadn't you?' The woman quietly laughed and then tousled my hair again. 'The lady's name is Rose. Rose Lipka. And mine's Mrs Bailey. So now you know,' she said, looking sideways at Margaret, a wry smile on her face.

'But that'sth my name asth well!' I said, astonished. I had never met another Lipka before. 'Lipka isth my sthur-name, Anne isth after a lady that my dad knew and Sthally isth for Stharah, which I can't sthtand. Stho, I'm Sthally Anne Lipka.'

'Is that right?' she asked in mock surprise. 'Well, well. What a strange world it is, dear. Ask your German grand-father about Rose Lipka. He might know more than I do.'

'I haven't got a German grandfather,' I said, realising that a stranger was repeating something that Mum had once said.

'I think you have, dear. Bill's family came over before the First World War I do believe. His name was Lipka at that point I think – I expect it was changed somewhere along the way.'

'Why would he 'ave changed 'is name?' said Margaret,

a touch more interested in the woman than could be good for us. This was my grandfather being discussed after all.

The woman looked down into my friend's wide-open black eyes and smiled. 'Because his father, your friend's great-granddad, had a shoe and boot mender's shop nearby which was smashed up during the First World War when the Germans were our enemy. Quite a few of the Germans got out of the East End at the time.' The woman then turned to me, saying, 'Ask your grandparents about it.'

'Isth that why I'm called a bloody German sthometimes then?' I asked.

'Course it is! Look at yer. If you're not a throwback I don't know who is!' She then turned away, shaking her head and quietly laughing.

'Well, I fink that'sth a fucking cheek, Margaret!' I said, not caring if the woman heard me or not.

Margaret drew breath and then, with a worried expression on her face, said, 'It's a good job it's not Sunday, Sal. You mustn't ever use that word of a holy day. Our Lady Immaculate wouldn't narf be upset over it.'

'I'm not a fucking German and nor is my grandfather! Fucking cheek.'

The figure of the woman merged into a group of shoppers without having any idea, I'm sure, that she had ignited the spark that set me on the path to root out a well-kept, hushed-up family secret about Rose Lipka. The fact that she was so certain that Dad's side of the family were foreigners had me fuming but I had no idea why. Probably all the talk about the war, which people still liked to moan about even though it was over and done with.

'I'm a true English rosthe. I'm not German,' I told Margaret. 'Lotsth of adults 'ave sthaid that to me that I look German justht costh I've got white hair. Fucking German. Fucking cheek.'

'I might be Italian for all we know,' said Margaret romantically. 'I'm a Roman Catholic. And lots of Italians moved to this country years ago as well. We might both be foreigners, Sal.'

'Well, I don't wanna talk about it no more,' I said, slumping down on the step next to her. 'It'sth none of uvver people'sth busthinessth what my grandfather is.'

Margaret pulled a rosy apple out of her pocket for us to share.

Even though I was only six going on seven I felt sure that something wasn't quite right. I thought about it for a minute and then realised where I might have seen the woman, Rose Lipka, before. In Grandfather's old photo album! She was younger in the picture but I felt sure it was her and I knew then that she was not someone to ask questions about at home or at Grandfather's house. I don't know why I felt that then but I did. I told Margaret, of course I did. But she said I must have imagined it.

I brought to mind the time I was sitting quietly with Grandfather by his small coal fire when he had as usual been reading a paperback and I was gazing into the flames. He had glanced up at me and said, 'Wouldn't you sooner be outside, Moggie?' (His pet name for me, meaning stray cat.) 'Playing with your little friends?'

Screwing up my nose, I shook my head and murmured, 'It'sth cold out and I fink it might sthnow.'

'And your coat's too short and threadbare so can't keep you warm. Is that it?' he said.

I didn't know what threadbare meant so nodded to be on the safe side. 'Anyway, Wheezy likesth me being 'ere, Grandfarver.' Hearing his name the old mongrel looked up at me and I patted the top of his head. 'Sthee wot I mean? Your dog likesth me better'n the uvver cousthinsth,' I said, hoping he would let me stay a bit longer.

He went quiet and thoughtful and then said, 'Open that cupboard door next to you and take out the old photo album. Give yerself something to do. But don't ask me who's who every five minutes. I'm reading.'

I promised that I wouldn't disturb him because a big step had been taken. I had been allowed to not only open one of his cupboards but to take something from it and look at old pictures. And this was something I loved to do. It pulled me into that private little world of his. Most of the photographs were old-fashioned and there were a few small loose ones at the back of the album – one of which was a sepia of Grandfather when a younger man linking arms with a woman and another of the same lady standing by herself.

I asked no questions at the time because of Grandfather's orders not to talk but the lady's face lodged in my mind, probably because those loose pictures were tucked away at the back, seemingly hidden. I recognised most of the people in the album but not the lady who I now suspected was Rose Lipka, the same woman I had seen in the Waste. On the back of the small photographs had been faded writing and that was the only thing I had asked my grandfather about. He had held out a hand, telling me to show it to him. Thoughtful, he gazed at the picture before he dropped it on to the burning coals of the fire, saying, 'It's all double Dutch.' He then went back to his reading and I just had to ask what double Dutch meant and he answered without looking up from his book, 'Never you mind, you nosy little German.'

I pushed my luck and asked him why people called me that and he said it was because of my white hair and blue eyes that gave me the appearance of a kraut. I had no idea what kraut meant but I had used up my questions so I went back to the photo album, which kept me quiet for ages. Later on, of course, I realised it was a nickname for a German. Deriving, I guess, from sauerkraut – cooked cold white pickled cabbage. Fair enough.

When I got home that day I went into the kitchen where Mum was peeling potatoes at the sink and said, 'Wasth I adopted then? Isth that why I've got white hair but Billy and Johnny 'ave got black and Laura's got brown? Costh I'm a bloody German?'

Her back to me, Mum slowly shook her head and chuckled, 'Don't talk stupid. With three children to look after I would hardly want to take on another one. Someone else's unwanted child. Especially one who wets the bed.'

This could have upset me but I had heard it too many times. I looked up at Mum to see that she was deep in thought, and said, 'Could you 'ave done wivout me then?'

'I could 'ave done without having any of you if truth be known,' she teased.

'Wot, Laura asth well?'

'No, not Laura. Your sister's a good little worker. She was washing up for me by the time she was your age.'

'But I can't reach the sthink properly,' I said. 'Could Laura when she wasth sthix?'

'She stood on a chair. And she runs errands for me. Eight years old and does a lot more'n you do.'

'Stho do I run errandsth,' I said, squinting against the sun in my eyes.

'Only on rare occasions. You're never in to ask.'

'But that'sth costh you sthend me out to play when I don't alwaysth wanna go out to play becausthe it'sth cold or a bit dark. But I would go for errandsth though if you let me.' I did like to run errands but in all honesty only so that I could wangle a threepenny toffee bar for me and Margaret out of the change without Mum knowing.

Mum sighed loudly and then told me to stop talking for five minutes and give her a bit of peace. This was something she said regularly and I no longer took much notice. I asked why my sister and brothers could go out in the hot sun without getting burned whereas I couldn't. She said I was a throwback from the German side of Dad's family and nothing like her family, the Ambrosees, who were from Romany stock.

After a short spell and then a smile from Mum, she said, 'You get enough attention at your grandfather's so you're not hard done by.' And there was no denying this. The three-storey Georgian terraced house was like a second if not a first home to me and a place where aunts, uncles and cousins gathered on Saturdays for a cup of tea and smoked salmon sandwiches. I loved being in the centre of things in the parlour below stairs. There was a spacious sitting room on the ground floor but that was kept tidy for grand occasions: parties and funerals and Christmas Day dinners and held little interest for me. But as for the parlour, I can still see the glow from the gas mantel on the wall next to the hearthstone and hear the hissing of Grandfather's coal fire and the lazy breathing of Wheezy, the black short-haired mongrel who I loved. When the door knocker went, Wheezy would bound up the stairs with not a second to lose to welcome yet another member of the family before returning to sit at Grandfather's feet, every inch the loyal pet.

The next time I was at my grandfather's and we were by ourselves I asked about Rose Lipka again and told him I had seen her in the Waste after she'd been shopping for errands. I also told him that she had spoken to me. Lowering his eyes, he pressed his lips tightly together and went quiet and for a second I thought his eyes were glistening more than usual. He said, 'You talk too much and wear me out, Sally. Off you go. And stop asking your elders questions about other people. It's not polite.' Of course that made sense and we left it there but I knew the old man well enough to think that he knew who I was talking about. Of course I could have asked any of the others in our family about the woman but I felt that to be wrong. I didn't even know if anybody else in the family knew about her. And why was it that only my dad, who was the eldest of his flock, was a Lipka when Dad's brothers and sisters, and Grandfather, went by the name of Lisbon? Margaret agreed with me that we had to find Rose Lipka one day and find out more. I couldn't wait.

I don't think any of my family, not even the aunts and uncles, who I was close to, knew about the times I sat in the small parlour with the old man and Wheezy. When I would wait until my time was up and he said, 'Off you go then. Don't want your mother worrying.' I always gave the same reply: 'All right, Grandfather. Sthee you tomorrer, eh?' He would smile at me and nod, knowing I might not be back for a week or so. The important thing was that I had spent time in his company and he never minded. He always offered me a piece of sharp cooking apple and strong cheddar cheese, but never a slice of raw Spanish onion, when he was having a snack.

What I really wanted to do and what I was still waiting for was permission to look inside the small green fitted cupboard to the left of the fireplace, next to where he sat in his small armchair. 'Rummage through the other one, Mog,' he would say, nodding at the cupboard to the right of the fireplace where the album was kept. I don't suppose there was much in his private one to intrigue a small girl but it was the fact that he used to draw breath whenever I mentioned it. Draw breath and slowly shake his head, as if I had asked him to open the glass cabinet to the crown jewels at the Tower of London. I expect he was playing on my young imagination, although, as I was to find out later on in life, he did keep all his private papers in that cupboard and, in particular, his birth certificate and his army book.

5
Rags to Second-hand Clothes

My nan, known to everyone as Lizzie, was tall and broad with a smiling face and light auburn curly hair and a wonky nose, which came from a fall years back. She worked at the Baron fish curing and pickle bottling factory on contaminated land in Assembly Passage where, incredibly, a German unexploded bomb still lies dormant to this day. The food processing premises where fish was smoked and cured was just a five-minute walk across the Mile End Road from Nan's house and the big light green wrapover apron that Nan wore had more than one use: it protected her frock from fish oil but the large pockets also safeguarded the smoked salmon or herrings when her shopping bag was full. She didn't pinch the fish; there was no need because the governors let the women working in the smoke and curing house have offcuts for next to nothing to discourage them from taking prime salmon.

The Hamish cucumbers in jars and crisp pickled onions, though, Nan and others in her smoking sheds did have to pay for. But my nan got them cheaper than anyone else could because she had a good brain and a quick hand and if she had had a mind to, she could easily have made her fortune in shoplifting. One of her mates who just happened to be a supervisor in the pickle bottling yard sometimes worked with Nan and the pair of them surreptitiously passed things to each other. Sixpenny bits went between them most of the time.

Some of the contraband was enjoyed at Grandfather's house on Saturday afternoons, when Nan loved to see all the family in her parlour enjoying a feast of bread and butter with a variety of smoked, cured or pickled fish, and some exchanged for other easy-to-come-by luxuries – scented soaps from a factory in Hackney and fancy lace nighties and knickers from a warehouse in Hounsditch, places where other aunts or close friends worked. An exchange of clothes between cousins would also take place at number 24, as Grandfather's house was known. Cast-offs from aunts went to cousins and from older cousins to younger. It was our own personal jumble sale with no money crossing the palm and more exciting than shopping in Wickhams, the posh department store with its Selfridges look-alike façade, not far from Grandfather's house. And of course most things could be purchased on the weekly, or, as in the case of my beautiful light grey and chrome pram, stolen. Everyone knew someone who worked some-where in that pocket of London and I have no doubts what-soever that my dad and my uncles had a mate in the loading bay.

With me, Grandfather was always gentle and kind but I think he must have ruled the nest with a rod to keep his flock in order because my aunts and uncles always respected him. Even as adults with children of their own they were answerable to him and took his advice. I don't think any of them would have thought to have cross words or ask searching questions because he was such a private old man. But so long as I could visit when I wanted I was content enough. And I especially enjoyed it on Saturday afternoons, once my uncles clocked off from the docks for the weekend and sat in the basement with Grandfather, talking and joking and sometimes playing a game of cards, expecting Nurse Sally to arrive with her nit comb.

And arrive I would and sit down quietly until my Uncle Harry or Albert would look at me and say, 'I'll give you a big penny if you comb through my hair, Sally.' I would then stand behind one of their chairs and begin my work, slowly going through Uncle Albert's short curly ginger hair first and then Uncle Harry's blond locks. Siddy, the youngest of the three, would simply watch and quietly chuckle and when I asked if he wanted his hair done, he would put up and hand and say, 'Not me, Sally. But I'll give you a penny for the show.'

I never found nits or fleas but I took my time and slowly hunted for any signs, pretending now and then to catch a mite and click it between my thumb nails. It never occurred to any of us that this grooming might have been a throw-back to our antecedents, the gentle apes. Grandfather didn't have much hair at that time but just like my Uncle Siddy he was happy to sit and watch as I behaved like the nurse who regularly came to our school to go over our heads. Once the door knocker began to go I knew that my aunts and cousins were arriving for the usual get-together so would stop and wait politely for my wages. Of course I didn't get just one penny from each of them, I got a threepenny bit or a silver sixpence depending on what was in their pockets.

When my Uncle Albert's back pocket was full from working at night as well as labouring in the docks for eight hours, I got a two bob bit or half a crown. I'm not sure what his night job entailed but little girls didn't ask such questions of their elders. He could have been blowing a door off a safe for all I knew. Apart from the money I earned I really liked the attention and felt loved in that house. 'Our Sally from the Alley' is what they called me and what they often sang. The strange, scruffy wanderer who couldn't sit still for ten minutes. I could stand though if I was combing hair. Pocket money had to be earned somehow.

When I banged the iron knocker of that front door one of my aunts would sometimes appear in the doorway with a finger to the lip before whispering, 'You'll 'ave to be quiet, Sally. Grandfather's in a quiet mood.' I felt sure that was just a load of bollocks to get rid of me, so I slipped past along the narrow passageway and down the staircase to the basement, where he would be sitting in his armchair, looking into the glowing coals of the fire or reading. I would tiptoe across the room, lower myself into the other armchair without uttering a word, and this never bothered me because I was quite content to sit and listen to the hissing coals and the breathing of the family dog by his feet. It was during those times with Grandfather that I discovered the reward of patience and silence. When he was in the right mood he would give me advice with just a few words, such as: 'You should never give to receive.' 'Only wish for a farthing more than you need.' 'Give with a good heart or don't give at all.' Sometimes he would end my visit by giving me a knowing nod and I quietly left to carefully close the door behind me until I heard the iron catch drop. He might not have spoken at length to me but I loved that silver-haired old gentleman.

But I preferred to be there when the place was buzzing, when my aunts were gossiping. I especially liked it when my Aunt Nelly took neatly pressed clothes out of a carrier bag for me. They were always spotless and mended with small stitches. Dad's other sister, Aunt Sarah, my smiling godmother, was another source of hand-me-down clothes. She was like a young mother figure and never forgot my birthday. Sometimes her card was the only one on the doormat and her small box of Milk Tray chocolates the only present.

Ripped hems and faded cast-offs which most of us children wore for most of the time didn't matter one bit to any of us and being cold in the winter and too hot in the summer was something that was standard at the time. We learned from our teachers' reporting of world events that worse things happened abroad and that children by the thousands were dying a slow death from starvation and disease from flies, so we thought we were the lucky ones.

Even though clothes bought from the rag-and-bone man, Mr Middleton, never squared up to the right seasons, we kids in the East End managed to dress ourselves decently from the second-hand clothes chosen from a pile. Wealthy people gave away their cast-offs to the travelling rag man when they were no longer needed, so in summertime there was bound to be mostly winter woollies and coats on the cart and lightweight clothes when it was freezing cold and snowing. But we weren't daft and could work it out for ourselves by keeping cotton frocks for summer and putting the mackintosh away for a rainy day.

Once the rag man returned from a round in a wealthier part of London to park up inside his shed under the Bethnal Green arches, he would come out into the light and whistle up to my mother so that she and her friend Alice Agent could have first pickings. Alice had a son called Kenny who I almost fell in love with – his bony knees showing beneath his short trousers put me off.

It was exciting to rummage through a fresh pile of clothes while steam trains chugged away noisily above us. Amongst the better items separated from the tattier stuff, which could pass as almost new, I once found a faded pink and white candy-striped frock with a tiered skirt that fitted me perfectly, and still remember feeling special at being able to choose my own dress.

Once when I was street-raking – hunting for anything useful or edible while playing with Margaret on a bombed site – my nan and Aunt Sarah caught sight of us as they walked arm in arm, and called out to me. We were scrabbling about in the remains of what had once been the cellar of an old-fashioned grocery shop on Cambridge Heath Road, sorting through some old rusty tins of corned beef. Nan told me to come away and that it was dangerous, but I was so thrilled with my find I held up a tin as she looked down at me. I said, 'D'yer want some of thisth, Nan? There'sth a load of bleedin' tinned food down 'ere going to wasthte. The tinsth are rusthty but that'sth all!'

'Come up out of there, you little cow!' called Nan. 'That's tinned meat from the wartime!'

'But it ain't bin opened,' asth it! It'sth rusty on the outsthide that'sth all! We could eat it!'

'Yeah, and one of them big rats that live down there could eat you. The pair of yer! Get out of there now!'

'There ain't no ratsth down 'ere, Nan!' I called back.

'Oh no? Well, I can see two bleedin' big black ones crouching in a dark corner with their eye on you!'

Of course that worked and Margaret and I were scrambling up and out of the bombed shop cellar. Arriving at the top, filthy and with a few new scratches, I grinned at Nan as I eyed my gold chain around her neck while she gently laughed at me. Then she said, 'You look like a little German orphan even when your white hair's filthy dirty. Does your friend know that you were the baby your father found wrapped in newspaper? A parcel that the Germans dropped during the war.'

'She ain't German!' said Margaret, who had been unusually quiet up until then. 'And even we know that the enemy would 'ave bin able to tell the difference between a bomb and a baby.'

I was momentarily silenced by all this talk and that second comment about me being a little German in just over a week and it made me wonder even more about Rose Lipka and whether she might have a part to play in unravelling why I always felt there was something I wasn't being told to do with our family. I couldn't be downcast for very long though, not with Nan and Aunt Sarah laughing and linking arms again and ready to go, with my aunt then calling back over her shoulder, 'Come down Grandfather's, you filthy little street-raker and I'll wash and curl your hair for you!'

My godmother was always trying to make something of me so that I didn't look quite the ragamuffin. Sometimes she stood for what seemed like forever, patiently heating iron curling tongs over the gas flame of the small, old-fashioned stove in the scullery of number 24 to spend an hour trying to turn my dead straight hair into long ringlets, much to the amusement of other aunts and uncles gathered there. I admit that I enjoyed being the centre of attention – it came as welcome relief from worrying about being a bit of an outsider at home, even though I hated corkscrew curls. I can still see my Aunt Sarah's smiling face when she used to say, 'Come and gimme a big kiss, Sally you scruffy little mare.'

Sometimes when the family all got together like that a song would start up and before I knew it they were singing a wartime favourite and I knew it was time for me to leg it.

But group singing was an important part of the camaraderie all over the East End of London and was no different to what I gather happened during the Blitz on London when families were in air-raid shelters. Mum sometimes told us kids what it was like when the siren went off and everyone had to run to the underground shelter closest to them and how everyone relied upon each other and clung together, sharing the same emotions: fear of death; of being buried alive.

That camaraderie carried right through to the fifties

when the same heartfelt songs spilled through open windows of the local pubs and taverns instead. People continued to sing popular war songs over and over until even we children knew the words by heart and thought that Vera Lynn was the most famous person in the universe. Come Christmas-time though, braving the cold, Margaret and I were the star act, giving a performance in the doorway of our local pubs and taverns.

I was a good songster, as was my best friend, even if we did sing out of tune. We looked forward to the festive season every year from when we were five until we were thirteen and found other ways to earn a living by working on Saturdays as skivvies in the local hairdressers and the hat-making factory in Cambridge Heath Road. For those eight years though, we made the most of our voices every Christmas, working hard for at least three hours each evening. We began our career by carol singing at every door in every block of flats on our estate. The following year and from then onwards we went further afield and trudged through shadowy back streets singing door to door. We entered dark Victorian tenement blocks, six to eight storeys high with no lifts. On Friday and Saturday nights around nine o'clock we wedged open the door of a local pub from which we could hear a piano playing, and sing as if we were giving our one and only performance that night. Our audience would be merry by the time we arrived, having downed at least a few pints of ale. Men and women, young and old, could not resist a pair of skinny bedraggled girls who knew every word of the age-old carols they sang. The cheek of our act really was irresistible. Margaret with her long, unruly black curls and beautiful, innocent, wide-open black eyes and me with my long, straggly white hair and 'butter wouldn't melt' gaze could melt hearts or prick a conscience or two.

To be fair, as well as playing on our ragamuffin cheek, we always tried to give value for money and sang until our throats were dry or a door was slammed shut in our faces. We didn't mind whose door knocker we banged on or whose bell we pushed. The closer to Christmas Eve it got, the more profit we made. Our earnings gave us enough to keep us going in small portions of fish and chips and sweets, with a little left over for Christmas gifts. Our most lucrative venues were a block of police flats by Harbour Square and the Jewish estate, as it was known locally, opposite the Blind Beggar, the old pub where Ronald Kray shot George Cornell in the saloon bar in true American western movie style. Other songsters didn't go into the Yiddish or police flats because the Jews didn't celebrate Christmas and policemen might have been none too pleased to have singing beggars at their door. How wrong they were. Our idea of going where no one dared tread paid off handsomely.

The newly acquired audience loved the novelty of us. One woman who opened the door to us was clearly moved by our rendition of 'Silent Night' and was almost in tears as she said, with one hand on heart, 'Darling, we're Jewish. We don't celebrate.' I explained that I realised this and thought it unfair that they never got to hear the lovely voice of the carol singer. The woman invited Margaret and me in to sing round the fire where we were given a hot drink, a biscuit each and a threepenny bit or a sixpence. Most of the policemen's wives did the same so we came away with a pretty good haul.

Fearing no one but certainly avoiding shady-looking men, we became quite brave in our attempt to cover as much ground as possible in our neighbourhood. In a back street not too lit up, lived Mr and Mrs Kray and their three sons. The family's terraced house was close to one of my brother's girlfriends, June. Reggie and Ronnie were mates of June's brother so were frequently in his house playing cards for money. I knew we were guaranteed two bob if we sang outside the window while the boys were inside gambling – and if they weren't in, June would come to the door and give us a couple of coppers. We would then promptly make our way round to Mrs Kray's house to carol there and sometimes we got lucky. Either Ronnie or Reggie would open the door and recognise us singers from previous visits, whichever one of them it was would then pay us half a crown not to sing any more. Once the door was closed firmly on us, Margaret and I would shout nice and loudly, our voices gurgling with cheeky laughter, 'God bless you merry gentlemen – we will be back again!' Of course at that time none of us had reason to believe that the twins would be quite so infamous.

From their street we would go wherever our fancy led us and on one particular evening it was across the Whitechapel Road into the back and beyond of the London Hospital. Dragging a reluctant Margaret (whose heart was set on being a nurse) away from the back entrance of the hospital, where an ambulance had just arrived with its lights flashing and a casualty on board for her to look at, we pushed on quite successfully. We knocked on the door of an old tenement house in Deal Street. It was quite dark with a somewhat gloomy atmosphere, so we agreed to sing only one carol at a few of the houses and then leave. We got no joy from the first door we knocked on but we persevered at the second, which had a light on inside the passage. If a house was in darkness we guessed that no one was in or that whoever lived there must be sleeping before going on late night-shift work.

We picked our favourite carol, 'Once in Royal David's City' and once I'd knocked on the door, we began to sing. We had an agreement that if nobody came to open their door we would presume they didn't have any pennies to spare, so would only give one verse of a carol and move on. On this occasion someone did come to the door – a man in his thirties who smiled at us and slowly nodded as he dug into his trouser pocket for loose coins. He held out two pennies and asked if we would sing 'Silent Night' for him. Margaret took the coins, thanked him, and then looked at me for reassurance as she began to sing like an angel. After just one verse a woman came through from the back into the gloomy passage and stood behind the man so that we only just had a view of her. But there was enough light for me to see her by and I could hardly believe my eyes. I felt sure it was the woman that we had seen in the Whitechapel Waste, the woman who'd been pointed out to me as Rose Lipka and who I had told Grandfather about.

Taken aback for a few seconds, I peered at her and then, still singing, stepped a little closer, only to see her warm smile dissolve. With her light blue eyes and greying hair she looked a picture in the lamplight. Margaret continued to sing but I stopped; my throat had gone dry. It could only have been a few seconds that we gazed at each other before she eased an arm in front of the man and slowly closed the door between us. With the tuppence in her hand my best friend looked at me as her singing voice trailed off and I turned and walked away, on the one hand disappointed and on the other pleased. At least I knew where Rose Lipka lived, even if she preferred not to see me. I was pleased that I had found this out by chance but sorry that she closed the door on us.

Sensing my mood, Margaret linked her arm with mine and we went home, discussing seriously whether I might be related to the old woman or not. Margaret thought that I was perhaps making something out of nothing and that there were probably lots of families living in our area with the same name as mine. I agreed but still I couldn't get it out of my mind or the photo I had seen in Grandfather's album. Deep down I knew by instinct, if nothing else, that we were linked by family blood and I wanted to find out more about her and determined that I would, somehow, do just that one day. I knew I might have to bide my time though – it was obvious that whatever the truth, the people who knew were in no hurry to tell me.

Before I had found my best friend Margaret I had little confidence. It was she who brought me out of my shell, saying that we had to stand up and fend for ourselves if we were to survive in an unfair world. That we were the unwanted children who had arrived after the Second World War that had been talked about on the wireless. We were two of the 'surprise babies' who became the unaffordable post-war children in homes across Britain, the celebration war babies. There were plenty of us in Stepney. We were a mixed bunch, those of us living in the East End, with varying backgrounds and religious beliefs and several coming from different parts of the world.

My school friends were mostly Church of England or Jewish, simply because there were more of them attending my school or living on the estate. Catholics tended to go to Catholic schools. I even had a Jewish twin, who lived on the fourth floor in our block and went to synagogue every Saturday. When we discovered that we shared the same birthday, we hounded our mothers to tell us precisely what time we had each been born. I turned out to be the eldest by four hours. I don't think he forgave me for rubbing it in. We did quite a bit of friendly chasing when we were young children and one day we had a fight that neither of us wanted. He called me names so I called him names back – or it could have been the other way round. In any case, I committed the worst crime of all. I called him a fucking Jew boy. He was so angry that he clenched my neck with both hands and stared into my face, his eyes bulging with fury. He suddenly seemed like someone else and I wanted to laugh. I only just managed to say, 'You are a Jew, Leslie. If you're ashamed of it then punch me; if not let me go.'

He looked puzzled but still held on. 'You called me a

Jew,' he said, his voice beginning to break. 'You're my twin and you insulted me.'

I said, 'But you are a Jew. I called you a fucking Jew boy. Hit me for swearing at you if you want and I'll kick you in the shin. But you can't hit me for calling you a Jew or a boy. I wouldn't hit you for calling me a Christian girl, would I?'

This had taken the heat out of the situation and he reluctantly let me go, saying he'd think about it. I don't know if it was the fact that we shared the same birthday or that we simply got on, but I really did feel as if we were related, as if he were a kind of a brother. To make up, I said he could come carol singing with me and Margaret if he wanted. I also said I would give him my complimentary ticket to the Forester's picture palace, where Mum was working as ice-cream lady in the afternoons as well as the evenings, for a short spell. I don't think I ever did give it to him though and I don't remember him saying he wanted to come carol singing, but at least I'd tried. The problem for most of my Jewish friends at that time was that there had been and probably still was some anti-Semitism around and so innocent remarks could sometimes be taken the wrong way. I think I had hurt Leslie's feelings and when I told Margaret about the incident she was none too pleased with me. Her mother and Leslie's were good friends but she promised not to tell her parents about it.

Margaret's family meant a lot to me and I was always in and out of their council cottage which I loved and they didn't mind in the least bit sharing with me. The garden where we pitched our small makeshift army tent, courtesy of her elder brother, was where we sat on drizzly days drinking our sherbet water, watching the rain and discussing where we would live once we were married with children. We both wanted the same thing: a cottage in the country, with tall colourful flowers growing up the walls, like the one on the toffee tin in Riddly's sweet shop window.

In Margaret's house there were carpeted stairs, which went right up to the attic room where her sister Julia slept and where I sometimes slept when Julia was away with her American friends for the weekend. It only happened twice but I loved it in that tiny room up in the sky. When Julia was home I squashed in next to Margaret in her single bed. I suppose I was bound to sleepwalk on those occasions because I had been doing so on and off since I stopped wetting the bed. I did get up in the night one time to go to the lavatory and in a half-asleep state I heard Margaret's mum calling out to me as I rolled around in her fur coat which was on the landing outside her bedroom.

She had believed it to be Damby the family dog playing around in the night. I answered her as easy as you like, saying that it wasn't Damby but me. She was none too pleased when she saw where I was and what I had over me as a cover. She patiently guided me back to bed. The next day she was laughing as she called up to my mother, who was on our second-floor balcony, telling her that I had used her precious fur coat as a bedcover, dragging it around on the passage floor. I think she was pleased to have one over on Mum who only had a fur-collared coat.

Margaret's brother George sometimes said that she and I were dramatists and we weren't sure what that meant so we went to Bethnal Green library to look up the word in a dictionary. I was quite pleased with the meaning and quite fancied the idea of collecting a few actors together and putting on shows. We started to think up plots and who we might choose to play certain parts in our four-storey block of flats, which made a perfect venue. We had enter stage left and exit stage right which led to the balconies either side. The concrete stairs made a good auditorium and the area by the lift, flanked by long windows, was our proscenium arch. I told the actors what to do, rather than write words down, because clean sheets of paper were a bit hard to come by. Margaret was the stage and entrance manager and charged other kids in the block a penny per ticket, which was no more than a small square piece of newspaper cut neatly. Of course hardly any of them paid but we had a lot of IOU promises.

We had the usual trouble with difficult actors: all the girls wanted to be the rich posh lady whose baby had been stolen and no one wanted to be the tramp who was trying to make a bit of ransom money on the side. I sometimes wondered why we bothered. The financial rewards were small and we knew we could make more money on seasonal work: carol singing or dragging a guy around pubs and picture palaces every November. I considered asking the new vicar once he arrived if we could put a holy Christmas show on in the church hall but never got round to it because I didn't attend Sunday school often enough and even then only if there was nothing else to do.

The one time I went into church to sing hymns, other than to a family wedding, christening or funeral, was with

Margaret and her older sisters. I was allowed to go even though I wasn't a Catholic. Her sister Helen gave me a scarf to wear and we went to their church which was close to the Toy Museum in Bethnal Green and I know where I would rather have been. It seemed an awfully long service and I wasn't used to standing on one spot for that length of time and thought Margaret mad for doing it so often. I did like the glowing candles though, because they reminded me of Christmas. But I never went twice. Despite and perhaps because of our differences, Margaret was the most important person during my childhood, and remains my best friend to this day.

6

Running Away From Home

Margaret and I were used to roaming all over the East End and by the time we were seven years old we were already venturing further afield than we were supposed to. We would take one skate each of her pair of rollers and covered a lot of ground in and around the East End, from Hackney, Aldgate, Old Bethnal Green, Shoreditch and Stepney to Forest Gate. We also found our way across the busy Commercial Road to the River Thames, going through dingy courts and smelly alleyways into Limehouse, St George's in the east and Wapping. Ancient riverside hamlets which were the backdrop to our lives and played an important part in the lives of thousands of people who had, over the centuries, arrived from various parts of the Continent. The Huguenots who came way back in the seventeenth century to escape persecution in France had made their way to Spitalfields, bringing with them their silk-weaving skills.

Irish farm workers who arrived later on in their droves formed a major part of the workforce during the construction of London's docks as did the Russians, Poles and Germans. Many settled in and around the dock area, Brick Lane, Bethnal Green and Aldgate, which with time were to become strong with a friendly Jewish trait. Margaret and I were used to treating this exotic mix as totally normal and were quite at ease in our neighbourhood.

We passed slum dwellings down by the river which were mostly decrepit two-up, two-down terraced houses accommodating families who were patiently waiting to move into brand-new places like ours, with all mod cons. These families living by the Thames had to put up with damp in their homes and rats running in and out of their back yards because vermin that lived by the Thames mostly nested in warehouses and came out at night to sniff around in the rubbish. There was always talk of grand improvements with tower blocks down by the dockside and a better standard of living for the Wapping people.

The older generation had seen worse of course and an ageing aunt of Margaret's, who we went to see now and then, told us all about it while we drank sherbet water she made especially for us. 'If the local council don't get a move on and bear in mind the downtrodden,' she said, 'fings could easily go back to what they were like. And then you young 'uns would know it.'

'We know,' said Margaret, giving me a warning look not to laugh at her old aunt.

'I go back to the nineteenth century. Poverty-stricken we were. All living in dire conditions, surviving on bread alone at times.'

'And onions and potatoes that you grew in your back yard, Aunt,' said Margaret, gently reminding the woman of what she had told us before.

'Oh yeah, that as well. At least my mother only had three children. Sometimes there was a whole family of five or six lodging in one big room with the passage and stairs belonging to everybody but looked after by no one. With a back yard choked with dust and filth, and a yellow sulphuric mist hanging over the lot of us.'

'But it's all changed now though, eh, Aunt?' said Margaret, eyeing a small plate of digestive biscuits.

'Help yourselves to a biscuit each,' said the aunt, not batting an eyelash. 'Of course, things have improved since the days when the narrow streets that we skipped through were black and muddy. When kerbsides were half filled with pools of dirty rainwater. That was where the trucks and barrows belonging to costermongers parked up, mind you.'

'I'm glad it'sth not like that any more,' I said, munching on my biscuit.

'No, you're all right, you children of the 1950s. Think yourselves lucky that you're on the beautiful council estate.'

Margaret and I loved going to that aunt as well as places we hadn't been to before and running away from home to find pastures new was often on the agenda. We actually made it as far as Stratford East once, over three miles away, our original destination having been Epping which we thought was in the heart of the country. We wanted to find rich people living in grand mansions who might charitably take in two innocent, unwanted, skinny children. Of course we used the only means of transport we had to get us there quickly – one skate each of Margaret's pair.

So, on one summer's day, excited at the prospect of a new life, we strapped them on and filled our pockets with jam sandwiches wrapped in sliced-loaf waxed paper that

Margaret's mother kept in the cupboard to use when making her husband's packed lunch for work. Half skating, half walking on our romantic journey of escape from our roots, we reminded each other why we were going and the kind of life we might be living from then onwards. We had to keep our wonderful goal in mind because blisters on our heels caused by the skates began to sting not that long after we set out. We stopped two or three times on the way to rest on low brick walls or a public bench to have a bite to eat and a drink. It being a hot and sweaty kind of day we got through our sherbet water far too quickly and, before we knew it, we had eaten over half of our jam sandwiches – with still a few miles to go.

Tired and somewhat defeated by the time we reached Leytonstone, we agreed that it might be better if we ran away later on in the year once we had worked out an easier plan. We realised that it would have been more sensible if we had slung the skates over our shoulders and bunked on to a train to Epping from Bethnal Green underground to skate around looking for somewhere to live once we got there. A touch defeated, we went into a police station, our skates clanking on the stone floor, and confessed that we were running away but had changed our minds and would like to be taken back home, in a police car.

'The fing is,' said Margaret, 'our mums and dads might go out searching wiv the neighbours or report us missing to Scotland Yard and at the Bethnal Green station.'

'I'll be in a lot of trouble wiv my dad if I don't get back sthoon. By police car,' said I.

'And we definitely will be in trouble if Scotland Yard

come out searching for us,' insisted Margaret. 'Especially if they put it on the news on the wireless.'

I could see that the officer behind the desk was listening intently to all we were telling him and felt sure that a ride home was on the cards. I was getting quite excited at the thought of it.

The policeman pursed his lips and looked from me to Margaret and spoke very quietly as he leaned over the station desk and looked down at our feet. 'And you skated all the way from Bethnal Green, did you?'

'We did,' said Margaret, 'and we could only stop once on the way cos there was only one public bench. I think there should be more than that for tramps coming in from the country. They need somewhere to sleep at night, don't they?'

'All that way?' he said, slowly shaking his head. 'All the way from Bethnal Green?'

We told him we had, each of us expecting to be taken into a room out the back to be given tea and biscuits.

He raised an eyebrow, impressed, and spoke quietly, saying, 'Well then, you can turn around and skate all the way back again, can't you. Just like Dick Whittington.' He then stretched, pulled his shoulders back and started to laugh at us. 'One of you could end up being Mayoress of London.'

We were incensed by his slack attitude and debated the odds as to what they would do to a policeman should it come out that he had turned away two seven-year-old girls who were later murdered or run down by a lorry on the way home, should such a tragedy happen.

Our lips pursed, our old spirit back, we clanked our way out of the station to then weave in and out of people on the pavement, growing more and angry as we skated on one foot, faster than we had done before, our skinny legs working nineteen to the dozen. We finally arrived home completely wiped out and our parents hadn't even noticed we'd been gone, so there was no emotional welcome *and* it was bath night. Something I hated and particularly didn't feel the need for since we had been swimming at the York Hall baths that morning. I didn't want to get into a tub of lukewarm water that had been used before me by my sister Laura.

Once I was in the bathroom, ordered there by Mum, I splashed the bath water about with my hands, washed my face and neck and sat on the edge of the bath and reread a slightly old damp comic left in there. Still disgruntled by our day of failed escape, I pulled the plug out from the bath and read the comic again. As far as anyone knew I had been in the tub for a scrub, dried and dressed myself again.

That was a day of drama and adventure all round, as it turned out. I went outside to play with the other children after my pretend bath and joined in a game of Cowboys and Indians and was so fired up I galloped at speed with one of the boys on my tail, closing in on me. I turned to look over my shoulder, to fire my invisible gun at him, only to see that he was gaining ground and when I faced the front again I collided with a tall metal lamppost to a loud reverberating noise in my head before everything went black. The next thing I knew I was in the arms of a stranger in the porch outside our flat, a cyclist, who happened along on his bike at the exact time of the collision to witness it.

Mum's voice was like a faraway echo as she shouted at the biker, accusing him of running me over. The motley bunch of kids who had shown the gentleman where I lived were rapidly telling Mum that he was innocent. I could only just hear Margaret's voice sounding as if it were coming through a tunnel as she said, 'That's my friend Sally Lipka! You better not 'ave killed 'er!' She hadn't seen what happened but had come outside, having been in for a pee, and seen me carried, limp and lifeless, as one of the boys had yelled to her, 'He's fucking well killed 'er! He ran 'er over wiv 'is fucking bike!'

I heard our street door slam shut and the kind stranger weakly defending himself as he gently laid me down on the sofa. I was semi-conscious and couldn't make out what was going on but could hear Mum accusing the poor soul. And all that the man wanted was to get out of our flat and back to his new bicycle before anyone stole it. He was in the thick of the East End after all was said and done.

I don't remember much of anything after that, until the next morning, when our doctor was calling my name and patting my face. I hadn't been asleep during the night as Mum presumed – I had been drifting in and out of consciousness. When I did try to open my eyes one eyelid slowly lifted but it felt as if it weighed a ton. The other eye was swollen so much that it was shut tight. Fixed shut. My temperature was taken and I could hear the doctor giving Mum a bit of a dressing-down for not calling him in sooner.

When our doctor spoke to me, his voice was full of compassion and this brought tears to my eyes. He held my hand and asked if I felt sick and I couldn't find the energy to tell him I did, so nodded and then closed my good eye. The doctor's voice was rather comforting. He spoke in a hushed voice telling me that he would return once surgery was over. He paid me a few visits during that week because he was concerned that I was sleeping so much. When I looked into a small shaving mirror that my brother Johnny eased into my hand to see that my injured eye was, as Dad had said, just like somebody's swollen bottom but black and blue and not pink I felt quite proud of it. We didn't have a television at that time and so I listened to the wireless to fill the empty silence in our living room during the long days of being in there by myself.

I got to like *The Archers*, laughed at *Hancock's Half Hour* and loved *The Glums* and *The Goon Show*. I was much better on the couch with the company of those people on the wireless than in my bed looking up at the ceiling with one eye in the silence, but I did miss my small bottle of milk I always enjoyed at playtime and my school dinners.

From the couch I could just hear Mum and her friend and neighbour Sarah gossiping in the kitchen. I waited until our neighbour had finished her second cup of tea and gone before I got up from my makeshift bed and went into the kitchen so as to be in the same room as Mum. As usual she was deep in thought so didn't take much notice of my being there, but at least I had gone from one room to another and that made a nice change.

Without turning to look at me as I eased myself down

on to a kitchen chair, Mum, with her back to me at the sink as she washed her work uniform, said, 'Why don't you go out and get some fresh air, Sally? It'll do you good.'

'I would do,' I said, 'but I sthtill feel dizzy and a bit sthick.'

'That's because you need fresh air and exercise. You've hardly got up from the settee since that man laid you there.'

'I know,' I murmured, 'that'sth why I came into the kitchen to sthee you. Isth it becausthe you want to wash the kitchen floor that you want me to go out? Or did you want me to run an errand? Or am I justht in the way?'

Mum didn't answer but kept her back to me as she gazed out of the window, probably wishing she was miles away from the drudgery she had to cope with.

'I sthuppose I'm being a nuisthance,' I said. 'Being around all the time but not well enough to run errandsth or that.'

Still locked in her thoughts, she filled the kettle to make a pot of tea as if she hadn't heard me, so I got up to leave thinking there might be a child in the grounds I could talk to. Someone else who was off school for one reason or another or that our fatherly caretaker might be in grassy area planting bulbs or forking the flowerbeds. I had just got to the street door when Mum called out to me, saying, 'Don't run down the stairs in case you fall!'

Warmed by this, I turned around and went back to the kitchen and stood in the open doorway and said, 'I thought you didn't like me because I'm alwaysth a pestht. But you mustht like me or you wouldn't care if I fell or not.'

Mum, still at the sink, her back to me, looked through the window up at the sky again and said, 'I'd be the one who would have to mop up the blood.'

And that was it. That's all she said. I watched as she then poured a little boiling water into the teapot and waited for her to turn around and smile and say she was joking, but she didn't and I think it was then that I realised she wasn't happy with her life or having to look after me. I went out of our flat and down the two flights of stone stairs to sit deflated on the step that led out of our block.

It was quiet and I could hear dried leaves scraping along as the wind gently blew them about. Nobody else was around – and there was no sign of the friendly Mr and Mrs Weeks. I don't know why, but that was the bleakest, loneliest time in my life. I sat on the step for a while looking at Margaret's house to see if there was a light on inside, but there wasn't. Mrs McGregor wasn't in. There was neither sight nor sound of one living soul. I wanted to go back upstairs to Mum and put my arms around her waist but she wasn't really the cuddling sort.

I had my pack of playing cards in my pocket and was quite good at patience but I wasn't up to it and was just going to go back upstairs and into my bedroom and my Cinderella tea set when I saw our neighbour Milly Cranfield, from the first floor, coming along. She was carrying her shopping bags. She stopped before going into our block once she saw me on the step and smiled down, saying, 'Hello, Sally love. That eye still hurting, is it?'

'It throbsth a bit, Milly,' I said, 'but it'sth all right. I haven't got no one to play wiv or talk to though and I'm not allowed to go to sthchool yet.'

'I should fink not, Sally love. Not wiv that bad eye. Come

on. Come and help me unpack my shopping and I'll see if I've got a drop of Lucozade for yer.'

'No, it'sth all right,' I murmured. 'I'm okay.'

She tousled my hair and smiled warmly down at me, saying, 'You're the prettiest girl in the block even wiv your bad eye. Do you know that?'

'I'm not,' I said. 'I'm sthkinny and my 'air'sth sthtraight and I've got a listhp.'

'Yeah, but what about them lovely blue eyes, eh? And that white hair. Put a fairy dress on and you could go on top of a Christmas tree.'

'And anyway my front tooth'sth not fru properly yet.'

'I can see that,' she said, smiling and giggling. 'Did you put the milk one under your pillow for the tooth fairy?'

'Nar,' I said. 'She never ever comesth anyway. Stho there'sth not really any point.' I pulled my old pack of playing cards from under the baggy sleeve of my cardigan and asked if I could go in with her to play cards.

'If only I 'ad the time, Sally love. Why don't you play flickers instead and get so good at it that you'll beat all the boys next time you play the game wiv 'em?'

'I could do, couldn't I,' I said, squinting up at her. 'That wouldn't burn up too much energy, would it?'

'I doubt it.' She chuckled. 'Is that what the doctor said then? You're to rest?'

'I fink stho. I can't remember. But I feel all right. A bit sthick now and then that'sth all.'

'Well, I'll tell you what,' she said. 'I'll go indoors and dump these bags and then fetch you a glass of Lucozade. Wot about that then?'

'Yeah,' I said, smiling. 'That would be good.'

So, our sunny neighbour with the hour-glass figure who had three children of her own lifted my spirits as she had done in the past at one time or another. With her short, soft, wavy blonde hair she had always been like a ray of sunshine and a mother figure to all the kids in our block. She had a smile to spare whether she was polishing her windowpanes or watering the flowers in her window box. The inside of her flat reflected her personality too – light, bright and cheerful and always smelling of lavender polish. Her husband, Arthur, was a gentleman, tall, slim and kindly, who sat at his sewing machine when not at work, fashioning matching coats and frocks for his three daughters. They were an unassuming, kindly couple.

I did practise spinning my cards from two fingers against a brick wall and became so involved that I forgot about everything else until I heard Mum calling me from our balcony on the second floor. I wasn't sure what she wanted so looked up at her and waited and I could see that she was waving me up and it looked as if she might be smiling. Mum could be straight-faced at times, it was true, but then, as she had told us, she was born for a better life than living in a council flat, washing up with water sprinkled with soda crystals to get the dishes clean before Fairy washing-up liquid became part and parcel of the kitchen sink. She told me to go back and rest on the settee and gave me a cup of weak tea and I felt loved again.

Drying sheets, shirts and our clothes before ironing must have been a bit much for a beautiful young-at-heart mother in her thirties to cope with. Mum was always at her happiest when dressed up, wearing red lipstick and a little powder, for a Saturday night out with Dad. Arm in arm, their backs straight, their heads held high, they went out to meet up with friends and family for a social evening. My parents loved dancing and because Mum was so ravishing, with her thick, dark wavy hair, deep brown eyes and natural tanned skin, the men, from what I heard, could hardly take their eyes off her. This caused trouble with Dad of course, but then he was just as bad when it came to flirting. Tall, broad and good-looking with fair hair and the bluest of eyes, the women were drawn to him. They were a match for each other any day of the week.

I can still hear the crashing sounds inside my head from when they returned late on a Saturday night from one of the dockers dances, after Mum had apparently waltzed romantically around the floor once too often with the same partner who happened to be very handsome. A furious row broke out over jealousy with Dad giving her a bit of a hiding and her giving as good back as they fought their way up and down the passage while we lay in bed listening and waiting for it to go quiet. They would then take a breather, having exhausted themselves, just before laughter from both of them could be heard. Not long after this, the squeaking of their bed springs meant that we could all go to sleep because all was well.

The next morning after one of their Saturday nights out we would wake to the delicious smell of sizzling bacon and knew that it would be Dad frying Mum a nice breakfast. Mum enjoyed those few times of being Lady Muck for a morning, while Dad cooked for her, and who wouldn't?

Sitting up in her warm bed eating her eggs and bacon with Dad still on the back foot. In a tiny way, I suppose she was ahead of her time when it came to the emancipation of women.

On those rare Sundays, after a blazing row, there was usually a nice atmosphere at home even though Mum might sport a bruised eye and Dad's face might be scratched. We kids weren't worried so long as love was back in the air and we could have our Sunday dinner in peace. In the afternoons, Billy, Johnny, Laura and I would play cards, I Spy, or a board game, while Mum and Dad had their Sunday afternoon two-hour nap in their bedroom. The following morning, a Monday, things would go back to normal with Dad up at the crack of dawn and out to work and my sister and I rummaging through the linen cupboard, where dry, unironed laundry was kept. We could always find ourselves something to wear for school and the creases didn't bother me. But Laura, being a neat person, began to iron her own things at a young age. If I could be warm in the winter and cool in the summer I didn't give a toss about my appearance – I was hardly living in an area where I would be teased over what I wore or how I looked. Most of us were in the same boat.

And from what I was to soon learn there was going to be another one of us in the Lipka boat. I had been told nothing about where babies came from so hadn't taken any notice of the fact that Mum was growing a belly. Being pregnant hadn't stopped her from working or looking glamorous, so there was no clue there to anything being different. She simply rested her ice-cream tray on her bump.

So I was in for a big surprise. It was, though, another of those times when I was poorly, resting on the settee in the living room suffering from recurring mumps and swoollen glands. I hadn't even reached my seventh birthday so the birth of a baby was the last thing on my mind.

I was lying on the sofa in the front room with a thin blanket over me waiting for my medication to work and feeling a little drowsy, and couldn't help wondering if something odd was going on. Our neighbour Sarah Damps had been coming and going all day long and so had a visiting nurse in a dark blue outfit. More importantly, Mum had been in bed all day and yet when I asked the nurse if she was ill, I was told that she wasn't. I hadn't paid too much attention at first when the midwife person paid a visit around ten o'clock in the morning, but with more toing and froing of women, our neighbour and my godmother, Aunt Sarah, popping in, I was beginning to wonder if Mum was dying in her bedroom as I lay on the settee.

Mum hadn't been one for cuddling me but she was still my world. I had a bandage around my head with poultice padding against my swollen neck and face and although it still hurt I was anxious to get up and go and see her in the bedroom, which no one had suggested, not even my nan when she came on her flying visit. She had popped her head round the door and asked if I was all right and that was it. She and my aunt were gone like the wind.

I got out of my makeshift bed and waited for the midwife to come in and take a look at me, as she had been doing, intending to ask her if I could go in to see Mum but she popped her head around the open door, smiling broadly, and said, 'Come and have a look at your baby brother, Sally.'

Baby brother? I thought she was mental. 'I've only got big brothersth, I told her. 'Billy and Johnny.'

'Well, now you've got another one to add to your list and he's beautiful.'

Peering at her I said, 'I fink you've come into the wrong flat. The woman next door might have had a baby, I don't know. But not my mum.'

The midwife held out a hand, saying, 'Come on, sweetheart. Come and say hello to the baby and to your mother.' She then pushed sweaty strands of hair off my flushed face and laid her cool fingers against my forehead and raised an eyebrow as she gently smiled. 'Well done, you, for resting all week. Your temperature is back to normal.'

Now I knew this was a good sign, because it was part and parcel of my ongoing complaint from as far back as I could remember, so if she could be right about that, maybe she was right about everything and there really was a baby in the bedroom? 'Did Mum sthay it wasth all right for me to get up off the couch then?'

The nurse nodded slowly and then placed a finger behind her ear and whispered, 'Listen.'

'Listhten to wot?' I whispered back.

'Just listen, Sally.'

So I did and that's when I heard a baby cry out. I was over the moon. 'Did sthomeone leave a baby on our doorsthtep?' I asked, ever hopeful.

'No,' said the midwife kindly. 'Come on into the bedroom and your mummy will show you the new baby brother that you've got.' She held out her hand again, coaxing me with a gentle smile. 'Come on, dear, there's no need to be frightened.'

I walked along the passage with her holding my hand, unsure as to what was going on because it had gone quiet again. Peeping around the bedroom door I saw that Mum was sitting up, propped against pillows in her bed with a bundle wrapped in white against her breast. I didn't know whether I was supposed to be in there or not because she didn't look up at me, so I went over to her chest of drawers, and looked at the midwife's utensils. I glanced sideways at Mum and the white bundle in her arms.

When she pulled her breast away from it and tidied her pink bed-jacket I couldn't believe what I saw. There was a tiny face of a baby with a mass of black hair sticking up from his head. I tried not to laugh because it hurt my glands, but I was overjoyed. I really did have a baby brother! A beautiful boy with dark blue eyes! Mum looked very tired and only just managed to smile faintly at me.

'Don't be shy, Sally,' said the nurse, 'say hello to your brother, Albert. Albert Henry James.'

I glanced up at her and slowly shook my head, saying, 'Albert?'

'That's right, dear. That's his name.'

'I fink we might wanna call 'im summink elsthe,' said I. Anything else but that old-fashioned name, is what I thought.

'Really?' said the nurse, with one eye on my mother. 'But a baby with the name of a prince is a bit special, isn't it?'

I looked at the baby with the name of a prince and

vowed that I wouldn't ever call him by it. The nurse asked if I wanted to hold Albert and this took me aback. 'I'm too young,' I said, 'and I'm ill.'

'Oh, you don't have to worry about that. The baby won't catch your swollen glands.' She smiled. 'You haven't got an infection, dear, so it's perfectly all right. Yours isn't an ailment that spreads from one person to another.' How right she was. It was many years later that I discovered that there lay the tiniest seed of a growing tumour in my lymph gland.

I was pleased about not having an infection then, of course, but I still wasn't sure what Mum would think about my holding the Albert. I glanced at her to see what she thought about it but her head was resting back on the pillows, her eyes closed.

I sat on the edge of the bed and lifted my bare feet up on to it to rest back as the nurse carefully placed the sleepy bundle into my arms. 'There. Now then, isn't he a little treasure, Sally? He doesn't look a bit like you but he's your very own little baby brother.'

'He'sth got black hair like Mum,' I said. 'None of my brothersth or my sthisthter 'ave got white hair like me. But that'sth probably becausthe I'm a bloody German.'

The midwife burst out laughing and then said, 'I shouldn't say that in front of your dad if I were you.'

I heard Mum groan, so peered at her face to make sure it was all right my being there but she slid down under the covers and closed her eyes. I gazed into the tiny baby's face and said, 'Hello, Albert Lipka. You wait till Margaret stheesth you.' It was like holding a real live doll.

When my best friend came home from school that day,

I was waiting on our balcony and directly she appeared I waved her up with urgency. My poultice bandage was still wrapped around my face from head to chin so I couldn't manage to shout but she saw me and was peering up at the balcony, puzzled. I urged her to come straight away.

Waiting for her at the top of the stairs, I was unable to contain my excitement. 'We've got a baby to look after!' I said. 'And it'sth a boy called Albert and it'sth got loadsth of black hair sthticking up.'

'Where did you get it from, Sal?' she said, sitting down on the stone stairs, worried. 'You didn't take it from outside a shop, did yer?'

'No, of course I never! Mum had a baby while you were at sthchool!' I sat down next to her and couldn't stop myself from giggling I was so happy.

Margaret looked all thoughtful and then slowly nodded her head. 'So that's why your mum's been fat, Sal. She was expecting to 'ave a baby. I fink she should 'ave told us. We know where babies come from.'

'No, we don't!'

'They crawl out of your vagina. My sister said.'

'What vagina?'

'The place where babies live till they're ready to come out. I've never seen one but I did ask Julie about it and it's at the bottom of us.'

'What – in our feet?'

'I don't fink so, Sal. How could it be? Perhaps it's somefing that grows when you're a lady. A grown-up?'

'Like hairsth under the armpit that your sthistersth are alwaysth shaving off?'

'Somefing like that, yeah.'

'But how did the Albert get into the fingamajig in the firstht place? That'sth wot I wanna know? Did he crawl up there? And if he did – why? It couldn't have bin very nice, could it?'

'No,' said Margaret, slowly shaking her head. 'I'll 'ave to ask my sister Julie when she comes in from work. She knows about most fings cos she's the eldest of us girls.'

'What if your mum'sth got one up there? We could have two babies to wheel around in our pram with sthtring for a handle, couldn't we?'

'I'll ask 'er, Sal, but I don't fink she can 'ave, cos she's not fat, is she? And your mum was before it came out. Anyway, we can share Albert. Take him wiv us when we go carol singing round the pubs. We'd get more money wiv 'im in our pram.'

'We'd 'ave to share between the three of usth though, eh?'

'Course we would, but he wouldn't get as much as us, cos he can't sing yet.'

'Wot if he criesth?' I said, already concerned for my sibling.

'Even better. They'd pay us quicker to go away.'

'Coursthe they would.' I grinned. 'You're not as fick as you stheem, are yer?'

Giving me her Catholic look, she narrowed her eyes and said, 'I'm intelligent, *actually*.' And then, 'So your mum is definitely gonna keep 'im?'

'Coursthe she is! We wouldn't give a baby away, Margaret McGregor!'

'I never said you would, Sally Lipka! How could you say such a fing?'

My best friend then flounced off down the stairs and left me to myself. I rushed inside our flat to ask the nurse if Margaret could come in and she thought that would be fine, but only one friend and only for a minute. So poultice and bandage or not, I screamed out for Margaret over the balcony for her to come up and see Albert. She was back in a flash, her cheeks flushed, and her big brown eyes sparkling. 'What's happened?' she said. 'Has another baby come out? Are there two of them?'

'No. But you're allowed to come and sthee it. Sthee Albert the newborn baby! The nursthe justht sthaid stho!'

Holding hands and quietly giggling, the pair of us went cautiously into Mum's bedroom to see that the baby was sucking at her breast and he had his eyes open. Mum then gently pulled her teat away from his mouth and smiled at him and then at us and she seemed like a different person. All soft and cuddly.

'That's it, you two,' said the nurse, smiling at them. 'Mother and baby need to have a sleep now. Why don't you go back into the living room, Sally, with your friend, and rest?'

'I will in a minute,' I said. 'I'm justht gonna sthee Margaret to the sthtairs. Isth that all right?'

'I should think so. But only five more minutes, eh?'

'I've gotta go in for my tea anyway,' said Margaret, all angelic, the good Catholic that she was.

We were beside ourselves once outside and on our own again. We sat on the stairs and planned the best way of protecting Albert when we took him in our pram to the shops. We eventually came up with the obvious. One of us could wait outside guarding him against kidnappers while the other was inside getting the errands.

Mrs McGregor, a week later, with a cigarette in the corner of her mouth, roared with laughter when Margaret asked if she would think about having a baby for us. 'No thank you,' she said. 'You two are enough to cope with.' She then said she was past all of that and so should my mother be. I thought it was a shame because I spent a lot of time in Margaret's house and it would have been nice if we had a little girl to go with the little boy.

Mum, Dad, my sister Laura and my brothers and I were all so taken with the new baby. It wasn't until the visits of the aunts, uncles and friends came to an end that life went back to normal and I wasn't too sorry. It was a strange spell in my life because I was forever being told by my relations that I was no longer the baby and that I was going to have my nose put out of joint.

Ours wasn't usually a home where hospitality waved its flag. Mum was always too busy to have her sisters-in-law coming round for cups of tea and a natter, so on the one hand it made a nice change with everyone coming and going and on the other it was all a bit too busy compared to what I was used to. I did happen to overhear, whether I was meant to or not, one neighbour say, while chin-wagging on the stairs to another neighbour in our flats, 'Anyone would think this was 'er first. Pity the parents didn't make the same fuss over that poor little cow.' Meaning me. My feisty spirit, which had lain fairly dormant when it came to other adults who weren't family members, crept to the fore and I wanted to tell them they were fucking old cows and to shut up. But I didn't. I clenched my teeth instead. It was *my* mum the cows were criticising after all was said and done. I called them both nosey old bastards under my breath.

Throughout this period of a new screaming baby in the home it was easier for me to be out of the way so I spent a fair bit of time in Margaret's house, which her parents had been lucky enough to get the key to when the estate was brand-new. Margaret's Uncle Dan had been working on the site when it was being built and had given her dad the nod to get in quick before all the cottages were taken. Their kitchen was bigger than ours with a table to sit six with a thick plastic flowery tablecloth that could be wiped over with a damp cloth, which was just as well because when her family were all out at work and we weren't at school we made toffee in the kitchen. We always ended up with sweet goo but ate it as if it were a delicacy and then let Damby, the overgrown black-haired curly poodle, who was never clipped, lick the sticky dish clean to hide the evidence. The saucepan would always give us away though. Margaret's mother saw only the back of our skinny legs disappearing out of the street door when she came home from work to find her kitchen smelling of smoke and burned sugar.

It was in Margaret's house that I first saw the miracle of the vacuum cleaner. Her working sisters and brother had clubbed together to buy the best present a housewife at that time could have wished for. I was there soon after its arrival and Margaret and I took it in turns to drag the Hoover from room to room sucking dust and Damby's curled-up dog hairs into its pouting bag. The house was spick and span for a week until we got bored with it and went back to playing in the streets. My sister Laura would have loved us to have one of those modern machines because, unlike me, she was more of a home girl, clean, neat and tidy and helpful around the house, while I was all over the place and mucked around in our grounds or on our green to one side of our flats.

It was there, on our green, that I had the experience that, after the scene in the cinema with the leering man, I knew deep down could happen again if I wasn't careful. I had been playing cartwheels on the grass with Margaret and at first I hadn't taken much notice of a man sitting on his bike, watching us. It was only when she went in for her tea and I was by myself that the stranger called out to me and then beckoned me over. He seemed quite ordinary, about thirty perhaps, slim and with fair hair combed back. He wore a belted gabardine mac and bicycle clips at the bottom of his trousers, and seemed pleasant and friendly when he told me that he was thinking about moving on to our estate because he thought it a decent place to live. He liked the fact that it was only a short walk from the park. He asked if I had seen the toffee-apple man that day and wanted to know if I liked toffee-apples. I shouldn't think that there were many of us children who didn't like them and even though little warning bells were ringing I didn't turn and run away as I should have done.

Smiling, he winked at me and said, 'Come on then, we'll

go and find 'im. He's probably on his rounds somewhere nearby.'

One voice inside my head was telling me to get away while the other was saying I was being too sensitive. After what seemed like an age of silence the voice of caution won out. 'I've gotta go in for my tea,' I fibbed.

'Shouldn't take long to find him.' The man chuckled. 'He can't be far away. We can take the route through the arches and along the cobbled lane next to the school and if we can't see 'im, we'll go to the sweet shop in Globe Road instead and buy some chocolate to make up for it.'

I knew the shop he mentioned so it felt right. He seemed as if he knew our area so it didn't feel as if I was talking to a stranger. 'I know the shop you mean,' I said, avoiding his eyes, 'but I'm not allowed to go away from the groundsth.'

He looked disappointed and hurt and started to make me feel bad. Gazing down at the floor, he sighed and then said, 'Well, if you like toffee-apples but you won't come with me it must mean that you don't like me.'

I told him that I did like him and this brought the smile back to his face again. 'Well, let's go then,' he said. 'We know each other now, don't we. I don't make friends easily because I'm a bit shy but I could tell you were different when I was watching you play with your friend.'

'I sthtill can't come wiv you,' I said, a warning voice from deep inside screaming at me to run away. 'Got to tell Margaret.'

'Come on. Up you get. On to my crossbar. Won't take ten minutes to buy toffee-apples or chocolate. We'll be back in no time with some for your friend as well. She'll be outside playing again by the time we get back.'

It didn't stop there. He went on and on, friendly and persuasive, making me feel guilty for not trusting him and he had such a lonesome look about him. As if he had nobody in the world to talk to. 'I saw some lads playing football in the square,' he said, sighing. 'I might go and see if they want me to referee a proper match for them. They looked friendly. I don't know many people. Sometimes it's nice to talk to people, don't you think?'

He carried on saying how much he liked our estate and would probably move in one day and might even take a position at one of the schools. He said he was a teacher. He wore me down so much that I eventually agreed to get on his bike and go with him through the arches. I was just about to climb on to the crossbar when the familiar voice of Milly from the first floor pierced through the air. She was strolling out from under the arches towards the flats when she spotted us talking and sharply called out to me. The stranger immediately rode away in the opposite direction as she made her way towards me, demanding in a motherly way to know if I had been going to get on the bike. I said I was and pleaded with her not to tell Mum or Dad.

She made a promise and kept to it, so I escaped an early night to bed for talking to a stranger and possibly a heavy hand to the leg from Dad should I have argued furiously that it wasn't fair to be punished for it, which I probably would have done. I more or less pushed the incident to the back of my mind, but one thing I never forgot was that

My dad when young, tall and blond with his brother, known as John Lisbon-Wood, who was killed in the Second World War.

A rare photo of my great uncle Bill and my second cousins outside Aunt Polly's house in Stepney.

A school photo of my friend Margaret, fourth from the left in the second row
from the front. Her teacher's name was Miss Dickybird.

Margaret hugging her new puppy
Damby outside our block of flats and
our favourite neighbour, Irene, getting
in on the shot.

Margaret all dressed up and
ready to parade in the
Catholic procession.

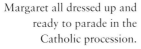

My adorable little brothers at Southend-on-Sea.

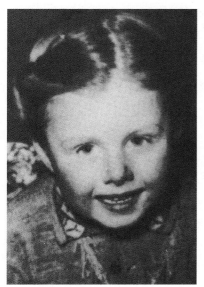

Me, at the age of four, when the
photographer came to school . . .

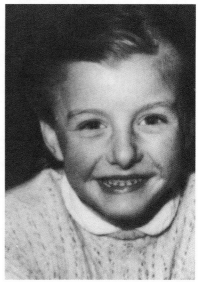

And my sister Laura, aged six,
on the same occasion.

I'm about ten in this shot, on holiday in Kent for hop picking.

Mum, Dad, and brothers Billy and Johnny enjoying life in Kent. Billy has cracked a joke and Johnny is trying not to laugh.

Family picture, hop picking. My sister Laura, leaning forwards with hops in her hand, in front of Aunt Polly and the Kentish measure-man. My little brother Albert and cousin Richard are next to him. My brother Billy is the tall man right in the centre of the back row.

Our proud netball team. We had just won the East London netball trophy for the third year in a row. Back from left to right: Barbara Witchels, Sally Lipka (me), Ruth Miles, Kathy James. Front left to right: Marian Aiken, Valerie Skinner, Irene Harris.

Me at thirteen in between brother Johnny and his friend, who I had a crush on.

Johnny's wedding. My sister Laura is in the car with our niece Lorraine, Billy's daughter, beside her. I am on the left next to the bride's sister Cathy – the one with the hourglass figure.

Johnny and Margo with best man Billy holding his little girl's hand. I am wearing T-bar shoes, which I adored.

Us girls having a whale of a time on the Costa Brava. I am at the bottom taking the weight and not giving a toss that I had forged my dad's name on my very first passport to get there.

We all dressed up to impress the sexy Spanish waiters. I can't remember too clearly but I think we all pulled that night. Mine was the most handsome and romantic, though.

Fantastic B&B weekend in cheap digs, Clacton-on-Sea. It was the infamous Bank Holiday when the Mods on their scooters battled with the Rockers clad in black leather. Us girls screamed with passion to the live band playing on the pier – Jerry and the Pacemakers.

The passport photo for my first, secret holiday abroad, which inspired the photographer in Islington to ask if I might be interested in modelling for him. I foolishly turned him down, thinking the worst of the innocent soul. I was sixteen at the time and had just started my first job.

our neighbour kept her word and didn't tell my parents. I decided not to tell my sister Laura about it, despite our pact, because the man had left me feeling as if I had done something wrong and that I was to blame; that I had invited trouble. I didn't even tell Margaret at first and when I did she went quiet and then said we had to be more careful in the future.

I didn't have nightmares over that man the way I had done over the fat man in the cinema but I was frightened to go under the arches in the dark afterwards. The problem was that it was en route to the nearest pub and Dad sometimes sent me out late at night for cigarettes just before closing time, with no time for me to go to the pub that was a little further away but in a more lit-up area. So often I had no other choice than to scoot through the dark on the errand.

The landlady, a tall thin blonde woman, would stand at the pub door and watch over me as I ran back home along the badly lit cobbled turning before I went through the arches. She told me more than once that I was to tell my father not to send me out at that time of night. I mentioned it once and he gave me a look that spoke volumes. I was his daughter and not the publican's and he knew what was best.

But even though I did have a few close encounters with men on the prowl for children, I wasn't taken away and murdered by a stranger as one of the girls in our neighbourhood had been. The terrible news of our little Kim Roberts, who often played in our grounds, made the headlines nationwide and sent shock waves through the whole country. Kim's lovely grandparents, friendly and warm, lived in our block of flats and no words could describe what the entire family suffered back in those dark days and there was nothing anyone could do to help them through it. Nothing.

Although most of us kids practically lived on the streets, playing in safety, we did look out for each other when it came to strangers but I guess no other kids were around for Kim on that day. I was one of the lucky ones when Milly Cranfield happened to be coming along with her shopping bag. But I was not off the hook. There was more to come. One wintry evening when Mum was working and Dad looking after baby Albert with Laura helping, I had been sent out as usual to get a separate shilling in case the electric meter should run down and leave us without light. Perfectly normal and not a problem because there was one person I could always be sure would let me have a shilling. This was a man who lived with his aged mother in a block close by to ours. He kept a small box filled with shillings and sixpenny bits and never minded my knocking on the door of his flat.

I was always a touch wary of his chummy nature and I wasn't sure why, but even so the lure of knowing for certain that I would get a shilling bit was a far better option than going door to door when it was dark and cold. On this occasion, when I suppose I was seven or eight, I knocked on the door and when he opened it I could hardly miss the fact that his flies were unbuttoned and his white pants were showing. It might have been a mishap but that happened to be the first time he casually suggested I went inside out of the cold while he searched through his jar of coins for a shilling bit. Alarm bells rang because usually he brought the jar to the porch where light from his passage glowed and let me take out the coin. I politely refused to go inside and felt my cheeks beginning to flush. He looked at me and his expression was different to usual. He was studying me with a strange look in his eyes. He finally shrugged and said, 'Wait there then.'

I felt as if I were in a kind of a trap but if I went away it would have been rude and I wouldn't have had Dad's separate shilling. So I stayed on the doorstep. When he returned his trousers were done up and we exchanged coins. I thanked him as if nothing worried me and ran back home never to return. Whenever I saw him after that, I politely smiled and said hello but didn't go to his door again.

A few weeks after the incident he was on the ground floor, about to get into the lift in his block of flats, where a new school mate of mine also happened to live. He held the door open and asked if I was going up. I said I always walked. He asked me why. I said I didn't like lifts. It was a lie and I think he knew it by the expression on his face but at least it ended there. I didn't go back to that block of flats again. There is no doubt in my mind that had I told my father about the mishap of his trousers he would have marched me to the man's door and pulverised someone who could have been totally innocent, without asking questions first. Of course I see this differently now. Any sensible man would not invite an eight-year-old into his home late at night, never mind the trousers undone. No, he had been luring me in with those separate shillings all right.

My third and most frightening brush with danger came

the following spring when a disgustingly rude man stopped me on the stairs of our flats as I was skipping down on a warm sunny evening to knock for Margaret while it was still light. Coming to a turning point between two flights, I was face to face with him and he was exposing himself and masturbating. Obviously I had never seen anything like this before so presumed that he was going to have a pee and had been caught out. Blushing madly, my neck burning, I looked anywhere other than at him as I continued to walk towards him on my way down the stairs and he said, 'Little girl, do you know what the time is?'

I looked into his face pretending I didn't know what was going on below and swallowed against my dry throat as I shook my head.

He smiled as he stepped in front of me, blocking my way, saying, 'Can you go and ask your mum? I need to know what the time is.'

I turned away, eager to go up the stairs and be safe from him but in my panic I suddenly and stupidly blurted, 'Mummy and Daddy'sth not in. They've gone to the picturesth.'

He reached out and gently took my arm and grinned at me while his other hand was busy on his penis. I didn't know what to do because he carried on talking as if things were normal. He asked which cinema they had gone to and what film they were going to see. I eased myself out of his hold and turned to run down the stairs when he pushed his hand up my skirt and tried to grab hold of me. I then ran for all I was worth and kept on running through the dark streets until I got to my grandfather's house.

Uncle Harry answered the door and all I could do was stand there trembling and crying. He swept me up into his arms and carried me downstairs and placed me on the armchair while he poured out a glass of lemonade for me. Once I was calm and told them what had happened all three of my uncles, Harry, Albert and Siddy, made me feel safe. Jackets were then pulled on and they told me we were going for a walk back to our flat and I was to walk ahead, with them following a short distance behind and if the man approached me again they would get him. They were so angry they could hardly speak. This time I didn't care what happened to the stranger. I wanted them to warn him never to come back again. Of course there was no sign of him and if he had seen me coming from where he might have been hiding in the shadows, my tall, broad and irate uncles would have put the fear of God into him whether they were keeping a short distance from me or not.

Once I was seen safely indoors after pulling the key on a string through our letterbox, I promised I wouldn't go out and they left, knowing that my sister would be in any minute with Albert who she had taken with her late that afternoon to a friend's house. I didn't stay indoors though, I went straight over to Margaret and Mrs McGregor insisted that I slept in her house that night. Sharing Margaret's bed, we talked about the incident and others that had happened to us and realised that we really did have to take care because it seemed that there were such types of men everywhere and we were beginning to fear all strangers.

7
Eight Stitches to My Leg

My being the youngest child before Albert came along, Dad sometimes took me with him to the docks when he was off sick from work to see the fellows in the wharf. The dockers at that time were on pitifully small sick pay and it was taken for granted that a man who couldn't work would visit the dockside, with one of his children in tow, to get some help from his colleagues. Those workmates who could only afford to slip less than five shillings into the man's pocket would press a half crown or a two shilling bit into the hand of the child – a sixpence even. The men knew that all coins given would be thrown in with the collection once placed on the kitchen table.

The last time I went with Dad to Canary Wharf was not long after baby Albert came along, when Dad had pulled a muscle in his back while lifting too heavy a load from one of the ships. The atmospheric buzz of the Canary Wharf was magical as were the smiles of red-faced men who were constantly on the move, unloading towering ships which arrived from across the ocean and loading others with cargo outward-bound. Men working long hours in the docks seemed none the worse for carrying heavy crates to and fro, their faces shaded from the hot sun only by the familiar peaked docker's cap.

Bananas, Canary tomatoes and Jersey potatoes were the kind of perks given to the men, and for as long as Dad was well enough to work they were our staple diet. These gratuities went some way to make up for the low wages and hard labour. Dad, tall and broad, striding along the grounds as he came home carrying a crate of fruit or vegetables on his shoulder, gave us all a sense of Christmas in summertime. Thanks to the bravery and determination of dockers prepared to strike over dangerous conditions, things had improved by then but all that came far too late for the grandfather I never knew. Mum told me that she was just fifteen years old when her dad, Grandfather Ambrose, had been involved in a horrible accident while driving a crane in Canary Wharf in the 1930s. Grandfather had told my grandmother and their adult children the day before the accident that the governors in the wharf were overloading cranes dangerously above the limit to cut costs. Sadly, he was proved right. Trapped inside the crane when it toppled over due to the heavy load, there was nothing he could have done to stop it plunging deep into the River Thames. Outrage amongst fellow workers meant that the incident was reported in the national newspapers and at least this publicity, together with the London dockers banding together in anger, did eventually change things for the better, but not in time to save my grandfather, who had only just reached his mid-forties.

On one of the times when Margaret and I went into the docks in Shadwell to visit a Catholic church just before Procession Sunday a spectacular horse-drawn funeral was taking place outside Walter's Funeral Parlour. With the few colourful wreaths of fresh flowers on top and a few draped across the two horses it was all quite regal and the scent of the flowers almost covered the dank smell of the dirt in the gutters. The funeral parlour, with its ornate exterior painted gold, purple and black, was quite mystical to us girls. In the window were two marble statues carrying torches and another figure of a woman in white holding on to a stone cross.

Once the funeral procession moved on we were straight into the undertaker's parlour to ask questions because we wanted to know if girls of our age, eight years old at the time, should we suddenly die, might be buried in the same stately manner. We could see two workmen through an opening into the back room hammering at a coffin who couldn't answer any of our questions while they worked because each of them held a mouthful of nails. So we left them to it and as we walked away I felt a wave of doom spread through my body as if a dark cloud had passed through it. Margaret, sharing the same thought, linked her arm to mine and said, 'Sal, we're gonna be put in a coffin and be buried one day.'

'I know we are, Marg. I was just finking the sthame fing. There'sth no way out of it, isth there?'

'No. It happens to everyone but not at the same time.'

I knew what she was thinking and that was the quietest we had ever been and I don't think we spoke a word all the way home. Everyone that we knew and loved was going to come to the same end and two men would one day be tapping nails into our mum and our dad's coffins. We didn't go back to that part of the river except for when Margaret was in the Catholic procession.

That evening, in my quiet of my room and feeling somewhat subdued, I lay on my bed and, partly to distract myself, turned my attention to something I had been doing more and more recently. Practising words without lisping. My name was the most put into practice. I was getting better at knowing where to place my tongue when using the letter 'S'. I created a whistling sound at first but soon discovered the best way round it. Over and over I would say words beginning with 'S' and eventually the lisp could hardly be noticed. A little cloud lifted from my shoulders. I wasn't the girl with a speech impediment any more.

Mum was back working evening shifts at the picture palace since Albert was almost a year old and being bottle-fed. So we kids were in Dad's charge again and I still seemed to get on the wrong side of him so kept out of the way for most of the time. I did try to change and be a good obedient girl where Dad was concerned but it never lasted long. Domesticity wasn't my thing whereas Laura, my sister, turned out a tastier stew than Mum did but we never let on. For her part, I suppose the fact that I was out more than in must have seemed unfair and got under her skin. We certainly used to argue at times and occasionally a little cat-fight would break out but these were few and far between.

On the evenings when he was in charge, Dad took no notice if we rowed and mostly sat in his armchair by the fire drinking cups of tea. He used to love to listen to the sport on the wireless, especially the boxing, but by then our first television had arrived in our sitting room and this made a big difference. The atmosphere changed immediately. Comedies and shows such as *I Love Lucy* and *Sunday Night at the London Palladium* brought life into our sitting room. Life and laughter.

Mum working at the cinema in the evening meant that Laura or myself walked Albert up and down the passage when he was teething or fretful and us who rocked him off to sleep. We would have walked all through the night with him if necessary and we sometimes put him between us in our bed to spend the night in our room, and in his own way our little brother brought Laura and I closer together because at those times there was a lovely warm sense of affection among the three of us.

I don't recall ever spending much time with Dad but some of the whacks I received when I was in a defiant mood are still etched in my memory. I don't think that Mum realised just how heavy-handed he could be on occasion. There was one incident that sticks in my mind when I refused to be sent from the warm living room to the cold bedroom for daring to refuse to go to the pub and get him ten Weights when I knew that he hadn't run out of cigarettes. I argued my strong case at such times but his counter-reply was always the same: 'I might run out – so do as you're told or go to bed.'

'No, I won't,' was my retort. And then, 'I could get murdered under them arches!' I stormed out of the sitting room and headed for my bed, firmly convinced that I shouldn't have to go out in the dark.

But I got no further than the passage when he came at

me like a lumbering bear, saying, 'If you swear at me again you'll get a good hiding.'

'I'd get one even if I never swore!' was my daring reply. 'And anyway Nan said that you goad me into it. So it's your fault! And I'm not going out to get your fags!'

His hand was heavier that time than it had ever been before and it left its mark. The next morning there was a red hand print on my thigh and I couldn't help limping even though I tried stubbornly not to. It was a Saturday and we were at home and together as a family. The flesh around the hand mark was tight and painful whenever I moved and so the tears welled in my eyes as I limped from my bedroom to the kitchen.

With a creased forehead and a suspicious expression on her face, believing, I suppose, that I was playing the part of an injured tramp, which I did do sometimes, Mum lifted my skirt to see what the matter was, if anything. She gasped when she saw the telltale welt marks in the shape of a hand and looked from my creased and pained face to Dad who at first quietly and gently said, 'I didn't do that.' As if even *he* was appalled by the thought of it.

But, if the hand mark fits and his did, there was nothing else for him to do but fill the tense silence by raising his voice and saying I had deserved to be smacked, that I was a troublemaker, always causing arguments. I remained quiet and passive through it all because I didn't want to give any reason for more trouble. At least all I had on that occasion was the flat of his hand and not the leather belt. Even now an icy-cold sensation shoots through me at the memory of myself curled into a ball on my bed as he, tall and broad, strode closer and I pleaded with him, quietly saying, 'Not the buckle, Dad . . . please, Dad, don't use the buckle end!' That penetrating sting that strikes to the core is something you don't forget too easily.

Worse things happened at sea though – and nearer to home. There was another child at our junior school who suffered far more than I did and for no reason. In the playground at school the children were saying that they were going to do something about the girl who was being repeatedly beaten by her drunken stepfather every time she went home. I followed them once out of curiosity if nothing else and hung back once we arrived at the flats where she lived and watched as she went into the block, like a lamb to the slaughter. She climbed a flight of stairs to the first balcony and once the front door opened and immediately slammed shut again we could hear the muffled drunken shouting begin and her stepfather's hollering was followed by her screams as he knocked her from pillar to post. I looked to the others, who were listening and gazing up at the flat not quite knowing what to do.

I whispered to one of them that we should tell someone but was told by more than one of the children that the girl had made them promise not to say anything because she would only suffer worse things if her stepfather was brought to the attention of the authorities. I had trouble getting off to sleep that night, at odds with myself. It seemed wrong to leave things be, but worse still to cause more trouble for the girl.

When I woke up the next morning my mind was clear

and all doubts gone. I went to school with a fixed determination and privately related all of what I had heard to my teacher who promised not to let on that I was an informer. I don't know what happened after that because such things were always hushed up. Apparently, as I found out later on, her backside, back and her chest were bruised from where he kicked and punched her. She hadn't attended swimming classes because she had handed in a note from home saying that swimming gave her bad nightmares because she feared she would drown. It was all codswallop but her stepfather obviously wrote a convincing letter.

Living in one the nicer parts of the East End I could enjoy the benefits of the local parks and gardens, the Children's Toy Museum and Victoria Park boating lake. Apprehensive though I had been at joining the juniors at John Scurr School, I had been pleasantly surprised on my first day to find the atmosphere warm and that we children were guaranteed a nourishing, tasty, hot meal every day with delicious puddings to follow. Apart from cabbage, greens and boiled fish I ate school dinners with relish and of course, like most children, I longed for those afters: home-baked fruit pies, steamed treacle sponge, spotted dick, apple crumble and custard. Second and third helpings. Those dinner ladies, just like the ones in the infant school, were so generous and sympathetic, but then they would be, they were mostly the mothers of the children attending the school.

Apart from school life, we street kids enjoyed ourselves on our Bancroft housing estate because of the way it was designed, with plenty of play areas and grassy knolls.

Living on the borderline which separated Stepney from Bethnal Green was a bit of a problem because even though the library closer to home was in Bethnal Green Gardens I wasn't allowed membership because our family postal address was Stepney and the Bancroft library was further away and too far to walk in the winter once the nights drew in. En route were dark alleyways and back streets where shadows could play havoc with an overactive mind and a place where shady dealings might operate without anyone taking notice.

The alternative arrangement offered to me was to sit in the silent Reading Rooms of the Bethnal Green library set within beautiful gardens where I could stay as long as I wanted and read whatever I chose to, so long as I didn't take any of the books out. It was a warm place where I could lose myself in other worlds, magical worlds of fantasy. I mostly read Enid Blyton's Famous Five books and discovered books by authors such as Charles Dickens which had been adapted for children and allowed me to easily conjure up a scene which I could slip into and play a part. The setting might be a grand house in the country or a sewer and living with rodents: the least thing could inflame my imagination.

The library became a second home. The smell of worn leather, dusty paper and polished wood was different to anything I knew and the silence had a special sound of its own. I had found a sanctuary where children were treated as if they belonged and where old-timers gathered to read the daily newspapers. Some, mostly the poor and out of work, were there to have a quiet read in the warmth during the winter and be nice and cool in the shade during a scorching hot summer. It was during one of those spells when I was lost in a book that I happened to glance up to see, once again, the mysterious woman who was somehow linked to my grandfather – Rose Lipka. She was coming out of the Reading Room where those who couldn't afford to buy a daily newspaper went to catch up on what was happening at home and abroad. She was wearing an old-fashioned grey two-piece suit with black trim on the collar of the jacket. I smiled at her but she didn't smile back. She turned away and slowly walked out of the library. A childish instinct urged me to go after her but common sense prevailed and I felt that I was bound to see her again in any case.

Margaret hadn't been with me on that day so there was no one to urge me on. The only small difference between myself and my best friend was that she loved to be busy and had an aversion to sitting still for too long except for when she was in church. She would have preferred me to go with her to the outpatients of any of our local hospitals instead of a library, when she would have loved to take temperatures, wrap bandages around bald-headed men and push old women in wheelchairs from one whistle-stop treatment room to another.

I was not the only one of us who loved to drift into a world of fantasy though; Margaret loved to seek out the unknown but she preferred for us to make our own adventure in the real world rather than read about it in a story-book as I tended to do. She wanted us to explore the paths other children dared not tread which, of course, I was more than happy to go along with. Dirty old unloved houses in the back streets were some of our favourite places. Properties which, for one reason or another, during our childhood were boarded up and running alive with vermin – which scurried away once we arrived.

We carried, dragged, or shoved bits of old furniture from one derelict house or shop to another in order to create a makeshift home in one room where we would light an assortment of partly burned white candles, which previous inhabitants had left behind. We burned them whether it was dusk or daytime because we needed to see clearly as we stepped over broken floorboards and tentatively climbed rickety old stairs. We might well have broken a bone or two had we not had the flickering glow of that free light.

That Easter holiday we had moved out of one old damaged house into another on a site just off Cambridge Heath Road and were making one of the rooms upstairs of a two-up, two-down our snug. We loved sitting by a cracked window to watch people coming and going outside. We were carrying up one of our best finds, a small mangy old sofa that we thought we could make look nice by throwing one of Margaret's brother's army blankets over it. Unfortunately, the sofa was heavier than we first thought and awkward to manoeuvre, especially once we were halfway up the narrow winding staircase. We were coming up to our eleventh birthdays by then, both of us still skinny, and my thin arms were unable to take the weight and so the back end, which I was gripping, slipped. The rusty old metal plate on the base hit my shin bone and gouged a hole. A grotesque open wound appeared but at first it neither hurt nor bled and so we continued our struggle to get our wonderful find to the top of the stairs and into what was to become the best of all our derelict homes.

We spent all afternoon hunting out enough bits and pieces to turn the room into a proper snug, even taking down the old filthy lace curtains which hung sadly at a small grimy window and we washed them in the back yard under an old-fashioned round brass tap, from which light brown water flowed before dwindling to a trickle. We re-hung our lace drapes once they were more or less dry and so, with our pretty curtains, our ancient rug on the floor and our bits of furniture, we were in seventh heaven, albeit a damp and smelly one. But then the injury to my leg began to throb and tingle. Margaret, eager to use her nursing skills, took a look at it and wound her quite clean handkerchief round my shin to stop an infection from getting in. Even though the wound only wept a little watery blood she insisted that we had to go straight away to our local doctor's surgery, next door to the Forester's cinema, where at that exact time Mum was working her afternoon shift.

Still feeling pretty cheerful and with our minds and conversation on how many stitches I might be given, we crossed the Cambridge Heath Road, without taking proper care and attention and only just managed to jump out of the way of an oncoming truck. I somehow managed to bang the heel of my other foot which hurt far more than the cut did. We slipped into the waiting room of the surgery, grubby, hungry and smelling of must, and sat down on a long wooden bench to wait our turn as watery blood continued to seep through the well-intentioned bandage.

Margaret spotted this and, becoming increasingly concerned, she whispered to me that she ought to take another look at my injury. I carefully removed her handkerchief to the sound of gasps from other patients as they saw the gaping slash and my shinbone shining through. It was mutually agreed that I should jump the queue and go in next to see the doctor. One Jewish woman fanned another who hadn't managed to get her smelling salts out of her handbag in time.

I just thought they were a little too eager to see the back of us and couldn't understand why. When the door into the surgery opened and Dr Brynberg said, 'Who's next?' he picked up on the silence and followed the traumatised gaze of the others. Even he, who had seen plenty of bloodshed in his surgery, was taken aback. I had shocked someone who had cared for me since I was born. He knew me quite well by then. The doctor beckoned me in, closed the door behind us and quietly asked where my mother was. I told him that she was on duty next door, in the picture palace. He cleaned my wound and put on a temporary dressing and told me that Margaret had done well but I was to go immediately to Mum and that she was to take me to accident and emergency at the nearby London Hospital, no more than a fifteen-minute walk away.

By then I was beginning to feel quite special, enjoying the drama, and still felt no pain in the leg. It felt numb and strange but that was all. We went into the foyer of the picture palace with a certain air of authority. My nurse Margaret was insisting that my mother be called from her duties immediately because we had an emergency on our hands. The manager raised an eyebrow as he haughtily observed my skinny friend with the long matted ringlets and dirt under her nails but Margaret simply pursed her lips and stared him out brazenly. He shuddered and pulled a strange face as he waved us in and told us to get one of the usherettes to show us to the staff room. I knew exactly where it was since we had sneaked in there a few times before.

Mum arrived looking as beautiful as Lana Turner in her smart white and navy uniform with pert little hat. She glanced at me, pulled back the temporary dressing and shuddered the way her manager had. 'Why can't you two stay out of filthy bombed ruins,' she said. 'Don't you think I've got enough to worry about, without all of this.'

'We was only making a nice place that we could go to so as not to be in anyone's way,' said Margaret, a touch defiantly.

'You've got a garden,' said Mum. 'Sit in that while the weather's nice.' She then pulled her purse from her pocket and gave me fourpence for our bus fare to the hospital and said, 'Get yourself straight home after they've bandaged that leg and *stay* there. You're nothing but trouble – both of you!'

Once outside we decided that taking a bus would be a waste of money since I could walk all right and apart from the strange throbbing in the leg I felt okay. We bought finger-sucking sherbet with the money instead and enjoyed this unexpected treat as we slowly walked through the back streets to the London Hospital.

Going up the wide steps I felt rather grown up. We found

our way to the waiting room and took off our grubby and somewhat threadbare coats, mine a light blue with the hem hanging down in places and buttons missing and Margaret's more or less the same, except that hers was red and fading. It was very warm inside the waiting room where we sat with grown-ups who had cut themselves or broken a bone. The drunks from the local men's hostel in Whitechapel had taken the bench at the back and looked comical with their rag bandages wrapped around their bloody head wounds or up against a punched nose. They seemed to be talking in another language, their words running into each other.

I removed the dressing from my leg so that all those around me could see just how bad things were beneath it and then passed over the brown envelope from the GP to the receptionist. A few minutes later my name was called. I had jumped the queue without trying and glanced nervously at the others waiting to see if I was about to be shouted at. Instead of which, I found compassion in people's eyes. Everyone was looking at me with a sorry smile. I limped towards the treatment room to the sound of a woman who was expressing her feelings loudly, saying, 'Talk about Orphan Annie.'

I didn't think much of that so gave her a sideways look to kill as I hobbled away. When the word 'neglect' was mentioned about these sorts of circumstances, I was fiercely defensive. I had never known any different so had nothing to compare my life with and I was used to just getting on with it. If I couldn't repair myself I knew that a nurse or a doctor could. It was that simple. The brisk nurse with no expression on her face glanced at my leg and then looked me in the eye, saying, 'You're limping on the wrong foot.'

I knew that she was hinting that I was playing for sympathy so looked back at her and curled my lip before saying, 'I nearly got run over and hurt my heel on *that* foot after it 'appened.' I used every bit of willpower not to tell her to fuck off and that I was no attention-seeker. I might have looked like Orphan Annie but I had more mettle than that. I gave her a black look and left it there. Other people weren't being mealy-mouthed but sympathetic so I could put up with one bruised apple in the bowl.

The second hiccup came when the nurse told Margaret that she was not allowed into the treatment room with me and that she couldn't watch while the skin on my shin was being sewn together again. Of course Margaret was none too pleased because she wanted to be in there to support me and especially since the room smelled of antiseptic, the essence being fragrant scent to her nose. Another kind and caring assistant nurse obliged by leaving the door open, so that the aspiring medical student could observe as a hooked needle was used to stitch my flesh back together. My best friend stopped looking and covered her face with both hands, though, when my screams echoed through the corridors of the London Hospital.

Before the skin could be sewn together again I needed to have an injection close to the wound. Unfortunately, being so skinny there wasn't any flesh over my shin bone and so when the stitching began I could feel it each time the curved needle pierced the skin and a knot was tied and cut, after each of the eight stitches. It was a wonder I hadn't broken every finger of the nurse's hand as I clenched and screamed. Once the local anaesthetic began to take effect it wasn't quite so painful and I looked through the open doorway to Margaret for sympathy and support, but couldn't see her. I wondered if she had been sent away by a fierce matron but then I saw her striding past, her hands covering her face as she cried. A few seconds later she was walking back again, still crying, her hands now over her ears, unable to bear any more shrill cries of torture from me. Everyone inside the hospital must have heard but I was Margaret's best and closest friend and she was suffering it with me just as I would have done if she had been on that table.

Once the stitching was over the nursed asked, in a whisper, if I wanted the needle and remaining thick black thread as a memento of a time when I was so young and so brave. I didn't want to think about it ever again, never mind keeping it as a reminder. Margaret might have done but I kept that from her otherwise she might have wanted to go back and retrieve it, collecting a few other bits and bobs from the nurse while she was at it.

Limping out of the hospital, a touch weak at the knees, a proper neat bandage on my leg, I could see that Margaret's eyes were puffy and red where she had been crying while trying so hard to be brave. I slipped my arm into hers and squeezed it. 'It's all right, Marg,' I said. 'It don't hurt me no more. I can't feel nuffing under the bandage. It's all numb.'

'I'm not finking about that, Sal,' she said, her bottom lip

curling under again. 'It's when you screamed out. It echoed right fru the hospital. Some of them women in the waiting area was crying and pressing their 'ands against their ears.'

'I didn't know I was that loud,' I said, looking left and then right before we crossed the busy Whitechapel Road. 'You'd better watch me carefully on the way 'ome though, in case I collapse.'

Her brown eyes wide, she looked at me in horror. 'You don't feel faint, do yer?'

'No,' I said, 'but I might, mightn't I?'

'Your mum should 'ave come wiv us, you know. That's wot the matron said while they was sewing up yer leg. I told 'er that we was neglected and she nodded 'er head as if she 'ad guessed that already. Then she sent me in the ladies lav to give my 'ands a good scrub. Bloomin' cheek. I did it though so as not to spread germs. I told Matron they'd better not cut your leg off from where it split open, while I was gone.'

'They wouldn't 'ave done that,' I said, icy cold at the thought of it. 'Them nurses were kind to me, Marg. One gripped my 'and while the lady doctor pushed the needle and thread in. Eight times altogether. Eight stitches and all knotted separately.'

Margaret broke into tears again and so we comforted each other for the rest of the way home. I described all that had happened in the treatment room, and how, even though I screamed, I never shed a tear, telling her that the nurse thought that it was from shock and not mettle. I had every right to boast – I screamed loud enough to bring the hospital to the ground. But I hadn't cried one tear.

'It was nine stitches, Sal,' said Margaret as we passed the pie and mash shop in Cambridge Heath Road and drank in the lovely baking smell. 'I know that cos that's 'ow many times you screamed.'

'No, it was eight,' I told her. 'Eight stitches and eight knots. The extra scream was when the needle went in before the stitches. The needle to make it go numb that didn't work. One of the nurses said my leg was all skin and bone wiv no flesh to inject. Fucking cheek.'

'People are always saying we're skin and bone but we're not as skinny as Keyhole Kate in the comic, are we?'

'I don't know,' I said. 'We could be. But it's nobody else's business anyway.'

We talked about all that happened in detail as we walked home through the back streets we knew like the back of our hands. Two girls, nearly eleven, one with long, unwashed, dead straight white hair and one with black, filthy, long curly locks, discussing whether it was a good idea or not for Margaret to be a nurse one day. She said she was going to have to think twice about it.

I had more than my fair share of cuts, knocks and narrow escapes during my childhood. There was one incident that I had brought upon myself, which caused the fire brigade to come out to my rescue. Margaret and I had been in the Bethnal Green gardens and it was one of those lazy Saturdays when the springtime sun was shining and the whole day stretched deliciously before us with nothing much to do. I suppose we were bored because I can't think of any other reason why I would have deliberately and slowly squeezed and eased my head through the park railings, copying a character from the *Beano* or *Dandy* comic. It started as fun, a lark or a dare, but it turned into an experience far more serious than we envisaged. It wasn't that difficult to ease and squeeze my head through the railings – but to our mounting unease it seemed impossible to get it out again. At first we laughed uncontrollably until tears ran down our dirty faces, leaving clean salty tracks. I drew a small crowd and enjoyed the attention, giving the other kids a free show, larking around and playing the fool, but as sure as the sun was shining, our laughter gradually ebbed away as it went behind the clouds.

One of the mothers in the park heard all the rigmarole and came over to see what the fuss was about. She tried to ease my head free but couldn't and it was then that I realised I could be in real trouble. Not only was I stuck fast but I was now facing at least a downpour and possibly a thunderstorm. My fears weren't eased either by the comment made by one of the other mothers who by then had gathered around me.

'Trouble is, she could be struck by lightning if the railings get hit. And it wouldn't be the first time. I've known this sort of a thing to happen before. The poor little sod whose booted foot was stuck just like 'er head is – burned to a crisp. Couldn't 'ave been no more than twelve years old. God rest his soul.'

The woman who had tried to free me and soothe my troubles gently asked where I lived but I had heard the remark and was really frightened at the thought of getting struck by lightning. I also knew that Dad would be livid with me for causing trouble, drawing attention to our family and wasting people's time. Margaret immediately weighed up the situation and said she would run home to fetch one of my older brothers, and before I could tell her not to leave me she was gone, running as if her life depended on it. Perhaps she really thought that mine did? People were steadily gathering around me and all I wanted was for them to go away and leave me to my humiliation with my head trapped and my bottom sticking out.

My brother Johnny soon came bolting to my aid and I recognised the sound of his pounding footsteps echoing on the cobblestones before I could even see him. Red-faced and concerned and out of breath though he was, still he managed a comforting smile. As soon as I saw him I started to cry. Pushing away the small crowd that were jostling around me, he climbed over the fence to the park side then kneeled down and looked into my face, breaking into a warm, soft chuckle. 'Silly cow, fancy going and doing a thing like this.' He then put his handkerchief to my nose and told me to blow. After he wiped my nose clean I managed to tell him, between sobs and gulps, that I was scared that I wouldn't get free and might be there all night and die in the dark or be struck by lightning.

'Course you won't, babe.' He quietly laughed, wiping away my tears gently with his thumb. He then tried to ease my head, which felt as if it had swollen to at least twice its size, through the railings. Johnny tried again but I screamed as my ears were bent forward and pressed painfully against the railings. He slowly eased my head forward again and I heard his defeated voice as he mumbled to my brother Billy, who had appeared on the scene, the words fire brigade. I knew then that this time my antics had got me into deep trouble. I hadn't given it a thought that something serious like this could happen in real life. Neither could I believe that what goes in cannot always come out.

Margaret, dutiful as ever, ran to the nearby telephone kiosk and dialled 999 for the fire brigade and once through to them was told that they had already been alerted. Our shopkeeper in the corner shop heard about my dilemma from one of his customers and had already made the call. Margaret was none too pleased about that but then other people, usually grown-ups, were always interfering with our lives one way or another.

I felt sure that I was going to be in trouble for causing such a disturbance and was frightened of the scolding I would get once home – that's if they *could* free me from the railings. It was as well that my Johnny and Billy were there to console me because when that huge red fire engine drove slowly along the narrow cobbled turning towards me with blue lights flashing, I felt my heart pound and my stomach churn with fear and anxiety. I don't think I had been so frightened in my life. This was official. This could mean that the police would arrive too.

One of the firemen looked at me and gently smiled. 'And what might your name be?' he asked.

'Sally Lipka,' I said. 'And I'm very sorry.'

'Don't you worry, sweetheart,' he said, 'it's what we're paid for. Now then, how on earth did you manage to achieve the impossible?' He was still smiling but I was too frightened to tell the truth. That I had done it deliberately.

Under pressure, Margaret came up with what I thought to be a plausible story. 'We was climbing over the railing,' she said, 'and my best friend slipped and her head went through one of the gaps and got stuck.'

'Is that right?' said the officer, clearly amused by her nervous ramblings and not believing one word of it. The fireman gave me a wink and then stepped away to speak quietly to the other officers.

Johnny saw how upset I was and wiped away the mucky tears on my cheeks and neck, telling me that I would be free soon and he would give me a piggyback home.

'But I can't get my head out, Johnny,' I wailed.

'Well, we'll just 'ave to take up the railing, won't we, darlin'?' he said, giving me a wink and stroking my hair.

One of the firemen then came and kneeled beside me and spoke in a soft voice as he said, 'Now then, Sally, we're going to place a metal bar above your head and between the two iron railings either side of you. Then with our magic crank we'll push them railings apart and you'll be free. How does that sound?'

'Will the police come?' is all I could think of to say.

'No. You don't need the boys in blue. You need proper rescuers.'

I looked from his face to my brother Johnny's and then to Billy, my eldest brother, for reassurance and he winked at me and smiled which helped a bit.

'You're the fourth little girl that we've had to rescue today,' said another fireman, which was a ploy to put me at ease I later learned. But I did feel safe in their hands and more relaxed once I knew the police weren't coming.

Eventually, with three officers on the job, the bars began to squeak as they were eased apart and even though I wasn't petrified I held my breath and imagined I was a stone statue as I closed my eyes tightly shut. Once I felt two warm hands around my head gently drawing it through the railings I breathed properly again, all to the sound of cheering from the small crowd which had gathered by then. A fire engine in those days was a crowd-puller. Once free, my body felt light – as if it might float on air – and my head seemed to be swollen and puffy like a balloon.

I floated away on my brother Johnny's back after one of the firemen told me never to climb railings again in case I did another somersault and got trapped. They knew what I had done and no doubt I wasn't the first to have pushed my head through a gap just to see what would happen. That night I kneeled by my bedside and thanked Lord Jesus and promised never to do anything that bad again, ever.

The telltale red marks on my neck, chin and cheeks from when I first panicked and tried to pull my head out of the railings myself, plus my tear-stained face did not go unnoticed by Mum when Johnny lowered me carefully down from his back. My brother explained it all and made the most of the exciting bit – the fire engine coming out specially to save me and the crowd that gathered to watch. Dad came into the kitchen and slowly shook his head, smiling, while Johnny told the whole story in a comical way so as to divert any scolding and make Mum and Dad laugh. He knew exactly what he was doing and it worked.

It wasn't easy to fathom at the time though. I had been a nuisance, caused a lot of trouble, and wasn't going to get a smack on the leg or be sent to my room? And I was being made a fuss of? I think I realised then that parents were strange people.

Margaret bravely came over and knocked for me an hour or so afterwards, but the novelty of my distress had worn off by then and Mum got to the door before me and told my closest friend that I wasn't allowed out to play because neither of us could be trusted for five minutes. That night I was sent to bed early to get over the shock, but I wasn't in shock or tired and I felt incredibly lonely in my room. To amuse myself I opened the top drawer of the small oak chest and withdrew the sheet of wallpaper and pencil that Dad had once given me as something to do when he had sent me to bed early. I carefully began to trace around a pattern just showing through the back.

I was pleased that I had been given this new pastime even though I knew deep down it was just another means of having me out of the way. I had got so used to this kind of thing that I took it as part and parcel of my life.

The next event that grabbed our interest was the preparation for the outdoor procession for the veneration of the Blessed Virgin Mary when bands from all over London marched into Wapping on May Day, and my best friend was going to be one of the Catholic girls dressed in a long white satin gowns and wearing beautiful headdresses decorated with fresh flowers and pearls, just like a bridesmaid. She was to carry a bouquet of flowers to match and her black hair would be set in perfect ringlets.

When preparations for Procession Sunday were being made I wasn't in the least bit jealous but proud of my friend. It was, after all, nothing to do with favouritism but religion. She was a Catholic and I wasn't. It was as simple as that. I was allowed by her sisters to see her in full regalia before the big day, and also watched while they tucked and pinned her dress into place as she stood on a chair in their sitting room.

Just about every one of us in the East End came out to see those once-a-year processions, when the pavements along Commercial Road were bursting with joyful crowds through which I would ease and wriggle my way to the front. Even then I only ever saw Margaret once or twice because I was swamped in a huge crowd of people cheering and clapping to the bands, and when I did spot her and screamed her name she didn't hear me, so slowly glided past amidst her group of girls.

East Enders in their thousands enjoyed the celebration, especially when the drum and fife bands marched through the main street to join up with the Irish pipers, playing their bagpipes, dressed in their tartan kilts. Fantastic music resonated through the streets as the bands marched through the East End, shoulders back and proud, with mace-bearers leading the way in their pinstripe suits and elbow-length gauntlets.

It was a glorious sight and a wonderful free show with the different music filling the air and resounding through the streets of east London, spectacular street theatre at its best.

Our hope was that one day Margaret would be crowned May Queen, but from what we gathered from her parents' and sisters' conversations, the May Queen and her maids of honour and ladies-in-waiting were usually chosen from St Patrick's Senior and Junior School which Margaret did not attend. It didn't seem fair because she followed all the rules necessary for the part: mass every Sunday morning and Saturday evening confessions. The only thing, and probably the most important, was that Mr and Mrs McGregor, her hard-working parents, were not that affluent and it would have been up to them to buy the more expensive long trailing dress with a matching train, long white gloves and new shoes. I was jealous of the May Queen but my favourites in the procession were the pageboys dressed up in white silk shirts, knee britches and black buckled shoes.

A few days after that grand annual event, once Margaret had come down from those heady heights, she was back in her faded cotton frocks and baggy ankle socks with hair all awry and scrambling through debris again. Back in the real world with me. We had the whole of the summer holiday off from school to look forward to and, better still, I had hop picking at the end of the break in late August.

That particular year, the day after the procession, I went to Grandfather's house and told Nan about Margaret being in the limelight and how I wished I was a Catholic so that I could have been in it too. She was in the scullery wearing her Baron's green overall and peeling a pile of potatoes ready for the evening meal for her family. She gave me a cup of weak tea and listened to my vivid account of the bands, the pageboys and the maids of honour. She didn't seem all that interested so I told her about my little mishap with my head in the railings while I sat on the stone and copper boiler in the corner of the small room.

Her chuckling and slow shaking of the head cheered me up because at last I had tickled her fancy and I had an audience – albeit one person.

I knew she would relate it to my aunts and uncles so naturally I embroidered it a little. 'My head was so wedged between the railings, Nan, that they thought they might have to cut it off,' I said.

She loved this account and exaggeration and I don't think I can remember having heard her laugh so much. She stopped peeling potatoes to wipe tears from her eyes with her big white handkerchief.

'You're enough to turn anyone into a Freddy,' she said, pushing the lid of her little blue tin open with her thumb and then sprinkling snuff on the back of her hand.

'I don't know what you mean, Nan,' I said, leaning as far back as I could before she sneezed. 'Freddy who?'

'Frederick Charrington,' she said. 'He turned into a bleedin' lunatic in the end, as will you no doubt. He spent a good deal of his life trying to stop men from drinking themselves into an early grave. Sent 'imself bonkers doing it.' She blew her nose hard and then sniffed long and free before pushing her handkerchief back into her apron pocket.

'Mind you,' she said, her eyes more sparkly, 'Frederick brought my father to heel when he was a young man all right. I never thought I'd see the day when your great-grandfather would go into a Mission hall knowing what the lecture was gonna be. But he did and was the better for it. He stuck to drinking just one small jug of ale a day after listening to Charrington. So maybe he wasn't so soft in the head, Mog. Maybe he wasn't.'

According to Nan, who had a gift for storytelling, my great-great-grandmother 'should 'ave got 'er claws into' Charrington. My great-great-grandmother was Nan's claim to fame. Apparently she was a stunner in her time. Nan flicked open her gold locket which always hung around her neck on my gold chain and held it out for me to see.

'She 'ad a lovely voice as well,' said Nan. 'Used to sing in the music halls. They don't make frocks like the ones that woman wore. Emerald green it was, all satin and lace. I wish I'd 'ave got my little hands on it when she died. Be worth a good few bob now. A museum piece that would be, Mog,' she said, drifting thoughtfully off to the past. 'A museum piece.'

'Was she a film star then?' I asked, lured in as ever by her stories, true or false.

'Course she wasn't a film star.' She chuckled. 'They never made films in them days I shouldn't think. No, she was a music-hall singer. On the stage, and better than some of the more famous ones.'

Nan told me, as she had many times before, how my beautiful ancestor started out singing in places like Lusby's, a music hall-cum-gin palace and then moved on to more salubrious music halls and rubbed shoulders with the rich. Nan then went back to peeling her potatoes, having fed my imagination. A quiet aura filled the room to the comfortable sound of the clock ticking. After a short pause Nan spoke quietly, saying, 'Your great-great-grandmother performed on the stage where your mother works. At the ABC picture palace.'

'She don't work there, Nan,' I said. 'She works at the Empire ever since she left the fleapit, the Forester's.'

'I know that, Mog. But it was called the ABC before it was changed to the Empire and the Empire is the same place that was Lusby's all them years ago. When it was a music hall-cum-gin palace before it was turned into a picture palace – or cinema, as it's now called.'

Since I had my nan to myself and she was in a talkative mood I broached another subject, one that even at my young age I knew was a touch taboo. 'Why have you and Grandfarver got a different surname to us, Nan?' I said, all innocent.

I watched as she slowly drew breath and shook her head, then looked sideways at me as she murmured, 'One of these days your nose will fall off if you keep asking questions.'

'And your ears will drop off if you keep on repeating yerself. Uncle Harry said that. He said you say the same fings over and over.'

'Oh, did he now?'

'Yep. And anyway I would only forget all about fings you might tell me about our name being different cos it's not that important, is it?'

'You're a crafty little mare.' She chuckled. 'Remember that I know from experience that you don't forget anyfing, Mog. Got a head like the vaults in the Bank of England, you 'ave.'

'Didn't Grandfather like the name Lipka? Is that why he changed it to Lisbon, Nan?' I said, believing I had got her talking.

'I couldn't care less one way or the other, Mog,' was her reply. 'It suits you though. Sally Lipka. Too much lip. Too many questions.'

'I know someone else who's called Lipka. A woman. Rose Lipka,' I said, a touch too confident.

Nan stopped peeling the potatoes and fell silent. She then dried her hands and sat in her chair in the corner of the scullery, facing me now, as she said, 'And where might you know that woman from?'

'Down the Waste. Outside Trinity Square where I play.'

'Where you're not supposed to play, you mean? Bin squeezing in through them railings again 'ave yer?'

'Yep. And do you know what? I saw a ghost in there once.'

'I bet it ran a mile when it saw you. So did she 'ave anyfing to say then – this Rose woman?'

'Nar. Not really. I've seen 'er a couple of times, here and there. A woman whose mother lives in this turning was there at the time and she said I was to ask Grandfarver about Rose Lipka.'

Nan slowly nodded and said she thought she knew who that might be. 'The local gossip.' She abruptly broke the spell of our cosy world of chatting and told me it was time to go home.

I eased myself down and off the copper boiler and gave Wheezy a hug. 'You know what, Nan – if you bought a lead for Wheezy I would take him out for walks.'

'Wheezy's too old to go roaming outside and quite content thank you,' said Nan. 'And he's a she.'

'She don't look that old. How old d'yer reckon that Rose Lipka is then?'

'That's enough of that, Sally,' said Nan, turning her back on me. 'I don't want you bringing that up again. All right?'

'I don't care about her anyway,' I murmured, sensing that it was time I left Nan to herself.

I left Grandfather's house and closed the door quietly behind me, following the golden rule.

Just after I had left Gran I realised that my stomach was rumbling and I was hungry. I had seven pence in my pocket for my pie and mash dinner so I started to make my way to the Whitechapel Waste. I got distracted from my goal of pie and mash when still in Grandfather's street; I passed an old door in the brick wall, which led into Bellevue Place. There was a fragrant scent of flowers wafting into the street from the gardens of the cottages inside. I thought about the time when Margaret had been taken short on our way to Wickhams, our posh store, and we snuck in there so she could have a pee. Since she was not unduly worried about it, I had one as well and we were caught with our drawers down by a woman who lived there.

The woman gave us a dressing-down and we vowed never to go into that secret garden again, but I couldn't resist the scent of those pink roses and I knew that I could reach the flowers which climbed up the old brick wall so lifted the latch and crept inside, gently closing the narrow door in the wall behind me. The private cul-de-sac was quiet, with forget-me-nots growing in the cracks of the paved pathway leading to a tall creeper-covered wall. These nineteenth-century cottages were almshouses rented out cheaply to people on low incomes. Behind the low garden fences were lilacs, roses and wallflowers and masses of forget-me-nots, all in the heart of Stepney and not that far from the busy Mile End Road. Other than us locals not many people knew what lay behind that old wooden door in the wall – a totally unexpected and beautiful corner in the heart of old east London.

'I 'ope you're not gonna pee, young madam,' came the voice of a woman from behind a tall flowering rose bush in her garden.

'I wasn't,' I said, the blood rushing to my cheeks. I wasn't sure if this was the same woman who had caught Margaret and me in there before. 'I came to look at the roses.' I then told her that my grandfather was her neighbour because he lived in Cleveland Way at number 24.

'Yes,' she said, with still no hint of a smile. 'I thought that I recognised you. You're Laura and Bill Lipka's girl. You've still got your granddad's Germanic looks, I see. Light blue eyes and white hair. How is the old man?'

'He's all right. He's not in though. He's at work. But Nan's in. I've just been to visit.'

'Your mother still working at the picture palace, is she?'

I nodded and then asked her why she wanted to know. I felt she might be going to report me for trespassing.

The woman smiled fondly at me then and said, 'Because we used to work at Charrington's together. We were good work colleagues me and your mum.'

I suddenly saw the lady in a different light. She looked friendly when she smiled.

'Did you want to use the lavatory?' she asked.

'No, thank you. I went at Grandfather's when I first got there.'

'I'm just taking my granddaughter up to the Art Centre in Whitechapel,' she said. 'You can come with us if you want to. I should think you're about the same age. She's nine. She's staying with me for a few days. For a little holiday.'

I was a touch surprised by this. People usually went away from Stepney to go on a holiday, not come in for one. 'Doesn't she like sand and the seaside then?' I asked.

'Course she does. But she likes coming here as well. It's a bit different from south London where she lives. Do you want to come with us to the Art Centre or not?'

'I would do,' I said, peering up at the woman. 'But there ain't no Art Centre in Whitechapel only an Art Gallery and I don't fink your granddaughter would like it in there because you have to be silent and the pictures are hanging too high for us children to look at.'

'I know that, dear,' she said, 'but that's not where we're going. We're going to the Art *Centre*, which is next door and above the Whitechapel railway station.'

I said there couldn't be such a place or I would have been in there with my best friend. Her granddaughter then came out looking clean and shiny with perfect plaits.

'Do you want to come to Whitechapel with us or not?' said the woman, shrugging.

'Yes, please. Even though I know there's no such place next to the station.'

'Stubborn little thing, aren't you,' said the girl's grandmother.

'Not really,' I said. 'But I've pitched my guy before bonfire night outside the station loads of times and I've never seen an Art Centre there. I was going up the pie and mash shop to 'ave some dinner, but if I come with you to 'ave a look at the place I can go from there, can't I? It's not far, is it?'

'No dear, it's not far,' said the woman.

So I decided I might as well go along and as it turned out I got chatting with the granddaughter, who was a bit shy but all right and quite chummy, and went straight past the pie shop even though my stomach was still grumbling. I think it might have been my stubborn streak coming to the fore. I wanted to prove that I knew Whitechapel Waste better than the woman did.

I was a bit put out when the grandmother proved me wrong. I could not believe that we had missed such a treasured place. Admittedly it was a small, unmarked, insignificant-looking door next to the entrance of the station but we should have known about it because we were street-rakers and proud of it. At the top of the stone staircase was an entrance door into my very own Aladdin's cave. I stood gazing in at the entrance of the spacious room which smelled of oil paint and wet clay. I saw three potters wheels, a stack of small squares of special lino for carving, easels and canvases, some clean, some work in progress. On a long wooden bench were big paste pots with brushes for making collages, together with an array of different colour paints in glass pots.

Pinned to the wall were paintings that the young students and children of my age had finished or were still working on. I glanced up at the lady and pinched my lips together before saying, 'Thank you for bringing me. How much is it?' Steeling myself for disappointment, I could only hope that my pie and mash money would cover my entrance fee.

My grandfather's neighbour smiled and told me there was no entrance fee and I could use any of the materials so long as I tried hard not to waste anything. She said I had to enrol properly and led me to one of the young art teachers who wasn't in a suit the way our teachers at school were, but wearing jeans and a black sweatshirt, with a little red neckerchief. On his head, sloping to one side, was a black beret. A young woman who was also an art teacher wore pedal pushers with little slits at the side and a blouse that looked more like a man's shirt except that it was orange and she wore black ballet shoes instead of the sensible ones that most teachers wore. I was mesmerised and couldn't stop looking at her. I still couldn't believe my luck at being allowed in.

I was properly introduced to the teachers, who were called tutors, who were not only friendly but helpful. The smallest grey apron was found that wrapped around my skinny body twice and was held in place by a tie belt. I found out that the tutors were fresh out of university. One was from Cambridge and one from Hampstead and both were lodging in rooms in Forest Gate. I had discovered a new world. I painted a picture of a boat on a river and this was pinned on the wall with the other children's paintings.

Thrilled by all this, I couldn't wait to tell Margaret. On the way home, so engrossed with my thoughts, I walked straight by the pie and mash shop almost without realising. I treated myself to a large portion of piping hot chips, sprinkled with salt and vinegar and ate them as I strolled home, the late afternoon sun on my face. I was smiling at the thought of what I had to tell my friend. When I arrived into our grounds I could see Margaret sitting on her front garden gate, swinging slowly to and fro. I had been gone for a good three hours or so and could see that she was miffed since we usually played together and I hadn't turned up. I tried to explain and even though she was listening she pretended not to be.

'I only meant to go to my gran's house to tell her about the fire engine and how I was trapped,' I said. 'But then when I came out I was hungry so was going up the pie and mash shop. I passed that green door in Grandfarver's turning and you'll never guess what—'

'I don't care,' said Margaret, looking around herself at nothing in particular. 'It's not my business what you do and what you don't do. I'll probably go round a school friend's house in a minute anyway.'

'I unlatched the green door to have a look at the flowers and the woman who caught us having a pee there that time came out and told me off! At least I fink it was 'er.' I realised that I had to embroider it a little if I was going to get her interest.

'You shouldn't 'ave gone wivout me then, should you? Or at least you could 'ave told me where you was going and 'ow long you'd be. You could 'ave fallen through old floorboards in a bombed house and be laying there with blood oozing out of you and rats running all round and sniffing your feet before they started to gnaw at your toes.'

'Well, I never fell, did I? And I'm all right. I don't know why you're in this kind of a fucking mood.'

'Don't you swear at me, Sally Lipka or I won't ever talk

to you again. I'm a Catholic and not supposed to listen to them words.'

'Well, if you're gonna be in your spiteful mood I'm going upstairs to our flat. I was looking forward to telling you what I found out and where I've been but not any more!'

'And I was gonna let you share what I've got in my pocket. Something that I could get into a lot of trouble for if my mum found out.'

We argued a little bit more about who was right and who wrong about my going off without her and then it finally came out as to what was needling her. In the pocket of her patterned cotton frock was a precious cigarette that she'd sneaked out of her mum's packet when she wasn't looking. I was seriously impressed – this was one of the bravest things that she could have done. We had talked about smoking and how we might get to try it out and I hadn't been there to share the daredevil excitement of Margaret's feat.

But she wasn't going to patch things up so I left her to her sulks. Margaret and I had many spats so I stormed off and went upstairs to our flat where Mum and Mrs Damps from next door were having a cup of tea in the kitchen and gossiping. As soon as they saw my face they went quiet, so I knew that whatever they had been talking about it was not something for my ears.

I poured myself a glass of water and drank it down in one go I was so thirsty. Turning around, I saw that the women bore an expression I had seen before. They were waiting for me to go away. I saw this as an opportunity for blackmail and asked Mum if I could have sixpence, saying that I wanted the money because I was going with Margaret to the gypsy fair which had come into town and set up near to where Aunt Polly lived, by the railway track in the back and beyond of Bethnal Green. She knew that the gypsies came twice a year but didn't know which month so I got away with that fib quite nicely. Mrs Damps said that sixpence wouldn't go far and pushed her hand into her deep apron pocket and pulled out a threepenny bit to go with it. It must have been hot gossip they were involved in, was all I could think.

I went to the lavatory and was out of that flat like the wind and on my way to Margaret's. I didn't give a toss about the argument any more. Mrs McGregor opened the door to me and said, 'She not coming out to play. She's in 'er room, reading old comics.' She then eased the door shut and I felt my anger rise. I hadn't done anything wrong as far as I could see and I thought it was a fucking cheek to be treated that way. I heard the window open above me and peered up to see Margaret.

'I'm not playing with you any more, Sally Lipka. I've got another best friend at school!' With that she slammed the window shut.

'Suit yer fucking self then,' I said and stormed off. Once again she'd made me swear like a trooper, knowing her mum would hear and knowing that I knew that Catholics were against swearing because of their strict religion and their Lady Immaculate.

So there I was, with ninepence to spend, but no mate to spend it with. I went to the sweet shop and bought an ounce of jelly babies for Albert and an ounce of pink and white coconut chips for myself and a *Beano* comic. I had every intention of going into my bedroom and having a lovely time. When I walked through the grounds on my way back, however, the contrary Margaret was back on her gate swinging slowly to and fro. I looked sideways at her to see if her lips were still pursed to find they weren't. But her nose was tipped slightly and I recognised the expression.

I guessed she was ready to make up but she wasn't going to beg. I marched over to her and offered the *Beano*, saying that I wanted it straight back once she'd read it. She took the comic saying that she wasn't a thief and always returned borrowed things. She then marched back into her house and I stalked off to our flat. Fifteen minutes later she was knocking on the door to return the comic and I couldn't help laughing at the silly look on her face. She began to giggle and that was it. We were off to wander about in the streets again, me giving her a detailed account of the Art Centre where I painted a picture but couldn't get the hang of the potter's wheel.

The following Saturday we went to the centre together and tried clay modelling and had a go at lino cuts which turned out to be my favourite pastime and quickly became my preferred hobby. Using a tool that looked similar to Mum's potato peeler seemed strange and hours slipped by like minutes when I was carving a pattern into a soft brown square of lino. I was given a plain white cotton tea towel to print on and loved easing a tiny paint roller through the special black paint in trays and gliding it across my linocut before pressing it on to my tea cloth. Once I saw the first square of my very own work printed, black on white, I was hooked. At the end of a Saturday session we were told about the life of William Morris and shown slides of his hand-printed wallpaper and fabrics. His name remained as familiar to me as Mr Riley in our sweet shop and Mrs Hogg in the grocer's. I had found another world and another hobby to add to those of reading and treasure hunting on bombed sites.

8
Drowning in the River

Every year between the ages of two and eleven I went with my family on a working holiday to pick hops in Kent. From as far back as I can remember I always loved it: Mum cooking over a camp fire, us sitting around it at dusk and best of all swimming in the nearby river during those wonderful hot, sunny Septembers. We lived in huts, slept on straw, washed in cold water and lived as I imagined those in working-class Roman settlements had done all those centuries ago.

The build-up to our departure from the East End to Kent was the most exciting bit. When I was eleven, however, and late August came round rumour had it that this was to be the last of picking hops by hand and rumour proved to be right. So that year was even more special than all the others before it. I could not wait to climb on to the back of the open-backed lorry which had been loaded with our belongings: a huge wooden trunk crammed with clothes, oil lamps, primus stove, candles and saucepans, crockery and food, a curtain for the room divider, bed linen and a rolled-up offcut of lino for the hut floor. On board were also a couple of kitchen chairs and a fold-up table.

By the time the lorry driver reached us he would have collected two other families, people we knew from previous years who, just like us, returned to the same hop farm every year. It was so good to see the same happy familiar faces waiting for us on the lorry when the migration of women as casual agriculture workers began. We were close in that we lived side by side for six or seven weeks, in huts in a field by a river, but once back in London, the season over, hop pickers rarely saw each other. We lived in different parts of the East End and there was a natural territorial divide and social calls weren't really on the agenda because most, if not everyone, worked a five- or six-day week.

During the run-up to us going away Mum was always happier than we saw her at any other time of the year. She couldn't wait to get into the open wide countryside and when she received her postcard from the owner of the farm inviting her family back to pick hops, drive tractors and collect fruit, she skipped around our flat with joy. This break from the East End, even though the living conditions were hardly palatial, was something that none of us wanted to let go of. Mum's sister, mother and brothers were not slow in telling her, on one of their infrequent visits to Stepney, how wonderful it was to live where the air was fresh and clean and not polluted with London smog and the smell of drains. She already knew this, of course, but she never bothered to point out that we got our annual dose of fresh country air for six weeks every year. To compare hop picking with their way of life, though, would probably have made them smile.

Mum got on quite well with the landowners of the farm who allowed me and a couple of friends to play in the farmyards with their sons now and then. My hop-picking friends were a boy called Bobby, who sang like a choirboy, and a girl called Viv who was as skinny as me and just as ragged except for her dark hair that was mostly cut by her mum using sharp scissors and a pudding basin. To replace street-raking in London we went scrumping for apples, pears, blackberries and plums from the farmer's orchards. We made a great trio and had lots of fun, missing for most of the time as we covered a lot of ground when we led each other to faraway farms to nearly always get back to the huts late with Viv and Bobby sometimes receiving a clout for having worried their mothers. Mum never punished me because she was used to my being out more than I was in and just like a bad penny – I always turned up when starving hungry or at bedtime.

Hop picking was mostly the work of housewives with husbands and adult offspring coming down on late Friday evenings for a weekend break. Visitors turned up in old cars, vans or trucks, while others came by train to Tonbridge and then a bus to the nearby village with a half-hour walk from there. Of course the men were bound to be more than ready for a pint of ale or cider at the local pub after their journey and a bite to eat, usually stew and a chunk of bread. Nobody spent much time in the huts because by day we were on the fields picking hops or in orchards working as apple pickers for the farmer – and swimming in our River Medway.

Come the end of a working day, the whistle blown, the women would stroll back to the common to cook over their own individual outdoor fires. It was quite usual to see smoke-blackened pots or kettles hanging on purpose-built iron poles over the flames. Later on as the night drew in, the glow of oil lamps shone softly from inside the rows of huts which were set on three sides of the green to create an enclosure and a village-like atmosphere, with the sinking sun reflecting on the sloping, corrugated black tin rooftops. There must have been fifty or sixty huts and at least thirty fires glowing in the dark with small groups sitting around them quietly talking or singing a ballad, which was often picked up by others until the sound swept right through the common, the song echoing in the still of the night. This was a comfort to us children as we lay half awake, warm and snug, in our make-do beds of straw-filled mattresses and hop-filled duvet-type covers and pillows.

The picking season usually lasted for six weeks starting in late August and ending in the first week of October. As the weeks went on, the nights got colder, and even though I was warm in bed wearing my navy blue drawers and vest, the way I did at home, the early mornings were cold and damp in those huts. To get around this Laura and I kept the clothes we took off inside our beds and pulled them back on again while still under our covers, first thing. Like everyone else we only had two or three sets of clothes with us, which were washed in a white enamel bucket of cold water, rinsed under the communal tap, wrung out and hung on a line to dry in the sunshine. Underwear was never a problem because most days were hot or at least warm and sunny enough to go into the river, so we swam in them and then let the sun dry them off as we ran about on the grass.

I loved our hut and my bed of hay where there was hardly

any evidence of bugs to be seen. Earwigs and spiders, yes, but no flat round bedbugs, which I was used to in our old house where they hid within the springs and beneath the old brass knobs on the four corners of a bedstead then came out at night. They often fed on my and Laura's flesh, leaving small round red marks as evidence for all to see.

A short distance from our common was a place sheltered by trees where the travelling gypsies pitched up each hop-picking season in their colourful wagons pulled by horses and ponies. The younger Romany lads could often be seen grooming their beloved animals and looking handsome in their white baggy cotton shirts with the sleeves rolled up, wearing faded black or gay patterned waistcoats. With their deep blue eyes and tanned skin they caught the eye of the ladies and were friendly and familiar with us Londoners.

The Romany women, soon after we settled in, came around to each hut selling their polished wooden peg boxes made by the men. Later they would return with handkerchiefs embroidered on one corner which had been made from white sheeting.

The hard-wearing, inexpensive rag rugs, created by gypsy girls, were the first items to be sold out and soon to be laid on the floor of our small makeshift homes. There was little doubt that the travellers added to the ambience as did we town dwellers. The colourful painted wagons, with their shades of yellow, green and red, and the gypsy girls, with their long faded coloured skirts swishing around worn leather boots, looked a picture. And for sure, some of them were just as beautiful as the Hollywood film stars with their lustrous black hair swept back from their tanned faces to show off their high cheekbones and penetrating blue eyes.

Mum had made good friends with a gypsy woman, Leila, who came over to our hut as soon as she heard we had arrived and went off with Mum to read her palm in private. Among other things that the gypsy predicted that year was that she would be a young widow and that there was going to be another man in Mum's life one day. A gentle man, who didn't flirt with other women, didn't bet on the horses and was solid and reliable, with his pay packet placed on the table each week. I remember Mum relating this to Aunt Polly whose hut was just a few doors away from ours and them both roaring with laughter, as if such things couldn't possibly happen!

Timeless scenery it was, with the hop gardens, orchards, barley fields, woods and the winding river. People toing and froing, lighting fires and boiling large black kettles as the smell of boiled bacon drifted through the air. Faggot firewood was always stacked high around an old oak tree with children dragging it to the outside of their family huts, ready for burning that evening. Later on when most were inside their makeshift dwellings the outside was reminiscent of a medieval village with smoke from the camp fires swirling across the common, filling the air with a smoky aroma. The best of all times for me was when the darkening landscape was still and peaceful against the orange glow of the sinking sun as it cast rays of warm pink light in the sky.

In the cold mornings the grass was always soaking wet

with dew but even so we took pleasure in having the early sun on our faces as we drifted towards the hop gardens, our wellingtons leaving imprints on the plush dewy grass. The women, wrapped in thick jumpers and coats and colourful knotted scarves on their heads, soon peeled off their top layers once the sun was well and truly up. The faded flowery and plain cotton sundresses might have looked out of keeping with the wellington boots to someone not used to that way of life

Sitting on those timber frames of a hessian bin with the sun streaming through the forest of hops, shielding the pickers from the hot midday sun, the women were content and happy to work while small ones slept in pushchairs or played together in the fields nearby. Most women wore cotton fingerless gloves to avoid being scratched by the bines when they were pulled. Even when the weather was against them, the pickers buckled down and sang as they worked. I don't know if it was from sheer tenacity that everyone did their bit to keep spirits up and pick at speed or their need to make some money for Christmas. Whatever the case it worked.

On Saturday evenings, of course, a good time was enjoyed by most of the adults at the local pub, where the landlord was just as happy as the jolly Londoners, the bell on his till dinging all evening long. During a tipsy stroll back to the common, singing under a star-studded night, there was bound to be a bit of mischief amongst the men who were in high spirits. It wasn't unusual for them to go out, torch in hand, silly and laughing like boys again, to creep to a nearby farm to pinch a chicken for the next day's dinner. Dad was like a different person during those weekends, more relaxed and likeable.

Once the men had gone back to London some of the women enjoyed a little freedom and fun with their apron strings looser than they might have been back home when their husbands were about. The setting was perfect for love – a haystack under a starry sky with the hoot of an owl echoing in the distance saw more than a few of our women slipping into the wild side of life with a Romany or handsome Kentish man. I'm sure my mother would have been no exception. She had gypsy blood in her after all is said and done. Her own grandmother, according to Mum, was from pure Romany stock and named after many of her ancestors – Rose Leigh. I wonder what the Kentish ladies would have made of it should they have overheard their men being referred to as a bit of rough from the mouths of cockney women.

The young, single and carefree also made the most of their time in that atmospheric bit of heaven, strolling in a country lane with a sweetheart by the light of the moon. Romance in the air was as natural as the flowing rivers and the cows chewing the cud. What better ending after a day of picking hops once the little ones were in bed than to push off the wellingtons and pull on the stockings. Carefully roll on the lipstick and then a little mascara, a pretty cardigan, a small handbag to then slip furtively away to the arranged meeting place, be it under the old oak tree or in a tunnel of hop vines.

In the mornings, once dawn broke, the pickers were woken by the sound of the baker going from one row of huts to another, announcing his arrival in a singsong voice as he called out, 'Wakey WA-*key*! Cakey Ca-*key*!'

He never failed to wake me up and I was always ready for a mug of tea and a fresh Bakewell tart to go with it, a treat that was never to be had in London. Once up and outside we washed our hands and face in cold water and soap using a small white enamel bowl. Towards the end of the hop season, with autumn set in, it was bracing but we were just as used to that as we were to having only one outside cold water tap and ten outside black tin corrugated lavatories to be shared between everyone.

My mother, not one for using communal lavatories, kept secret the small brick privy she found for herself – a proper outside flushing lavatory, immaculately clean with a supply of tissue toilet paper to hand. This bit of luxury happened to be located in a country yokel's cottage garden, a few minutes' walk down the lane, behind a tall hedge. The first time Mum trespassed she wasn't in the least bit concerned whether she would be caught out or not because she had no intention of using the public lavatories. She then made friends with the Kentish woman whose lavatory it was, who invited her in for a cup of tea and a chat. None of us particularly liked using the communal lavs, especially after the first week, when they were no longer fresh as a daisy, so most of us eventually wandered off, toilet paper in hand, to a remote part of the river or woods, where no one passed by and where there was long grass to hide in.

I loved picking hops off prickly stems into our bin and stopping for a picnic lunch of tea from a flask and cheese sandwiches. With fresh air and the bittersweet smell of the hops all around us, the sun shining through the vines, it was lovely. I was mostly away, though, playing by the river before the whistle was blown to mark the end of the working day. Mum, just like the rest of the women, was always tired and ready to leave the hop fields to sit outside her hut with a fresh cup of tea.

Back at the huts the women lit their fires and cooked their stews. There might not have been much meat in the stew but there was plenty of barley to fill bellies and a variety of free root vegetables, dug up from fields before dark the previous day by us children. I expect I knew the taste of parsnip and turnip before I knew their names.

My handsome brothers were like magnets where the young fresh country girls were concerned and we hardly saw much of Billy and Johnny once they had finished a day's work and eaten their meal. It was late to bed for them and up before the crack of dawn where Johnny was concerned. He could always be found at the river's edge, fishing. There he would stay until it was time to clock in as the pole puller's mate, using a long, thin, wooden pole with a hook on the end to free the tangled tops of the hop vines caught on the wires high in the sky above us.

Tall and broad for their age, both my brothers secured seasonal work in the fields without a problem and had good singing voices too. It was they who often started up with a song while working that would set off the rest of the pickers, which sometimes turned into a competition with two songs on the go from two different fields. Those who sang loudest sang longest. Laura was a good picker and I was good at disappearing when friends signalled to me from their hiding place amidst the thick vines to run as fast as our wellington boots would allow in search of adventure, which was never far off. Neither was danger – of one kind or another.

From the age of seven I had regularly been sent with a shopping list to the village roughly a half mile away so by now, four years later, I was more than used to it and liked walking in quiet country lanes by myself, especially a long, gently curving one that led to the local shop and was hedged high on either side to protect the orchards from being spoiled by children scrumping for apples. It was a long lane for a girl to walk by herself but at least I could pick blackberries to eat on the way. I also collected soft fruit which hung on branches that leaned over the hedges that surrounded the farmer's Victoria plum orchard. And as an extra bonus when I arrived in the village shop, the woman who owned it and lived above would give me a glass of weak orange juice

During that final year of hop picking on one of those shopping expeditions on a Saturday morning, while my family were picking in the fields, a green van pulled up beside me, and the driver asked me if there was a shop close by where he could buy a bottle of lemonade. He must have seen my empty shopping bag so might have guessed where I was heading. Walking alone in my black wellington boots that rubbed the back of my legs sore and wearing a faded flowery cotton frock, hair long and scraggly, pale skin flushed from the sun, I must have looked like a sitting target for men of prey. I peered at the stranger as he quietly laughed at me and repeated his question, saying, 'Well, is there a shop or isn't there one?'

Very frightened because of my experiences with the man on the bike at home and then the man on the staircase, I did my best to look natural and brave as I said, 'There is one but it's at the end of the lane and across a road.'

He nodded and thanked me and then glanced up at the sky, squinting. 'Looks like the sun's going to be out for the rest of the day. I should say it's going to get hotter, mind. Hot and sweaty. Don't you think so?'

'I don't know,' I said. 'It could do.'

He pushed his head out of the van window and looked back to the hop fields in the distance, saying, 'I expect that number two field is almost bare by now.'

'Mum and Dad 'ave just move on to field four,' I said.

He raised an eyebrow and said he was surprised that my father was there for the picking. I told him that most fathers came down at the weekends.

'I never knew that,' he said. 'Well, there you are – I've learned something today and from a girl. A pretty girl at that.' Then, looking at my face, he sucked in air between his teeth and winked at me. 'I bet you sixpence that you've got friends down here in Kent that you'll miss once you go back?'

'Not really,' I said, 'my best friends are in Stepney. I don't miss anyone from here when I'm back in London.'

'Not even a boyfriend down here for the picking? One of the lads? I don't believe you.' He chuckled and raised an eyebrow higher than I had ever seen anyone do.

'I haven't got a boyfriend,' I said. 'I'm only eleven.'

'Don't you come that old soldier with me.' He laughed. 'I don't believe you. A pretty little thing like you. I should think those boys are always chasing you for a kiss.'

I could feel myself blushing as I told him I had to be getting on my way to the shop.

He did the trick with the eyebrow again and said, 'I can see you're blushing, so I reckon you must have a boyfriend who kisses you now and then. I bet you show them yours and they show you theirs.'

I knew what he meant and I knew I was in trouble. I was in an isolated lane and it was as far back to the hop fields as it was to the shop ahead of me. I felt frightened, trapped and vulnerable.

'Come on,' he said. 'Get into my van. I'm going to the shop and so are you. I'll give you a lift.'

That's when I knew for sure he was one of them, one of the strangers to run from. I politely turned down his offer and began to walk onwards in the direction of the shop. As I continued bravely on my way, trying not to look worried, my heart pounded fit to burst.

The man drove slowly beside me, his van door slid back. 'It was me catching on what you and the boys do together,' he said, carefully steering the van with one hand. 'That's why you won't get in next to me. You show them yours and them showing you theirs. Is that why you don't you want a lift? You want to play with them, do you?' he jeered. 'Are you meeting one of the little boys so you can go under a bush where no one can see you?'

'I'm not meeting anybody,' I said. 'I've got to get my mum's shopping.'

He continued to drive slowly and menacingly by my side, persisting with his dirty talk and leering looks. And it got worse. Some of it I didn't quite understand but I was scared and desperate not to cry. I wanted my elder brothers but my instincts were screaming at me not to let him know that I was frightened. So I tried my best to look brave and nonchalant as I strode forward, my chin out and proud as if I were in a race, while all the time a voice inside was warning me not to run just yet. I hadn't realised how long that lane was until then. He carried on like this until we reached the crossroad where the shop was.

'You're a dirty little girl.' He laughed. 'Showing the boys what's inside them drawers of yours. Letting them put their hand on it.' He turned left and drove away.

I ran to the shop, pushed open the door, and burst into tears. The next thing I knew I was on the shopkeeper's chair while she telephoned the local police station and I was being eyed with suspicion by a customer. The country woman obviously saw me as one of 'them' from the common that brings trouble to Kent. I pleaded with the shopkeeper not to call a policeman, telling her that I would get into trouble with Mum and Dad if I went back with someone in a uniform. She gave me a puzzled, sympathetic look and continued to turn the small handle of the old-fashioned black telephone on the wall. I was told to wait there in the shop until a bobby on a bike arrived.

Once she replaced the receiver, my hands were sweaty and trembling so I gave her my shopping list to read rather than reel off the errands we needed. She slowly filled my dark red shopping bag while speaking quietly to the other customer. 'This isn't the first time this has happened in this village and it's time somebody did something about it.'

'Well, it's a bit of a coincidence that it should happen while the cockneys are here, wouldn't you say?'

'No, I shouldn't say that. I shouldn't say that at all. I know for sure that this kind of thing has happened during the times when the pickers are not up from London. You would be surprised what I hear in this shop.'

The customer sniffed and then gave me a quick once-over as if I were something the cat had fetched in. 'Well, what has reached your ears hasn't reached mine so we'll leave it at that, shall we?'

'If you ask me, I think it's a delivery man from a completely different area looking for children out on their own.'

Feeling hot and clammy, I got up from the chair and offered the money for the shopping and as the woman took it she said, 'Don't you worry, sweetheart. You'll be safe now. You sit yourself down and wait for the policeman.' She then went out the back to pour another glass of weak orange juice for me. The country customer in the shop was still glancing at me with a contemptuous expression as if I had done something bad. So I left. I felt sure that the man in the van would have gone from the area by then.

Halfway along the lane, walking as fast as I could with the heavy shopping bag, a policeman arrived on a bicycle and stopped to ask if I was the girl who had been accosted. Now it was really getting serious and try as I might I couldn't stop myself from bursting into tears. He got off his pushbike, took my bag of shopping, looped it on his handlebars and then patted the top of my head, saying, 'Don't you be frightened, pet, no harm will come your way. I'll see you back safe and sound to your family.'

'It's all right, you don't 'ave to,' I said, wiping my face on my sleeve. I felt sure that Mum and Dad would be so angry with me for causing trouble and turning up with a copper.

After what seemed like a long, slow walk, with neither of us saying a word, we finally arrived at the hop field. I led him to the tunnel where my family were picking at their bin. Others saw me coming with the policeman and word soon swept through the hop fields like wildfire, inflamed with the gossip of Chinese whispers. Dad appeared out of the shade, tall and broad, with other men around him who had stopped what they were doing and were glaring at the village bobby on a bike. No doubt they thought I had pinched something from the shop and had been caught and brought back after a reprimand. If that had been the case the caring copper would have been told to go away in no uncertain terms, not too politely either. I felt myself going cold when the officer, short and to the point, quietly explained to Dad what had happened to me. Then came the questions from Dad, firing like bullets, one after the other, with no consideration for me and the way I felt inside. There didn't seem to be any sympathy, just anger. This was why I hadn't wanted the shopkeeper to call the police.

When Dad ordered me to tell him exactly what the man said to me I mumbled, as I fixed my eyes on the ground, about do I show the boys mine and so on.

'What else did he say?' asked Dad, a touch amused by this.

I covered my face to hide my tears. It was all getting so much worse.

I was thankful for the quiet but stern tone in the policeman's voice as he said to Dad, 'That'll be enough, sir, thank you. You can see she's upset.'

The look he received from my father spoke volumes. Had the country officer not been wearing that uniform, he might well have suffered a black eye or a nosebleed. The policeman impassively turned to leave, saying that he would be back the next day to ask me a few questions that he needed to know the answers to. What, for instance, was the colour of the van and was there lettering on the side? But Dad wasn't going to have any of that. He wanted to know there and then every detail about the van and what the man looked like. I was ordered to try and think and tell the policeman everything I remembered. Aware of the trouble I was causing I couldn't think straight so I said whatever came into my mind to get it over with. That there was writing on the side of the van in gold lettering and that was all I could remember except that the man was ordinary and wore a light brown cotton overall coat that most delivery men wore in those days.

By then I felt worse instead of better and I wasn't sure why, since I was back with my family. I knew it had some-thing to do with the way Dad was reacting though. He was exercising complete power over the policeman. It was as if he thought it more important to find the man than make me feel safe and protected. Cold and shivery under the midday sun, all I wanted was to go back to the hut with my sister who I could see was upset for me. It was true that we were very different personality-wise and that we hardly ever played together but she was protective towards me when necessary, within the confines of our school and in the streets, and that was what I wanted right then – someone to look after me, make me feel safe.

The policeman had noticed my obvious unhappiness and suggested that my parents took me back to the hut and tucked me up in bed. He then pushed his bike away, swung a leg over and peddled into the distance. I watched until I couldn't see him any more and hoped that he would come back the next day, but I didn't know why. As I turned around to look up at Dad I muttered that it hadn't been my fault that a dirty man had talked to me in the lane. He never said a word but gave me a look to let me know he could do without a copper turning up on his doorstep. Dad was not someone who often broke the law but working in the docks he, like other dockers, sometimes picked up stolen goods for sale on the cheap. And this did not sit well with chummy policemen appearing at the door asking questions, no matter what the reason. Coppers were coppers after all was said and done.

Dad relaxed once the officer had gone and told Johnny to take me back to the huts to unload the shopping, saying that he, Mum, my sister Laura and little Albert would follow up later.

That evening, a Saturday, my elder cousin Mary and my sister Laura were given instructions to watch over me while the grown-ups were at the local pub with other hop pickers.

Since it was the weekend and Dad was visiting, we girls were to sleep in one of the spare black tin huts that were kept for weekend visitors. Once they had tucked me up in bed, Mary and Laura went into a friend's hut to play Monopoly, taking Albert the toddler in his beaten-up old pushchair. I was by myself, but this time not in my familiar bedroom but in the dim light of a candle burning in its tin holder in the corner, alone and vulnerable. I was frightened of who might come in. Very frightened. I lay there watching the door for ten minutes or so without being able to sleep before I pulled back my covers and tried to lift the small iron latch on the hut door. It wouldn't budge. I kept trying because I couldn't believe that anybody would have wanted to lock me in, but I just couldn't make the latch shift. In the end, I was so terrified, I kicked and banged with my fists and screamed for someone to let me out.

No one came because no one heard. At first I was afraid to raise my voice too loudly in case I got into trouble but that went by the wayside once panic gripped. I was like a wild animal screaming and kicking the door for all I was worth. Eventually one of our neighbours from a pink painted hut close by came to let me out. She was carrying an oil lamp and must have seen the look of sheer relief on my face.

'If one them lads have locked you in there, Sally, I shall hang, string and draw them.'

'I don't fink it was one of the boys. I never heard anyone out there. But I thought I would suffocate because there ain't no windows in the tin huts.'

'No. That's because they're mostly kept for the adult

men who come up at weekends. They're usually so drunk they wouldn't notice in any case. Come you with me, my dear, and we'll soon have you snug in a rug.'

I walked beside this angel of mercy, wondering what I could say in order to not let her get angry with anyone. I had had enough for one day. She led me into her hut and sat me down and then put a tartan blanket around my shoulders and proceeded to make me a mug of cocoa with milk already boiled. 'Leaving you all alone in the dark and locked in after what you've been through. What were your parents thinking of?'

'I wanted to go in the black tin hut,' I said. 'I felt nice and warm and cosy in there.'

'I'm sure,' she said and then smiled gently at me. 'Come on. Come outside and sit round the fire. I shan't make a fuss over it.'

I felt my shoulder drop as I relaxed. 'I think my cousin and my sister might have put the twig in the catch so I wouldn't go out in the dark and get lost or something.'

'That's exactly what they did do. At least it wasn't the boys being cruel.'

As it turned out it had been my cousin Mary and sister Laura who had pushed a strong twig through the outside latch, so that I wouldn't go outside. Which wasn't all that bright since I was hardly a child of five. There was talk of them both slipping off to meet up with a couple of boys, though, so I suppose they hadn't been thinking all that clearly.

Mum and Dad eventually strolled back with other happy songsters, having enjoyed their Saturday night out in the local pub. Neither of them were pleased at being given a lecture by the woman who had taken me in. Mum in turn gave Mary a telling off. She was older than Laura by almost a year and was meant to have known better. I loved Mary, who was a favourite cousin and I knew she had done what she thought best by fixing the hut door shut to protect me. All I could think was that had the woman in the shop not called the policeman, nobody would have known what I had been through in the lane and things could have gone back to normal. Some part of me knew that she had been right, though, by boldly going in where others feared to tread; the man, after all, could have been the husband or father of somebody she knew. One thing was for certain: all in all I seemed to have caused too much trouble for one day and as I finally lay back in bed that night, with my sister next to me, I asked Lord Jesus if he could please stop men from wanting to torment and steal children away – and me in particular.

A week later, on the following Saturday, Dad and a few of my uncles and their friends were on the lookout for that green van, one that delivered to local houses on that particular day in that particular area. They had been doing their homework, but I had no idea what was going on, because I was at our bin picking hops with Mum. Laura came running up to our bin, out of breath, and said I was to go immediately back to the huts. When she managed to get out the full story between pants we learned that Dad and the others were holding a man hostage.

My first fear was that they might be holding the wrong man and have harmed him already. There was no time for worrying over this though. I ran as fast as I could in my wellington boots. I could hear supportive cheers and advice from pickers at their bins, telling me not to be shy at pointing the finger at the bastard. Word as usual swept through like lightning and it was all a touch scary. The only thought going through my mind as I ran to the common was, Please don't let it be him. Please, God, don't let it be him or they will hang him from a tree and be hanged for it themselves. Behind me was a trail of other children wishing to be part of the action and drama.

When I arrived at the van, the small and skinny driver was shaking and begging for his life as the brawny dockers surrounded him. The expression in his eyes as he looked into my face was full of terror and I felt he was pleading with me. I knew I was to sound as if I meant it when I muttered, 'This isn't the man.' I would have said it whether it was him or not, but it wasn't him, so it was easy to sound certain. I couldn't think straight so I just kept saying it wasn't him. The London men finally relaxed, gave him a slap on the shoulder and a message to pass on to the other drivers, which hardly needs explaining.

The delivery man got into his van, still trembling with fear, and drove off, never to be seen in the area again while the hop pickers were about. Dad took me to one side and spoke quietly, saying, 'If you dare to talk to strangers again and bring the police to our door you'll get the hiding of your life.'

'But it wasn't my fault,' I said, not in the least bit scared of him. 'You should 'ave gone to the shop instead of me and it wouldn't 'ave happened, would it!'

By the expression on the other men's faces I could tell that they agreed with what Dad was trying to get across, but they were also giving me a reassuring look or a faint and fond smile. One of them gently ruffled my hair and said, 'She'll be all right now. Safe and sound with us watching out for 'er.'

The men were on my side so I could breathe a sigh of relief. I knew then that I wouldn't get a smack on the leg for bringing trouble to the door and then cheeking Dad in front of the other men, who had clearly found my daredevil stance a touch amusing. I climbed into my bed that night having learned a little more about the twists and turns of life.

A week before the end of the final hop picking something far worse happened which affected every one of us, man, woman and child. A young engaged couple visiting their relatives for a weekend were swimming in the river close to our old-fashioned wooden bridge where it was shallow in parts and deep in others. The girl had auburn hair and a Hollywood-style swimming costume and looked like she'd stepped out of a fashion magazine. I had been scrumping from a Cox's orchard nearby with some other children and was making my way back to the river with the hem of my skirt pulled up to create a carrier for my rosy apples when a high-pitched scream pierced the silence. Then there were more urgent screams for help: the young woman's fiancé was yelling at us that his girlfriend was drowning and he couldn't swim. I can still hear him pleading as he yelled out to us children, 'Get help. I can't swim and she's drowning! Get help!'

Dropping our apples, we sped over to the river when really we should have run to the huts yelling at the top of our voices. As we got closer we saw that the girl was in the water struggling and waving her arms frantically. Even though she was a strong swimmer she could do nothing about the cramp that had gripped her legs. One of the lads ran back to the huts shouting that someone was drowning and all we could do as we stood on the bank of the river was look on, helpless. It all happened so quickly that we hardly had time to take it in. I could swim very well by then but I was hardly a stout girl and it had been drummed into me by our swimming coach during lessons at the York Hall baths that only adults, and preferably a qualified life-saver, should go to the aid of someone drowning

Unable to stand by and watch helplessly, the girl's fiancé went in to try and save his beloved, preferring to give up his own life than lose her, I suppose. He looked petrified as he waded in from the shallow, sloping part of the river towards her, holding out his hand and screaming for her to take it. He lost his footing and within seconds they both disappeared under the water to come up again, clinging on to one another before going below into the depths. Help arrived finally in the shape of two strong men who went in to the rescue as we children were ushered away.

A few minutes later all was quiet and an eerie silence was spreading, no one saying a word. Some of us children sneaked back to see what was going on. I was horrified but the curiosity was just too much for me. The couple had been pulled out of the river and were lying face down on the bank. Two adults were pushing and pummelling the water out of their lungs and trying to breathe life back into the couple to the sound of the river gently lapping under the blue sky. Slowly and in silence we all walked back to our huts, hoping the life-savers might be able to do something for the couple. There was a heavy atmosphere clouding the usual pleasant, lazy scene.

I sat down by our small camp fire where our big black kettle was steaming and moments later I saw the couple being taken away on stretchers, thick red blankets over them as they were carried to the lane and to the waiting Red Cross ambulance. They both lay still, the only difference was that we could see the man's pale face but a red blanket was covering the young woman from head to toe. She was dead. I ate my tea of two doorstops of bread and dripping from my white enamel plate with the blue edge and wondered why God hadn't been able to save the young man's sweetheart. Once I had eaten every last crumb I took my plate to the communal tap and scrubbed it clean with a bunch of wild hops snatched from the hedgerow. As I dried it on my cotton skirt, I couldn't ignore the heavy sickly feeling inside.

The girl tried so desperately hard to survive because she so much wanted to live. As much as I loved hop picking down in Kent I wanted to go home. There was no singing round the camp fires that night and no calling for absent children playing in the dark to come in for bed. They were already inside their huts truly wishing that the day hadn't been.

Mum was washing the crockery and cutlery in a small bowl of hot soapy water outside our hut and I thought she would be pleased that I had already cleaned mine for her. I held it out and she took it from me without a word and placed it in the bowl with the others. Her mind was on the tragedy too. Leaving her to have some peace and quiet, I wandered back over to the riverside by the old bridge and sat on the bank staring at the place where the girl went under and couldn't believe that it had happened. There they had been, happy and beautiful and swimming . . . and then she was gone.

9
Food, Glorious Food

Hop picking, living in huts and working in the fields was over, not just for our family and friends but for everyone. Mechanisation had by then well and truly arrived and machines were already in action on other farms taking on the work of people. Our tragedy in any case meant that none of us would really want to go back to our bit of Kent countryside with the haunting memory of that girl who was sunbathing one minute and drowning the next over-shadowing our time there. It was over. No more hop picking for us.

With the catastrophe behind us, over the following winter Mum began to think about the next year and caravans by the seaside, Leysdown, Clacton, Ramsgate, while I was looking forward to becoming a teenager. In August 1959 Dad had got himself a car, a second-hand shooting brake, which we piled into one Sunday to follow one of my uncles, who was driving his lorry with the rest of our extended family aboard, my two elder brothers included. We were on our way to Southend for the day. A kind of family beano I suppose.

My mother didn't think much of the place, which was buzzing with people in kiss-me-quick hats and littered with ice-cream wrappers which also spewed out of overflowing bins. The beach was pebbly and congested with people from all over London sunbathing cheek by jowl. I loved the Curzal but it wasn't much good being at a funfair watching everyone else enjoying the rides with no money in my pocket. We kids had each been given two shillings and sent off to enjoy ourselves but that was also to buy our meal of the day – a huge portion of chips in paper sprinkled with vinegar and salt.

With no pocket money to my name and no way of earning any, I made the most of the beach and collected winkles in Albert's colourful bucket before we made sandcastles together. Laura and I took turns to look after him at the seafront. Needless to say the adults were in the pub after a bit of fun in the Hall of Horror so we had time to kill and no money to spend. I loved the Laughing Policeman but, even so, there was only so long that one could stand and watch as people came and went, pushing a penny into the slot meter for the same old repetitive show.

After that first experience of the sand and sea I knew for sure that I much preferred to swim in rivers and sunbathe on grassy banks. But, since swimming down in Kent for five or six glorious weeks each year had come to an end, I was going to have to make do with the public swimming baths all the time. But I had my imagination to fall back on and could draw on this whenever I wanted to be in my most favourite place in the world, the hop farm.

My imagination could help me stave off hunger, my frequent companion, when young. One day, after I had searched our pantry to find that the cupboard was bare, I lay on my bed and conjured up an imaginary plate piled high with light golden hot chips, which our neighbour, Milly, often served to her three daughters as soon as they came home from school. Not only could I see the hot food in my mind's eye but smell it too – salt and vinegar as well. I could easily visualise myself picking up a hot golden chip and popping it into my mouth and could actually taste it. I would then summon up a thick slice of fresh warm bread, spread with best butter, piled high with my crispy chips then folded over to make a melting sandwich.

This had somehow satisfied my stomach and stopped me from feeling hungry and also rendered me a touch on the sleepy side so I played this new game when I was in bed at night and the more I practised the better I got at it. I could satisfy my rumbling stomach by bringing to mind an entire roast dinner, providing I took it all very slowly. I needed to start at the beginning to make it work and go through the motions in my mind of shopping at the butcher's and the greengrocer's for supplies. I would then think my way through the procedure of standing in the kitchenette preparing, roasting and serving the meal on to my enamel plate, as I had seen Mum do when I was sitting at the small kitchen table watching her.

I then very slowly ate my fantasy meal and could actually taste all the different flavours and satisfy hunger at the same time. It was a brilliant discovery but I didn't always have the patience to go through that sequence, so on such occasions when I rummaged in the kitchen cupboards for something to eat, to find only a packet of Bisto, flour and barley and half a bottle of Daddy's brown sauce, I paid a visit to Aunt Polly who could always find me some food.

I was completely at home in her house because my aunt had looked after me so many times before I had started school when Mum worked at Charrington's. I was still close to and fond of my cousins, as I was of my aunt and uncle who taught me to play cards and board games at an early age and gave me my first old worn-at-the-edges pack of cards, so that I could practise by myself. By the time I was seven I had mastered the games of trumps and pairs, so when I was at home playing cards with my sister and elder brothers Johnny and Billy I didn't do too badly, thanks to the lessons from my cousins. Occasionally Dad would join in with us and those times are my best memories of him.

He always seemed to be more chirpy and relaxed when we were all together as a family than on the evenings he was childminding Laura, myself and Albert, while Mum was at work at the cinema. When we did play cards round the table Laura preferred to watch us and keep score and had a quick brain for figures. Her favourite lesson at school was maths. Maths and reading history books were her two pastimes and especially reading anything to do with our local history in borrowed library books. So on quiet Sunday afternoons when we played cards after Sunday dinner, with Laura keeping score in between reading about old London, I was a happy, contented girl.

Later in the afternoon, sometimes Billy or Johnny would take the local history book from Laura and flick through, testing my sister on historical facts. She could nearly always reel off the answers, having learned them by heart and mostly got eight or nine out of ten and sometimes full marks. I loved those Sunday afternoons when after dinner

Mum and Dad often were in the bedroom having a two-hour nap. Listening to Laura, I could easily be carried off into the past and see myself in the streets in Dickens's time, singing next to a chestnut seller for my supper. She could make everything sound like a story and would tell us about filthy overcrowded streets in east London a hundred years before our time, when there had been disease from the squalor of the slums, and the reason why Victoria Park, in Hackney, was created.

The gardens were seen as a place for people from all classes to come and breathe in fresh air during leisure periods. In reality, though, such luxury was only afforded to the wealthier people who had time for measured walks in lovely surroundings, but later on the park was taken over by the working folk who appreciated it more than Queen Victoria, who opened it, could ever have imagined. Margaret and I certainly did. We had been going there for years at Easter and summer breaks from school. Playing on the swings, feeding the kangaroos, on the penny paddle boats and, best of all, swimming in the Lido, the open-air swimming pool. This cost tuppence to get in and when we had no money and were strong enough, we, like the older boys, managed to climb over the tall surrounding wall and bunk in free.

My eldest brother Billy had left school around about this time at the age of fifteen and was employed full time so there was a little more money coming into our house and the cupboard was more plentifully stocked. My survival instincts by then had grown, and so on my regular weekly shopping expeditions to the butcher's shop for

Mum, I earned a little income on the side. She always wrote on her list the price that she wanted me to pay the butcher for our Sunday joint. The butcher working in our local shop, being a close family friend, served us generously, the joint being weightier than the allowance. Mum wasn't the only one to earn out of this. If, for instance, she wrote sixteen shillings for a leg of lamb, I would ask for a leg of lamb at fourteen shillings and slip two bob in my shoe. I got away with this for months and was never found out.

I always used the florin to buy a family-size chocolate or jam and cream Swiss roll, which I kept hidden in my drawer and Laura and I ate it during the week when we were hungry or fancied something sweet to eat. This was our secret and one that I once told to Nan who was strolling along, arm in arm with my godmother Aunt Sarah, on her way to the market. Stopping to say hello with a smile on my face she asked why I was looking so chuffed with myself.

'Cos I've just made half a crown, that's why, Nan. It's in my shoe.'

'What d'yer mean?' she said, hardly able to contain her laughter. 'Been running errands for the neighbours, 'ave you, Mog?'

'Nar. They never treat you even if you do go for 'em, Nan. I've bin caught out like that before. Fuckers never give me a penny for a chew for going. Nar, I've bin a bit more clever than that. I've hid a bit of the money out of Mummy's change in me shoe.' She and Aunt Sarah started to chuckle so I told them how I wangled the money out of the Sunday joint fund and how it was my own idea. I then got carried away and told her about other little tricks of mine.

'You'll be in trouble if your mother finds out,' she said, still trying not to laugh. 'Two and six is a lot of money, Mog.'

'But it's not really money though, is it? It's a thick slice of roast meat less, that's all.'

'I s'pose that's one way of looking at it.'

'And I'll tell you summink else as well while I'm at it, Nan. I pierce a hole in the bottom of a tin of peaches and drink the juice. Then I turn the tin upside down and on Sunday Mum opens it with the can opener and she's none the wiser.'

'You mean she don't notice the fruit's dry?'

'Well, she does, yeah, but she blames Higgings, the corner shop. Says she's gonna give 'em a piece of 'er mind one of these days.'

'I wouldn't like to be on the other end of that, Sal,' said Aunt Sarah, pinching her lips together. 'Wouldn't want your mum telling me off.'

'So you know what I 'ave to put up wiv then? Dad's worse though. He's a bucking fastard at times.'

'All right,' said my grandmother, containing a smile. 'That enough of that. You can twist the words around as much as you like but it means the same thing. Go on 'ome and try to be good. Your mother will annihilate yer if she finds out what you've bin up to.'

Their quiet chuckling turned into raucous laughter as they walked away, having promised not to tell on me. It wasn't the only secret we shared. Nan had once caught me and Margaret bunking on the underground train at Bethnal

Green which we often did. She thought this was funny too
and swore not to let Dad know if I agreed not to take too
many free rides in case the guard caught me without a
ticket. But Margaret and I had often slipped past ticket
collectors and had become experts by the time we were
twelve. We often rode from Bethnal Green underground to
Redbridge in Essex where we slipped out a side gate to go
and play in what we thought was the heart of the countryside.

The pair of us liked nothing better than to take off our
shoes and paddle in what we thought was a narrow river
and over the years it became a favourite pastime. We didn't
discover until our final free trip there when we were eleven
going on twelve that our narrow river, which ran alongside a field often filled with daisies and poppies, was actually part of the sewer system. Happy as sand girls,
Margaret and I hadn't taken too much notice of an old
man who was shouting from a distance and waving his
arms frantically at us, yelling at the top of his voice for us
to get out of the water.

He had a slight country accent so it wasn't that easy to
make out what he was trying to tell us, but the one word
he did repeat, over and over, was poliomyelitis. Once we
picked up on this we stared at each other, horrified, and
then scrambled up the small bank. As we started to walk
towards him, he backed off and then ran away as if his life
depended on it. We put our black plimsolls back on to our
wet feet without even brushing off bits of rotting wet leaves
and ran to the train station to get home as soon as possible
so that we could sit in the bath and scrub away the polio.

Once safely on our estate again we split up and I crept into our flat and the bathroom to run a lukewarm bath, knowing that Margaret would be doing the same in her house. I sat in the bath peering at every tiny fly and minuscule slug which came off my feet and legs and floated to the surface when Mum suddenly opened the bathroom door and demanded to know why I was taking a bath when it wasn't bath night. She looked from my flushed face to the grimy bath water and shuddered before leaving me to it, pulling the door shut behind her. Once out and almost dry I went to my and Laura's bedroom and stayed there, keeping out of the way until the symptoms showed themselves.

It was the second half of the 1950s and polio was continuing to be a big problem right across Britain even then. We didn't know all there was to know about it but we knew it was serious, so the next day, Margaret and I went to the library to look up the word poliomyelitis in the medical dictionary. With a little help from the librarian we read enough to be fairly certain that we could actually die from it or survive but be paralysed for life if the outlet from the sewer had been full of the bacteria. We made a vow that if only one of us got the illness the other would take care of the unfortunate one forever and not leave the invalid in a wheelchair outside shops for too long.

We went immediately to the nearby Bethnal Green Hospital only to find a disinterested attendant on duty sitting in his little room and peering out at us through his special window which slid open and shut. 'If you've come to visit someone,' he said, 'you can come back later once you've scrubbed your face and hands and washed your hair. You look like you're running. Alive.'

'Fucking cheek,' said I. 'We ain't got fleas! And we ain't come to visit no one. We've come to let you know that we've caught polio as a matter of fact.'

'Go home and have a good hot soapy bath then. The pair of you.' He slid his little window shut and that was that – he was gone from view. But since we couldn't see him and he couldn't see us, we pushed open the heavy swing doors and went off to explore the wards in search of patients recovering from polio. All we found though was a geriatric section, so related our story to a group of old folk who were getting ready for an afternoon sleep and left to the sound of their laughter.

'People these days don't care, Sal,' said Margaret and we walked out of the hospital arm in arm. 'We could be dead and gone or paralysed for life and they wouldn't worry. We'll just 'ave to leave it to Our Lady Immaculate. She'll watch over us.'

'And Lord Jesus,' I said. 'He'll want to be in on it.'

'You'd better not start taking the mickey out of my religion, Sal, or we might break up for good.'

'I wasn't taking the mickey,' I said, my fingers crossed so she couldn't see.

'I'm not sure about you, though. You never go to church, that's the trouble. You don't put yourself out for the Lord in any which way.'

'You could say the three Hail Marys for me again, couldn't you?' I said, a touch of plea in my voice. 'Like you've done before?'

'I s'pose so,' she said. 'Anyway, we'll 'ave to leave it to our Lord to decide if we're to die or not.' As it turned out, neither of us were in the least bit ill – which was a bit of a comedown in a way.

With Albert going on five there were now seven mouths at home to feed, and with Dad and my older brothers' huge appetites, my sister, my mother and me, there was only just enough dinner to go round at times, so if any of us were late to the table, and I often was, the food would be gone before you could say, 'Where's mine?'

I remember one of those occasions when I had stayed out playing for too long and came in starving hungry and created blue murder when nothing had been left for me to eat. I caught a look of warning from Dad but still said, 'It's not my fault for not being here at the time you decide to dish up dinner! You could 'ave put some on a plate for me!'

'That's enough of that,' Dad warned.

But did I stop? Oh, no. I told him that it wasn't right or fair not to save food for a growing girl. The expression on his face spoke volumes. He knew I was taking liberties because my elder brothers were there and so I was not in fear of the belt. I then left the room and slammed the living room door loudly before calling out to him, a touch too foolish for my own good, 'You selfish bucking fastard!'

This was serious and I knew it. Dad and I were often at loggerheads and I cheeked him and he belted me and round it went. This was all quite normal, but I'd never said anything quite this bad to him in front of the others before.

I knew that I had no choice other than to get out of the flat, pronto. So off I went but instead of going downstairs where he might follow me I went up to the next floor and sat quietly on the stone staircase waiting to see if he came out. He didn't, so I crept back and pulled the key on a string through the letterbox and went into my bedroom and scrawled a note on a sheet of paper ripped from a school exercise book meant for homework. I then stole into the kitchen and left the note. 'You never feed me and Dad hates me. I've run away for good. Look after Albert. Love Sally.'

I made myself a thick jam sandwich to take with me and left the flat to fly down the stairs and away. I pictured a grand house where I felt sure I would find work as a scullery maid's help or in the kitchens where a maid below stairs might make me a sandwich once I got there. I wanted to find a place from which I could write to Margaret and tell her to join me if she wanted. Since Dad and my older brothers were playing cards for pennies with Albert watching them and Laura curled in an armchair, reading a paperback, I felt they wouldn't miss me for a while. Mum was at the Empire on her evening shift, in the spotlight selling ice creams.

It was beginning to get dark and had just turned seven o'clock but I wasn't in the least bit scared. I ran through the dark arches and along the cobbled unlit turning until I was out on Cambridge Heath Road and pushed on until I arrived at the Bethnal Green Hospital where I sat on a bench in the glow of a street lamp to eat some of my sandwich. I intended to carry on walking in the same direction until I came to the countryside, to a grand house, where there might be a bunk bed for a stray who was all skin and bone and took up little space. So as not to have to answer awkward questions as to where I had come from, I decided that I would pretend to be deaf and dumb. This ingenious new idea really appealed to me and I wondered why Margaret and I had not thought of it before to gain sympathy.

Carried away with my fragile dream and fantasy, I hadn't noticed the fine drizzle of rain until a flash of lightning struck in the distance and the sound of thunder rumbled. Before I knew it, the heavens opened and the rain poured down, forcing me to take shelter under the porch of the hospital where I stood wondering what I should do next. At first I didn't think there was much choice other than to keep on going because I had left that unequivocal note in the kitchen. It hadn't occurred to me that there might be a hiccup such as a torrential downpour.

It did eventually ease off but I knew that I was going to have to go back home and put off my departure until the weather picked up. I ran in the rain like the wind towards home, pleading with God to not let anyone at home have spotted my farewell note. By the time I reached our block of flats I needed to sit down on the stone staircase I was so out of breath, with a painful stitch in my side. Sarah Brown from next door arrived, shook her umbrella and told me I should be indoors. So as not to cause any waves I followed in her footsteps, my heart pounding, rain in my hair and trickling down my neck.

Quietly opening the letterbox and pulling the key on a

string through, I let myself in and crept along the semi-dark passageway and into the kitchen where I saw to my relief that my note was where I left it. But my brother Billy heard me come in and opened the hatch door between the kitchen and the sitting room and glanced casually at me before closing it again. I could hear whispering and quiet laughter. I was hoping that this was just because of the way I looked, like a half-drowned puppy, long straggly hair soaking wet. I scrunched the note in my hand, took it outside to the rubbish chute to get rid of it and then went back into the flat and into the warm living room to casually sit down by the new electric-bar fire with the imitation flame.

No one said a word, but just carried on with what they were doing, the guys playing cards and Laura reading. I later learned the silence was all part of their plan, to simply ignore the fact that I had gone and come back again. I was back in the fold safe and sound and they could afford to smile over it. When Billy glanced at me, his lips pressed together, laughter in his eyes, he only just managed to speak without chuckling, 'All right, darling?'

'Why shouldn't I be?' I said, feeling better straight away. 'I'm hungry cos I never got any dinner but I won't starve.'

'Course you won't, babe,' said Johnny. 'I'll open a tin of Heinz spaghetti in a minute and we'll both 'ave some on toast. That do you, will it?'

'S'pose it will. I'm not fussed,' I said, shrugging as if nothing was out of the ordinary, even though I was sitting there, soaking wet and hair still dripping.

I was less scared of being punished and somehow the

steam seemed to have been taken out of the situation. Dad and my brothers carried on with their game of cards and Laura her book. Nobody mentioned a word until I went into the kitchen to make a pot of tea at Dad's request. I hadn't been in there a minute when he came in, glanced at where I left the note and then looked into my face and spoke in a very quiet, stern voice, saying, 'Don't you ever write things like that down again.'

I was subservient for a few days after that and kept out of the way when I could. Naturally I told Margaret about my failed attempt to leave.

'It serves you right, Sal,' she said, 'for not taking me with you. We're supposed to stick together through fick and fin until the good times come. That's what we always said.'

'I was gonna write to you from the mansion where I would be working. I planned to put in a good word for you as soon as I was settled in.'

'You can't get work till you're fifteen and anyway I still don't fink you should have gone off by yourself like that. We've not left school yet. We can't get a legal job till we've reached fifteen.'

'We could if we worked below stairs in a mansion.'

'I'm not working below stairs anywhere! I'm gonna be a nurse!'

'Well, there wouldn't 'ave been any point in taking you with me then, would there? See? I knew what I was doing. The fucking weather ruined all my plans!'

'Your plans weren't worked out properly if you ask me.

You did it on the spur of the minute. We'll be earning a living in a few years' time. That's when we'll go off together and share a nice furnished flat and be independent. The same as my Julie's gonna do.'

'Have fun and as many boyfriends as we like and perhaps save to go to America where your Julie's going one day,' I said, sensing a glimmer of hope. 'She'd let us stay with her, wouldn't she, Marg?'

'Course she would. As soon as we've left school and can earn a wage, we'll go out there. To New York.' It all sounded so wonderful but we had years to go before that dream could come true. In the meantime there was still home, Dad and school to contend with. Pipe dreams would have to wait.

10
A Sad Farewell

Not long after my attempt to run away my grandfather died. He passed away in his sleep, having suffered a heart attack in bed. He hadn't been ill that I knew of or poorly, he simply had one fierce attack and that was that and everything changed forever at number 24 Cleveland Way. It was quiet and Wheezy was sad and miserable and it was strange to see my grown aunts and uncles crying and hardly able to speak. I was not allowed to look at Grandfather lying in his coffin in the parlour on the first floor nor attend his funeral, and obviously I wasn't best pleased about this.

Dad told me that that kind of a thing was for adults only, but I thought I had as much right as anybody to see him before he went to his last resting place. I sat for what seemed like hours on the stairs waiting for the chance to slip into the room when no one was looking but it never came. There was always someone coming or going. None of them listened when I tried to explain why I needed to see the old man, to say goodbye, and kiss him on the cheek. Aunt Sarah squeezed my arm and said, 'Grandfarver's with God in 'eaven, Sally. Where we'll all be one day. Floating abaht.'

I know this was supposed to give me comfort but it was all bollocks as far as I was concerned. My grandfather would never have wanted to float anywhere. If his spirit did leave the body once he was dead he would have been off and away and be done with. For this reason alone I wanted to see him just once more in the flesh before they screwed down the lid, because I was going to miss seeing him peel a cooking apple or slicing a Spanish onion to go with his cheddar cheese – never mind that he would no longer be there to give me his words of wisdom.

I also, of course, had lost my favourite quiet place to go to, his little room with just the three of us by the crackling coal fire, him, his dog and me. I felt sure that Wheezy understood how I felt. I could tell by the way she looked at me and sat by my feet on the landing while I sat on the rickety old stairs waiting. I whispered to the dog that I would find out where her master was going to be buried and take her to that very spot on a lead one day.

When the day of the funeral came round, Dad and his brothers carried the coffin majestically on their broad shoulders out of the house, as if they were carrying a king. At least I managed to get close enough to touch the coffin and say goodbye. Standing amidst neighbours and friends who were outside in the street to pay their respects to an old neighbour and friend, I watched the procession of family in black come out of number 24 and recalled what Mum had said earlier that day: 'It's not an occasion for children. Stay with your cousins and don't make a fuss. You won't be the only grandchild who's not going to the cemetery.'

Of course she was correct but the sense of right and wrong wasn't something to think about just then. I did as

I was told and stood silently by the black railings and was pleased to see how many neighbours were out. I also saw the woman Rose Lipka again. She stayed back, almost as if she were hiding behind other people as she stood next to the man who had been in the house with her at Christmas-time when Margaret and I were carolling. The man who had given us tuppence to sing his chosen song. Her brother. I was too sad to care who they were on that miserable day when an occasional shake of the head and pursing of lips were the only movements from those watching and saying goodbye to an old gentleman of few words. A proud man who always returned a smile and doffed his cap. A family man who kept himself to himself. My grandfather.

His snug below stairs took on a different ambience for a few days after the funeral and was filled with relatives drinking tea and discussing the service, the flowers and the turnout of old friends and workmates. No one sat in his chair and I couldn't understand why so I wove my way through the packed room and was just about to sit down when my godmother, Aunt Sarah, told me I wasn't to use it. I looked up at her tear-stained face as she murmured, hardly able to get the words out, 'That's my dad's chair.'

Her gentle husband, Uncle Sailor, came to my rescue, saying that the old man wouldn't mind if I sat in it but this was enough for my aunt to burst into tears. My Great-Uncle Bill, Nan's brother, was close by and he smiled at me before wiping his eyes with his large white handkerchief. He then said, 'Go on then, Sally, he won't mind if it's you.'

I eased myself into his chair for the first time in my life and made myself comfortable, placing a hand on each side on the wooden arms. I looked into the small Victorian fireplace where no fire burned. It wasn't a cold day but even so there had always been a small coal fire glowing when the old man was alive. Nothing about the room was going to be the same again; already it was overflowing with people drinking beer and sherry which I had never known to happen before.

Sometimes the conversation was hushed and sad and then there would be a burst of laughter when someone cracked a joke to try and lighten the mood. Then it would go quiet again until someone spoke about loss and another tragedy worse than ours. There was always someone who knew someone who had died younger and more tragically than Grandfather. It was like watching a film from my seat by the unlit fireplace. I wondered what he would have made of it all and couldn't help smiling now and then. I knew he preferred to be in this room by himself and had little time for social gatherings. But it didn't matter any more what people were saying about anything really. My grandfather was dead.

A few weeks after the funeral my eldest brother Billy brought home the love of his life to meet us. He had already been in and out of love many times with pretty girlfriends, few of whom crossed our threshold. One or two of them lived somewhere on our estate so I knew who they were, whereas others I met only once or twice when Billy could not, or did not want to, go on an arranged date. On those occasions I was given a sixpenny bit to go to the meeting place and give a message to the girl waiting for him that he was unwell or working late. A lie for a sixpence seemed a fair deal to me.

But all this stopped once Billy met the girl he wanted to marry, the girl of his dreams. Blue-eyed and pretty was June from Hackney. My brother's James Dean image changed slightly and he became all soppy and sang love songs when he was in the bathroom. The couple were engaged a few months after us first meeting her and it wasn't long before wedding plans were being made – and I was to be a bridesmaid and wear a long white satin frock with a pale blue silk sash and flowers in my hair. In my cut, tight curly permed hair which I hated. I had never wanted curly hair and I was hopping mad but there was no point in losing my rag over this because as my godmother had said to me, 'The damage is done now, Sally love. So you'll 'ave to lump it.' She was smiling at the time.

I was the youngest bridesmaid and Albert the only pageboy, who, when trying on his white satin and pale blue outfit looked as if he were getting ready for a Catholic procession. Our local church, St Peter's, was the venue for the wedding and the reception was held in the church hall with approximately a hundred guests for a sit-down meal. Arrangements were put into place fairly quickly because June was bursting out all over, pregnant with Billy's baby. Relatives, in true East End tradition, rallied round. Aunts and friends on both sides of the family helped with the preparation of the food and the beautiful fresh flowers were courtesy of a close friend of the bride, who owned a florist and was chief bridesmaid.

Once the moment arrived, apart from my permed hair, I found that I liked being a bridesmaid, all pretty and carrying flowers. I glided down the stairs of our block of flats to step into a relative's highly polished old black car with white ribbons, there especially to take Laura, Albert and myself to the church. Most of our neighbours were watching and I loved all the attention, pomp and ceremony and dressing up like a princess. The next day, however, I was just as happy to be back in my old clothes and not having to worry if I got them dirty or not. I never wore my lovely frock outside again but I used to put it on to wear in the house until the fateful day when I was cavorting around our living room and spilled a cup of tea down the front. Off it went to the wash bag and returned a size smaller.

It was strange at home once Billy moved out, quieter and with a little more space for the rest of us. He hadn't moved far away so we saw him each Saturday when he came to visit and behaved as if he still lived at home with us. On one of those visits, while he was in the kitchen sharing a pot of tea with Mum and Johnny, chatting and quietly laughing, Albert, Dad and I were in the living room enjoying a game of catch with a soft ball. Albert was four years old and I was eleven and a half.

It was a lovely quiet family game we were having which made a nice change. But then Dad misjudged his aim and threw the ball over my shoulder to disappear behind the sofa. I leaned over the back to retrieve it to the sound of my little brother laughing because my backside was sticking out while my arm was stretched to the full, my hand feeling for the toy with Dad giving me instructions saying, 'Further along, bit more, bit further, bit further,' and then there was an almighty bang and a white flash and I was catapulted across from one side of the room to the other.

I crashed against the wall to collapse into a heap on the floor and the next thing I knew I was in my eldest brother Billy's arms and I could hear Albert crying and saying I was dead. His voice sounded as if it were coming through an echoing tunnel. I might have enjoyed the attention if I wasn't trembling and shaking so much. When I could finally manage to speak I was hysterical, yelling at Dad to pick Albert up and get him out of the room, insisting that there was a rat behind the sofa, a rat which had bitten off my arm. I turned to Mum, who was standing very still and glaring at Dad. He was saying something about forgetting that he hadn't put black tape over the bare wires that connected our television set to a socket behind the sofa. Mum was not impressed and it showed on her face. Dad shouted, saying it wasn't his fault and that he had forgotten about the black tape and that he had warned me enough times about going anywhere near that spot.

I went to bed early that night of my own accord.

I I
Farewell, Margaret

I had always been close to my little brother Albert from the moment he was born and loved him dearly and being his nursemaid had never been a problem, but as he became more active with age I didn't always want to listen to his never-ending, long-drawn-out stories of what had happened during the day while I was at school. So as a compromise, before I went across to Margaret, I would sit in the kitchen and let him talk nineteen to the dozen while I slowly sipped a mug of tea. It was much easier to let him get everything off his chest in one go with all my undying attention. Of course I knew that he would relate whatever story he had to tell to Laura once she came out of our bedroom having finished her homework, but he was so earnest about things that I had to make an effort and try to look as if I were interested.

My only escape from him was to retreat to the lav and read a comic in peace but even this was no real escape. He would simply stand outside the door chatting to me through the gap where the hinges fixed the door to the frame. But to give him his due he hardly ever whinged or cried and he was a good boy, but he just couldn't stop talking. There was one time he suffered in silence when I couldn't forgive Mum or Dad for not taking him seriously when he was in dire pain. Albert, just a few months after my brother's wedding, had at the tender age of four and a half fallen over while playing in the grounds of our estate and hurt his arm. When I came in around nine o'clock that night, having been over at Margaret's playing Monopoly, I could hear him crying in bed.

Mum was working her evening shift and Dad had felt that his son was being a bit of a crybaby but he was very wrong. My sister Laura heard me come in and rushed to tell me that she had been in and out to our little brother and had tried telling Dad that he wasn't making a fuss over nothing. 'Don't barge in and make Dad angry though,' she said. 'That won't get us anywhere. I think I should run to the Empire and get Mum. What do you think?'

I glanced at our kitchen clock and said, 'There's no point. She'll be home in about fifteen minutes if not before.' I told her that she should have gone down to Milly Cranfield, our neighbour, or Mrs Walker, a kind and beautiful woman who lived on our balcony who had helped us out before and would have known what to do.

'Dad wouldn't want us to do that, Sally,' she said, then signalled for me to go with her to check on little Albert. I followed her along the passage and could have wept myself when I saw his pale little face twisted in agony from the pain. I sat on the edge of his bed and patted him while Laura gently wiped his tear-soaked face with a cool flannel.

'I could go into Sarah Damps next door and ask if we can use 'er phone to call Dr Brynberg. Mum's got the emergency number down somewhere,' I offered.

'We'll have to check with Dad first, Sally,' she said, a look of worry in her eyes.

'I'll go and talk to 'im,' I said.

'Well, whatever you do don't swear or get his temper up. You know what you're like.'

I smiled and laughed quietly at her for Albert's sake. 'I promise I'll keep on the right side of 'im.' I then left them in Albert and Johnny's bedroom and went into the living room, controlling my rage.

Dad glanced from the television to me and smiled. 'Make us a cup of tea, Sal? I'm gasping.'

'That's what I came in to ask . . . if you wanted tea or cocoa. I'm gonna make some for me, Laura and Albert.'

'Not with milk you're not. There's not enough.'

'I know. I only ever put a little drop of milk in.' I waited a few seconds and then added, 'Albert's arm don't half look bad, Dad. It's swollen at the elbow.'

'Mum'll be in soon. She'll know what to do for the best. Probably put our crepe bandage on it.'

'You don't think we should phone for the doctor then?'

'At this hour? Don't talk silly. He'll be all right.' He then leaned on his elbow, shielding his face with his hand and watched his programme. I knew from experience that this was a signal for no more chit-chat so I went back to the bedroom to report to Laura that we had no choice but to wait for Mum to come home.

When she arrived, tired and ready for bed, she looked at Albert's arm and was of the same opinion as Dad. She gave my brother a cup of cocoa I had made and an Aspro. Our parents thought it was best to leave things be until the morning and then call a doctor if all was not well. Laura tried to get it across to Mum that our brother needed the doctor that night or should be taken to hospital but all that came of this was a pat and Albert being told what a brave little boy he was. He wasn't being a brave little boy, he was a boy in a great deal of throbbing pain who had a high temperature. His sorry voice and the agony on his face still haunt me. I can see his pale green eyes pleading with me to do something to make the excruciating pain go away. But there was nothing I or Laura could do other than to keep the aspirin going every three hours. Our brother Johnny was not due in until very late because it was Friday night and he was out with his mates pulling the girls at the Two Puddings dance hall in Stratford East. When it was time for me and Laura to go to bed, we kissed him goodnight and just before I turned the light off he said in a broken voice, 'It really hurts me, Sally.'

The next morning Albert was taken to hospital because of the bruising, swelling and inability to move his arm. His eyes were red and puffy from crying into his pillow that night trying to muffle the sound. His arm in fact was broken at the elbow joint and for a while he was seen as the bravest little boy in the world. He was rather proud of himself after the event once it had been seen to but it wasn't good enough. Our bravest little boy in the world had been in dire need of attention through the long dark hours of that awful night.

Later on that year it became clear to everyone that there was another baby on the way. Two in fact. The one expected by Billy's new wife June and another by Mum. This time of course I knew why Mum had gradually ballooned and the following January at the Bancroft

Hospital she delivered a fourth son, our angelic, adorable, baby boy who was christened Gary, after a film star and not a prince like his brother Albert had been. Our new cuddly chubby baby had light gold hair which stuck out exactly the way Albert's had, like a feather duster. His eyes were a soft hazel and within days my little brother was smiling at me. I loved him to bits.

Gary was spoiled and fiercely protected by all of us and in retrospect I can't help wondering if our little Albert was eased out into the cold once Gary came along, without us realising. If so, then it would have been a double blow for him when Billy, his wife and their new baby Lorraine moved in with us. They had been living in two furnished rooms which were small and cramped, and on a visit to see his eldest son Dad had been far from happy with the conditions they had to put up with. At that time in the late 1950s it was almost impossible to find decent rented unfurnished accommodation.

The continuing regeneration of the housing programme throughout the East End saw more old properties razed to the ground but not enough flats being built in time to replace them, so there was no real alternative for Billy and his family other than to move into our three-bedroom flat until a decent place was found for them. Dad's act of generosity in insisting they move in with us enabled me to see him in a different light. Mum had to be persuaded – and who could blame her?

Patiently sitting in the chair in the kitchen Dad pulled out all the stops to charm Mum into letting their son come home with his family in tow. I heard all of this by eavesdropping or from making an excuse to go into the kitchen to get a drink of water. Once in there I deliberately caught Dad's eye and gave him a wink and a secret thumbs-up sign, which made him smile. Suddenly we were communicating and for the first time in my life I wanted to give him a hug for fighting my eldest brother's corner.

So for a few months there were eight of us living in our flat, Billy and his family in one bedroom, Mum, Dad and baby Gary in another, Laura, myself and Albert in the third, and my brother Johnny sleeping on a sofa in the living room. It was a very difficult time for all of us and especially for Mum. There were two newborns and rows of napkins drying on a washing line fixed up in our bathroom and on the back balcony as well as the communal laundry line in the grounds. There were two babies crying to be fed and sometimes in unison, by day and by night. This all proved too much, understandably, so occasionally sparks flew between herself and her daughter-in-law. It was testing time for the young married couple too.

Thankfully after several months a flat was found for Billy and his family in Ravenscroft Buildings in old Bethnal Green overlooking Columbia Road flower market. Once they had moved out of our house, Johnny moved back into the end bedroom with Albert, while Gary remained in his cot in the corner of Mum and Dad's room and things settled down nicely again. During this time Mum had secretly gone to see our doctor to get something for her nerves. When he saw the state she was in he, according to what Mum told me, was very worried, and so he prescribed medication that would brighten her mood and which did in fact cheer her up no end. The name of the tablets he thought suitable was purple hearts. While she was on these, I heard her sing out loud while she was washing up or cleaning windows and this was something very new.

Having just arrived into our teens that summer Margaret and I were no longer rummaging around old bombed houses but used the last of our daredevil cheek to take free illegitimate rides on public transport away from Stepney, often using a red double-decker bus instead of the under-ground, where we were too familiar to the ticket inspector for comfort. We had long since found a way to dodge bus conductors by sitting on the upper deck when they were below collecting money and then going downstairs once they came up.

We achieved our dream of going to the West End and Oxford Street at Christmas-time that same year to see for the first time the famous Christmas lights. I think it was the exciting atmosphere that added to the spirit of the season that ordinary people loved. It certainly was the case with me and Margaret. We were happy as Larry just to be there, in Oxford Street, clutching on to our paper bags filled with hot chestnuts.

Looking at ourselves in a full-length mirror in one of the store windows within all the brightly lit grandeur, Margaret said, 'Ere, Sal, I fink we must be poor, you know.'

'We are hard up, Margaret,' I said as I munched on a chestnut and stared at our scruffy reflections. 'But we'll be rich one day.'

'When we come up on the pools, Sal.' She smiled, parroting her mother.

'No,' I said, 'we probably won't win our fortune – we'll earn it even if we have to work our socks off. I'm not gonna be poor all of my life, Marg. I'd rather be a thief.'

'Nor do I wanna be poor. But we can't be certain we'll marry a rich man, can we? So we'd better start finking about what jobs we should train for. I fink I might be an archaeologist,' she said. 'We've found plenty of old stuff already so we must be quite good at it.'

'I thought you wanted to be a nurse?'

'I do. But nurses don't get paid much, do they. We'll just 'ave to see how fings work out.'

Our interests seemed to change the minute we became teenagers. We were thirteen and found that we quite liked boys and they seemed to be taking a fancy to us. We still borrowed their bikes when they weren't looking and sometimes disappeared with them for an hour or so which was hardly difficult since they always left them leaning against a wall if not in the bike shed. Peddling off at speed, side by side, was brilliant. When caught we paid for the loan with a kiss so it was a double treat in a way. The bike shed, which was originally built for prams and pushchairs with six cubicles, was taken over by the men and boys for their pushbikes. I imagine that it must have been noisy in there at times and a disturbance for the neighbours living in the ground-floor flats either side of the sheds.

Margaret and I enjoyed a good view from her bedroom window of the kissing place and saw who came and went and if we had told all there was to know, there would have been a few cuff or cat fights between the married people in our block of flats. It was tempting at times to stir things up for a bit of fun. But we never did. There was our lovely old couple who lived to one side of the bike sheds who were getting on and yet I don't remember them ever complaining.

The pensioners, Mr and Mrs Weeks, owned a wind-up gramophone and sometimes we could hear their 78 records of classical music through their open doorway. Sadly, the lovely old gentleman became poorly during the following bitterly cold winter and passed away. His partner of a life-time, Mrs Weeks, was clearly heartbroken and missed him dreadfully. It seemed so quiet and strange once he was no longer part of my little world. Everyone was used to seeing him chatting and smiling and watching the world go by. From the day he died his widow, my lovely silvery grey-haired lady, wore black or grey with a spray of pink silk flowers pinned to whatever she wore. She was lonely and lost without her husband and it showed.

When I knocked on her door, the way I had done before at a certain time of the day, she opened it and looked at me as if she didn't know who I was, or simply didn't want to be reminded of times gone by. Times when the three of us would sit in her lovely old-fashioned living room listening to the wireless or the old gentleman telling me a story from one of their books while she got on with her embroidery. Even though she looked at me as if I were a stranger, I knew that she knew who I was. After her short pause she would say, 'Not today, Sally dear, the old lady's a bit tired.'

She wasn't lonely for too long and although it was sad for us, I think that her passing away was probably for the best where she was concerned. So lost without her best friend, the beloved husband, she became weaker in mind and fragile in spirit and was probably ready to join Mr Weeks. She believed in God, guardian angels, and heaven – and a little of this rubbed off on me. On the day she passed away, I had been playing in the grounds with the other children when one of them said they could smell something strange coming from my old lady's flat.

I went to the kitchen window and could smell it too. It was horrible and it was strong. I peered through the glass pane but I couldn't see much through the net curtain so I went to the front door and knocked twice. I got no answer so I pushed open the letterbox which I immediately had to draw away from because the smell of gas filling the passage was so awful. I knocked again and waited but there was nothing but an eerie silence with only the faint background sound of her radio playing soft light music. I knew that something was badly wrong. Looking around I saw my sister Laura who was chatting to Milly, our neighbour, so I called out and waved her over.

She sauntered towards me not realising the urgency but once she got closer her eyes widened. She too could smell the gas. I nodded at the window and whispered that I thought that our lady was inside even though she wasn't answering the door. Milly parked her bags by the wall close by and peered in the window standing next to Laura.

'I can only see her bandaged legs, Milly,' Laura murmured. 'She's lying on the floor.'

Margaret's dad, Mr McGregor, was in his front garden watering his roses so I called out to him and as he got nearer to us he was obviously concerned because of the smell. He looked at my sister who shrugged sadly back at him and I think we all knew what had happened but didn't want to believe it. Margaret's dad went directly to the front door and with one good kick it flew open with a crash. We were ushered away and an ambulance was called. My lovely old lady had slipped on her kitchen lino and hit her head on the floor before she had time to put a match to the gas jets in the oven.

People said it was a nice way to go and that she would have just drifted off to sleep and I thought they were probably right, but still I didn't want to see the neighbours gathering or the police in and out of her home so I went upstairs to our flat and into my bedroom. I knew I would never see her alive again. I lay on top of the bed thinking about her and Mr Weeks and I felt a warmth seep into my chest as tears tricked down my cheeks. I looked about the room and took comfort from the fact that nothing was different in there. I then felt a warm golden sensation sweep through me. I thought about the collection of old-fashioned beads Mrs Weeks had given to me and the bits of lovely lace and silk material and dried my eyes as I whispered, 'Goodbye, Mrs Weeks. I hope you found your husband up there.' I don't know why but at that moment I felt that she had already found him. That they were together and, not only this, they had come into my bedroom to say goodbye in their own way and sent that warm, golden, loved feeling right through me.

I got off my bed and went to knock for Margaret who was still watery-eyed and we went up to the attic bedroom.

Even from up there we could hear that things were happening in the grounds below. People were coming and going and we didn't want to be part of it. We attempted a game of snakes and ladders but it was no use, we hadn't the heart for it, so we went to the park instead. We sat in the shelter next to the library and watched the park keeper tidying his treasured flower gardens and asked him if he could snip off a red rose for us to place on our old lady's doorstep.

The keeper was a rather a strict man who kept wild children in order and was obsessed with stopping them from spoiling the trees and gardens, so we didn't really think he would believe us when we told him why we wanted the flower, let alone say yes to our request. But the man bore a different expression to usual as he listened to us, slowly nodding his head and rubbing his chin. He told us we could choose a rose each, which of course we did and he carefully clipped off two blooms from his prize bushes. Margaret chose white and I chose red and each were perfect with a lovely scent. He told us to put them in a milk bottle filled with water and a little white sugar so they would last longer. We went straight home to follow his instruction only to find that somebody else had had a similar thought. There was already a bunch of wild flowers on the wall in front of the ground-floor flat. Within days it was covered with more picked flowers from neighbours. But the thing about our neighbourhood was that life never stood still and before too long there were other characters in our block for me to wonder about and puzzle over.

Directly above the old couple's flat and beneath ours a

new set of people had moved in, three women and a man called Arnold. They turned out to be the noisiest people on our estate, if not the entire area. From our sitting room we could hear their shrill voices bickering as they watched a favourite television programme. They seemed to prefer to screech at each other rather than talk normally like everybody else. They were odd in many ways though. As well as cursing each other they would cast wicked spells out loud, so that most of us in the block could hear and they would threaten each other with a big shiny kitchen knife. But in a way, this peculiar and sometimes affectionate Jewish family were a cameo of the vanishing old East End of London characters.

From what we could make out the women were sisters and Arnold was married to one of them. But there was a contradictory story that he was actually a brother to two of them and was the lover of the third who he had never got around to marrying at all. No one really knew or cared. Arnold was short, chubby and balding and no oil painting, but was at least unassuming and a rather gentle man. The expression on his face when coming home from wherever he worked said it all really – the poor soul had no idea what to expect from the three women that evening.

He would stroll through the grounds at exactly the same time each day with a slightly crumpled folded newspaper under the arm of his flowing grubby mac. He always had an expression of deep contemplation, and was at pains to have the world believe that he was a studious gentleman who could read, even though some of us knew he couldn't, if his ageing sisters were to be taken any notice of. They often shouted that he was no better than them and couldn't read a word written in his bloody newspaper. But he ignored them and often stood on the balcony with his treasured, out-of-date copy of *The Times* resting on the cement flower boxes which held only damp dirt, while in the background the three sisters would be screaming at each other or him, from within the flat.

Predictably, they would come in and out yelling their side of a particular argument at him while he browsed through the fragile pages of his paper. Sadie was tall and lean with thinning dead straight grey and black hair to the chin. With her overly large hooked nose and big brown eyes she was quite attractive. When she was quiet, she was very quiet but when disturbed by one of her sisters she was extremely loud with a high-pitched, shrieking voice. Her most used and I suppose favourite line, when addressing any one of them, was, 'Why don't you bloody well get out! Pack your bloody things and go!'

This of course was a deliberate opening for the night's operatic. Out one of the sisters would come, waving a frying pan or a broom shrieking that this flat was hers and *she* bloody well paid the bloody rent!

'You don't pay the bloody rent, you bloody well deliver it to the bloody rent office!' was a familiar retort. 'We all put our bloody share in and I put in the bloody most! And you can leave my bloody digestive biscuits alone! Buy your own bloody biscuits!' was another typical flow of words from the sister who smelled of witch hazel and natural hair grease beneath her scent of Evening in Paris.

Short and lean with rounded shoulders, Julia was the

most graceful of the four. Her hair was regularly dyed black and pulled back in a neat, tight bun. Sometimes she spoke in a terribly posh accent, mostly when she was using the iron banister on the staircase to practise her ballet movements, with one leg stretched high to give a private viewing to any poor soul who happened to be coming up the stairs. The third woman, quiet and sultry, was Becky, who enraged them all by saying nothing at all but shaking her head in despair. This was the one who might have been a sister-in-law, or Arnold's wife, or his lover, or the third sister. We never saw them arm in arm out walking. In fact we never saw any of them together other than on the front balcony. Sometimes they sat out there perfectly normally, chatting together, calmly looking down at the grounds below, or up at the sky, as peaceful as if they were in the front pew of a church. But it only ever took one tiny thing to spark them off and then pandemonium would break loose with each of them waving the carving knives again or jabbing the air with scissors and threatening to kill each other.

They didn't last that long on our estate. Becky was the first to trundle off and disappear in the wee hours of the morning with no more than a bulging, battered suitcase. When she went she took Sadie's rose-scented talcum powder and every single night for a week Sadie came out to broadcast, screeching, 'She's a bloody thief and she ought to be bloody well locked up! She took my ablutions! I'll bloody well kill 'er!'

Arnold, licking his finger and turning a page of his treasured copy of *The Times* on the balcony by himself, would ignite a little spark if it got too quiet, calling over his shoulder, 'It wasn't talcum powder! It was DDT! Dis-in-fect-ant Dust-ing Tal-cum. There's a difference.'

'It was bloody talcum powder! I bloody well know the difference! It cost me a bloody fortune! Evening in bloody Paris! I'll bloody well kill her!'

Arnold was hardly ever that bothered by any one of them and would simply turn a page of his newspaper. Occasionally we might hear him call out to the girls inside, 'Oil shares are down by threepence!' This in the next breath would be followed with, 'I expect she's gone there then! To Paris. To have an evening in Paris. Lots of evenings in Paris. She can afford it. She took all her money with her! Mine as well!'

The free shows they gave us were not to last though. The council were on to them for something, possibly not paying rent. For everyone else on our estate, a proper bath-room with a gleaming white bath and chrome taps was a dream come true, but this lot didn't sit in theirs to soak away their troubles. From the moment they moved in they had the coal man shoot bags of coke into it. In the proper outdoor coal cupboard they stored a collection of old toot, brought with them from wherever. No one knew whether they went to the public baths, unable to shake a habit of a lifetime or whether they bathed at all, but none of us got too close if we could help it. The mad motley bunch brightened up grey days and evenings though, even if some-times they would scream at each other for over an hour.

I don't know if the local lads had anything to do with them deciding to up and leave us or whether the council had offered them a place elsewhere, on an island perhaps, for safe keeping. The boys, my brothers included, would creep up to their door every so often, if all was quiet, and carefully position a grey rubber mouse so that it was nibbling a brown rubber spiral-shaped turd on the doormat. They would then knock on the door before scampering off to wait in hiding for the shrieks, as one of them opened and then slammed the door shut again.

When it eventually came round, moving-out day for the family took a week. They used big old prams instead of a removal truck, wheelbarrows and battered suitcases. In fact they pulled or shoved anything on wheels that they could find on dumps to transport their possessions. The last thing to go was an old mangy armchair on wheels, one of a pair. Arnold, sitting squarely in it, held a huge overflowing cardboard box which contained his wardrobe of clothes, with Sadie pushing him. They didn't look that bothered about moving on. In fact they seemed quite pleased with themselves. They had moved home several times by all accounts.

Once their flat was fumigated, cleaned up and given a fresh coat of paint, our new neighbours moved in. My little brother Albert couldn't have wished for a better family to be living beneath us. Mr and Mrs Lakenby and their two children, Joan and John, were a stark contrast to the brother and sisters before them. Albert and John were the same age and became so close as to be like brothers, with Albert spending more time in his friend's home than he did in ours.

John had the face of a choirboy on a Christmas card and the nature to go with it. His parents treated my brother as if he were their own son and when they were giving sweets as a treat they were shared between the two of them.

More than that, John's mother not only kept the door on the latch for Albert but fed him a proper meal as well. I don't know what they made of the way Dad summoned Albert from our flat, directly above theirs, in the evenings. Come rain or shine, when it was time for our newly acquired, adorable pet Pekinese dog, Fluffy, to be taken for his evening walk, Dad would bang three times on the carpet-covered stone floor with the poker. A lazy way of giving his young son the message to come up before Mum came home from her evening shift at the Empire. Having a dog in the flats was against the rules, of course, but since our dog was small and Dad was taller and broader than the caretaker, nothing was said.

Margaret and I had covered a fair bit of the East End during our childhood and so had branched out in another direction to the south of the river to an open-air swimming pool which we discovered was easier to bunk into than our Lido in Victoria Park, though not as nice. We thought nothing of walking through Rotherhithe tunnel from the east to the south and for five or six times this passed off without incident. The last time we ventured through what we considered to be just a long subway, though, we got a bit of a scare. A lorry slowed down beside us and the driver told us through his open window that we were not only risking our lives but could cause an accident and be in trouble for it. He behaved like a strict father, I suppose, and told us to climb up into his cab. We didn't mind one bit and were grateful for the lift so his headmaster stance was well worth the ride.

We sat in his cab, Margaret next to him and me by the door, enjoying this new experience of being so high up and at the front of a lorry. Alarms bells started to sound, however, when I noticed the change of inflection in his voice, from gently scolding to soft and chummy as he spoke quietly to Margaret, saying something that I couldn't hear but made her giggle. I felt he was using the same kind of tone that the man on the bike, earlier on in my childhood, had used on me. He then furtively gave Margaret a sweet and not me. She thanked him and then said, 'What about my friend?'

'You give her one,' he said, giving Margaret a wink as he passed her the small white paper bag. 'You can have the lot – I'm not that keen on barley twists as it happens. I only suck 'em if my throat's a bit dry and it's not.'

I took a sweet but said nothing until we came out of the tunnel into the light when I said, 'Thank you very much for the ride. You can pull up now and let us out.'

'No, mustn't do that, it's too dangerous in this bit of the road. Too much traffic. We can go further along where the road's less busy. Then you can find a safe place to cross over, a nice easy country road.'

'That don't matter,' I said. 'We're from Stepney. We're used to crossing busy roads.' I nudged Margaret for a bit of backing but she was sucking two barley sugars at once.

'Trouble is,' said the man, 'should a policeman see you not using a zebra crossing, you could get into serious trouble.'

Peering through the front window I could see a good safe place where he could easily pull up and told him so.

He quietly chuckled, insinuating with an expression that I was a dimwit.

'I think I know what's best, don't you? I've been driving a lorry on this route for years.' He then smiled at Margaret and spoke quietly, saying, 'Shall we drop your friend off and go for a drive in the countryside to look at baby deer?'

Margaret's expression immediately changed to one of full alert. With sweets in her mouth I had to answer for her. 'We want you to stop and if you don't I'm gonna open this window and scream for help. We're not fucking stupid and we're not little kids.'

I could see by his expression that he was weighing things up. He then tried the old chummy father routine, saying, 'Now don't be silly. I'm trying to help you. Wandering around in tunnels by yourselves. I don't what your mothers would think if I was to tell them. Anyway, there's a packet of chocolate buttons in the glove compartment. Get 'em out for us. I love chocolate buttons, don't you, girls?'

'Never mind about that,' I said, angrier with him than scared. By now I think I had had enough of the fucking man to last a lifetime. 'Pull up now!'

'Ooooh dear, a right spoilsport your friend, ain't she, sweetheart?'

'No,' said Margaret, spitting the sweets into her hand. 'She's right. We're expected by an aunt at the swimming pool and she'll phone the police if we don't arrive soon.'

'You don't have to break your Catholic rule of not telling lies just because of him, Margaret! If he don't stop the fucking lorry I'll scream at top voice out of the window!'

Sighing loudly, he pulled into the verge. He looked studiously at me and then at Margaret once we stopped and then reached across and opened the passenger door. 'Go on, you fucking little tarts. Get out of my fucking lorry, you pair of pissy drawers. I can smell the stench from 'ere! Go on – fuck off!'

We were out of that cab like a shot and still he kept on, his face red, a leering smile on his face. 'You pair of fucking child whores! You stink! I wouldn't want my cock anywhere near one of you!' With that he pulled the cab door shut and roared away.

In silence we stared after him until Margaret said, 'My drawers don't smell. I put 'em on clean four days ago.'

We enjoyed our swim in the open-air pool but we didn't stop long. We weren't our usual selves and we wanted to go home. Back to our side of the tunnel but not go through it. Not then or ever again. So we jumped on a double-decker bus intending to dodge paying our fare as we had done successfully many times before. However, the lady conductor was on the ball and confronted us in a loud and stern voice and stood watching as we went through a charade of checking our pockets.

'I know I put the two threepenny bits for our fare home in my skirt pocket,' I said, blushing bright pink.

'You did, Sal,' said Margaret. 'When your mum gave us the fare. I saw you put it there. It must 'ave fell out when you was changing into your swimming costume in the cubicle.' Another lie from my friend. One was bad enough but two in one day was scary.

'I've seen you two before,' said the woman sternly. 'And

I'm telling you now, if you come the Old Soldier with me again, I shall not only put you off my bus but report you to the authorities.'

'I'm very sorry,' I said, feeling worse for coming on this journey by the second. 'We've never lost our bus fare in our lives before.'

'No, I'm sure you haven't,' she said, to the sound of quiet laughter from a couple of other passengers. 'Don't try it on again or I'll call a copper.'

There was nothing more for us to say so we kept our mouths shut and sat in our seats looking out of the window. Once we were off the bus on our side of the tunnel, Margaret said, 'I don't fink we should go back over the river again, Sal.'

'No, Margaret. We won't. I fink them days are over.' We both knew it but it was hard to accept. At thirteen we were now proper teenagers and no longer street kids.

'The bus conductors on our side of the river are much more friendly,' Margaret quietly murmured and we both realised that we had turned a corner as far as being irresponsible children was concerned. We were at the difficult in-between bit. No longer a kid, but by no means an adult. And there were other things bringing on changes too. Both of us girls, even though we hadn't admitted it, were beginning to make new friends from each of our schools and that twin-like bond that we once had was slowly stretching like an old soft elastic band. Stretching and weakening before it pulled apart. Margaret seemed to be growing more thoughtful and quiet and a touch distant and I had started to roam about on my own, wending my way back to Aunt

Polly's and to my cousins and to a girl I had seen who lived close by.

I don't know if I was subconsciously looking for a new friend to bond with or it was just coincidence that on my next visit to Aunt Polly the girl I had seen quite a few times before, who looked to be the same age as me, was playing two balls against the wall of her house. Stopping to let me pass she smiled and said hello and told me that she was Josephine. She had light blonde hair, blue eyes and in fact the only real difference between us was that she was wearing a spotlessly clean frock and socks and neat pony-tail with ribbon whereas I was as grubby as ever. She looked angelic but my wariness of her soon disappeared when from her mouth, after we had nodded and said hello, came a not so angelic voice.

'It's like looking in a fucking mirror looking at you,' she said. 'Where d'yer fucking live anyway?'

'Bancroft Estate,' I said. 'Why? What's it to you?'

'Ain't nuffing to me, is it. You can fuck off for all I care. I've seen yer round this way before though.'

'My aunt lives up the turning,' I said, not sure which way to go with this one.

'I thought that'd be it. You can come in for a cup of tea if you want,' she said, playing her two balls in the air. 'It's up to you. But I'm going in for one and a fag.'

'Wot about your mum? Won't she mind a stranger coming in?'

'Course she fucking won't. Silly cow. She's at work anyway.'

'All right then,' I said, 'I will come in. My Aunt Polly wasn't expecting me or anyfing.'

'Wipe your feet on the mat,' she said, looking down at my grubby plimsolls.

I offered to take my shoes off and she looked aghast. 'Not wiv the state of them socks you won't. Bet they smell like old sweaty cheese.'

'No they don't, fucking cheek!' Who did this girl think she was?

We talked while she made a pot of tea and I felt strangely comfortable in her company, as if I'd known her for years. The little sitting room which led into the tiny kitchen was all spotlessly clean and homely with small plants in pots on the windowsill. Something I had not seen before. I asked her what school she went to and that's when I discovered that come the autumn term she would be transferring to the same senior school that I was attending, Cephas Street Secondary Modern.

'Got expelled from my uvver school, didn't I,' she said, drawing on a Woodbine cigarette from a packet of five. 'Too fucking long at that place I was.'

'What school was that then?' I casually asked.

'Mind your fucking business. What's it to you anyway?'

'I just wondered,' I said, unable to contain a smile. I began to chuckle as I looked into her face which suddenly broke into a grin and before I knew it we were both cracking up with laughter. And from that moment a new friendship began. She was rebellious, but only when told to do something she couldn't see any point to, or when blamed for something she hadn't done. She didn't pout or sulk but just refused point blank to go against what she believed was right. Most of the time she was good and got on with her own life; she didn't argue with other children, or me, she just said what she thought and left us to make of it what we would. I had never met anyone who could make me laugh so much without even trying or knowing she was being funny.

When she swore it didn't sound like swearing, it just rolled off her tongue in a singsong kind of way as if it were a normal part of her vocabulary. Josephine didn't give a hoot for the establishment, rules or regulations if there was no sound reason to them and wouldn't think twice about crossing over a class divide if the need arose. She would have walked into Buckingham Palace had there been reason to do so. To her, rich posh people were only posh because they weren't born in the slums – it had little to do with brains or graft.

We saw more and more of each other and I learned about her life at home, which was quite different to mine. She was the youngest of three girls and her sisters were away and married, living in other parts of London. Her mother, Hazel, was a lovely, gentle woman who took a liking to me. She would often feed me a meal, even though she had to work all hours to make ends meet, going from one office cleaning job to the next. Josephine was always in clean ironed clothes, hair brushed out and hanging loose or in one long plait and wore clean white socks or luminous pink or lime-green ones. In the early evenings or rainy afternoons, the three of us sometimes played cards or board games by the fire in the tiny sitting room, drinking a mug of Horlicks and eating the best bread and butter pudding in the world. Josephine's dad was hardly ever around and

I asked no questions because she referred to her dad as him – the old devil. So I guessed there was not much love lost there either.

Her soft-natured mother, who I came to be very fond of, sometimes ached from working long hours. She also seemed a touch on the lonely side at times, especially in the late afternoons or early evenings when Josephine and I went in from the streets to find her sitting by her tiny coal fire with only the wireless for company. She was still a beautiful woman in her mid-forties and from the photograph in the best room it was clear that she had been a stunner when she was young. The picture of her in the 1930s as a bride in a long, trailing, ivory silk gown and flowing lace veil was overwhelmingly lovely and she looked every bit the model bride, someone who was suited to the front cover of *Vogue* magazine with big, pale blue eyes and soft, wavy, fair hair. And yet here she was alone for most of the time, keeping the home fire burning almost single-handed.

One sunny afternoon when the three of us were playing a board game at her small wooden drop-leaf table, I sensed Hazel studying my face. I wasn't my usual self that day; in fact I was a bit off colour and trying to ignore the reason why. When I winced in pain for a second time during our game, my eyes screwed tightly shut, she asked what the matter was and I told her that my bad arm was throbbing. She looked at the baggy sleeve of my cardigan and then carefully drew it back.

She glanced from my arm to my face and back to the grubby, makeshift bandage which was no more than a strip of torn-off old sheeting through which pus had been seeping for days. She asked me how long the bandage had been on. I said I couldn't remember but it was probably about two weeks and I was waiting for the scratch to heal.

She spoke in a soft voice, telling me that it looked to her as if it might be more than just a scratch and asked how it had happened. I confessed that I had pinched one of the boy's bikes from the grounds at home and scraped my arm along a rough wall, when I made a clumsy turn. Then, with my arm throbbing painfully, I couldn't hold on to my tears any longer. Up until then, apart from Margaret, nobody had taken any notice of it because it was hidden under my cardigan sleeve.

Examining my arm below and above the rag bandage Hazel slowly shook her head, saying, 'We'll have to get that looked at, Sally love.' She then pulled herself up from her chair and told Josephine that they were going to have to go with me to the casualty ward at the local Bancroft Hospital. I was quietly relieved that someone was doing something because I knew that it was getting worse. The three of us walked to the hospital which was close by and once we arrived I sat with Josephine while her mother spoke in a hushed voice to a nurse who looked over at me while she listened to all that my carer had to say. I turned to my friend, hoping she would say something funny to make me laugh the way she so easily could. But even she wasn't smiling. The nurse then beckoned me over as I wiped another telltale tear from my cheek.

Stroking my straggly hair she smiled into my face saying, 'Let's take a look at that arm then, shall we?'

I followed her into a treatment room dreading what I knew was about to happen. The bandage had to be removed no matter what. She gently peeled off my cardigan and took a closer look at my arm and brushed my cheeks with the tips of her fingers, telling me that they would soon have me feeling better and that I was to wait while she fetched a doctor. A few minutes later she was back with a friendly Chinese man in a white coat with stethoscope around his neck. He said hello as he drew another chair up close to mine, but his smile dissolved when he saw the extent of the problem: the little flesh that was on my thin arm had almost become one with the strip of white ragged sheeting.

He spoke in a caring voice, telling me that they would take off the bandage but would soak it with a lotion first to soften it. I can still hear myself screaming as they peeled off that bandage after it was soaked in antiseptic. I can't believe that I didn't pass out or die on the spot. A quiet debate between the medical staff followed while I, probably as white as a sheet, lay on the treatment bed, wishing it was all a horrible dream. I could hear them talking about whether or not I should be kept in overnight, which I would have liked because I didn't want to move, or walk, or go to bed at home. I wanted to stay in that safe, warm antiseptic place. But it was decided that I could go home. I still had to have my arm treated and an injection of penicillin. Thankfully, the ointment on the bandage didn't sting or hurt but seemed to soothe my raw and smarting flesh.

I was given a letter to give to Mum. The tender care shown at the hospital couldn't stop the agony I went through, but it helped a lot, as did the lovely clean proper crepe bandage on my arm which reached from my wrist to my elbow. I was given prescribed tablets in a small bottle and an appointment card for my next visit. Josephine was waiting for me in the reception room and her mum was by the door chatting to, of all people, the woman who went by the name of Rose Lipka. She clearly recognised me from our previous fleeting moments and smiled gently before taking her leave.

Too traumatised by what I had been through, I couldn't have cared less who she was or where she came from. The truth was that even in other circumstances I might not have taken too much notice. Since my grandfather died my reason for knowing more about the mysterious Rose felt less urgent. I had grown used to my family's habit of keeping the secret and part of me felt that perhaps it really was just a coincidence that this lady had the same name as me. The curiosity hadn't gone away, but it felt less vital to know who she was.

In any case, I was thoroughly distracted by the pain. Thanking Hazel for looking after me, I was pleased that she urged Josephine to walk me home. My friend did her best to cheer me up and tried to make me laugh by pointing out odd characters on the way. She had heard those screams of mine echoing through the halls of the outpatients and I knew that deep down she had been affected by them. But it wasn't in her nature to talk it through. It was done and dusted as far as she was concerned. If I had started to go over it I feel sure she would have said, 'Oh, fuck off talking about it. It's over and done wiv. Put it behind yer!'

It just so happened that all I wanted was to be indoors, on the settee or in my bed. I felt very tired and even for a hardy street kid it had all been too much. I later learned that had I not been taken to the hospital by Josephine's mother I might well have lost a hand and a part of my arm because gangrene had set in. The scar is still visible and looks like a wide ladder in a nylon stocking. Mum, with all her other responsibilities to worry about, couldn't have realised that a serious problem was growing beneath that rag bandage and she was none too pleased with the letter from the hospital, which, I can only presume, gave her a bit of a dressing down. She asked me why I hadn't told her that my arm had been hurting and I knew it would be pointless telling her that I had cried in pain with it once in the kitchen when she was there having a cup of tea and reading her horoscope in the newspaper.

Unfortunately, my two best and closest friends, Margaret and Josephine, never hit it off. They didn't argue, they just didn't speak. So I lived a kind of double life, spending time with my first and very best friend and then slipping away to see Josephine, sometimes staying over at her house for a night here and there. But horizons were expanding by then for both me and Margaret, who was making new friends at her Catholic school. She was going places without me after school and sometimes at weekends and I was seeing more of the girls who attended the seniors and who lived close by. Life was going quite nicely, but of course such times don't last forever.

I was in for another shock from out of the blue although it was far worse for Mum than it was for me. One evening, after being at Josephine's house, I arrived home ready to curl up and watch television but wasn't allowed into our front room. So I shuffled into the end bedroom where Albert was playing with a Hornby train set, passed on from a cousin, and I asked if anything was wrong. He said that people were in the living room with Mum and that he was hungry. Baby Gary was blissfully asleep in his cot and looked like an angel. I kissed him gently on the cheek and then went into the kitchen to make toast and cocoa, which of course went down a treat with Albert.

Curious as to who was in our home and why voices were being kept down low, I eavesdropped once I had put the kettle on the stove and lit the grill. With my ear close to the small serving hatch between the two rooms I could just hear my Uncle Harry quietly talking to Mum, and knew from the tone that something was wrong. I couldn't hear Dad's voice so went back into the end bedroom to ask Albert if Dad was home from work. He wasn't and that was unusual for that time of day. Back in the kitchen, my stomach turned over when I heard the words 'police' and 'prison' mentioned. It seemed that Dad had been arrested on the way home from the docks when one of his work-mates had been pulled up in Commercial Road, with Dad a passenger.

The driver of the lorry had stolen goods on board and Dad was unlucky to have been given a lift on his way home the day he was picked up. The man, a docker by all accounts, was under surveillance and the police had chosen that day to catch him red-handed. Since Dad was in the cab of the lorry with him, he too was taken in for questioning and kept in one of the police station's cells overnight. Our flat had been searched by the police earlier and of course they found no stolen property.

The code of silence between men working in the docks meant that the driver's accomplice, who had been dropped off before Dad was given a lift in the lorry, was not expected to come forward, believing that since Dad was innocent he would be set free. But this, it appeared, was not going to be the case and my father was possibly facing a prison sentence of eighteen months for a crime he hadn't committed. It was up to him to prove himself lily-white rather than the dock police having to find him guilty, I think.

As far as the authorities were concerned, Dad was caught red-handed in a lorry with stolen goods aboard so he was as guilty as the other man of the crime. He was in a trap unless the guilty man came forward of his own accord. The meetings in our living room went on day after day with a horrible atmosphere in our home. Dad's brothers and workmates were coming and going, leaving a small collection from the dockers most times to tide Mum over. It was a worrying spell. After one of her visits to Dad in prison where he was being held on remand, Mum told my elder brothers Billy and Johnny that she had to talk to Dad through a glass window. This puzzled me because in all the comics and free films I saw at the picture palace, people locked up were in a jail behind bars, not glass.

Eventually, Dad's brothers did break the unwritten law and gently persuaded the guilty man to come clean and hand himself over. A full confession followed and Dad was released without so much as an apology at the time. But the vision of him smiling as he strode, a free man, through the grounds where Laura and I were waiting for him made up for everything. I walked cautiously towards him, holding my precious baby brother Gary in my arms with little Albert walking alongside me. Dad swept Albert up into his arms, saying, 'Daddy's home for good, son.' He then put him down and took the baby from me and carried him back home to our flat.

The following Saturday night there was a celebration party in our flat with relatives and my parents' friends and talk of solicitors and compensation. For a week or so Dad was like a different person, always in a good mood, until life went back to normal and there was no further conversation about the arrest, life in prison, injustice or compensation. The whole experience had been like a roller-coaster of emotions all round. Even though Dad was innocent, the shame of being arrested and placed in a cell left a smear where I was concerned. There had been a piece in our local paper reporting the incident before he had been found innocent and set free and children in playgrounds could be spiteful. But I gave as good as I got and only had one fist fight with one of the loud-mouthed girls, in which I came out a touch bruised but not shamed.

Shortly after that episode another two smart men in suits arrived at our front door one day and were ushered into the front room by Mum. I pressed my ear to the wall but this time it was from my bedroom I eavesdropped. I couldn't quite make out what was going on because the men were talking in hushed voices but as soon as they left I was straight into the living room to see that my parents were not in despair but relaxed and smiling. I later learned that Dad received an apology from the plain-clothes officers. Dad hadn't caused any fuss over his arrest and no doubt he knew that right would out, one way or another.

It transpired that in a sort of unofficial piece of compensation, the police were going to turn something of a blind eye even if there were rumours that he was harbouring filched goods in our flat taken from the docks. This of course gave Dad the opportunity to become a fence for a while, selling on items which others had passed to him. Similar to Gran and the smoked salmon scenario except that the items were non-perishable so evidence could not be eaten.

In Dad's wardrobe for a space of time were small items and trinkets that had been imported into this country by the crate-load, with a crate going missing now and then, which was a normal everyday event in the docks. Up until then my parents and brothers, like most others where we lived, chose not to steal but never turned down anything going on the cheap, if it happened to be what they wanted and could afford. Cigarette lighters, ladies watches or other small pocket-sized goods which made lovely Christmas and birthday presents.

The shelf in his cupboard in his bedroom was like a little treasure trove for a while and our flat became an even more sociable place, with friends and relatives popping in when they were looking to buy something classy on the cheap – a gift for a loved one perhaps or something for themselves. Dad made the most of it while it lasted, playing the businessman, and so for a short spell of a year or so we were guaranteed more than just jam on our bread every day.

12
No More a Child

Even though I had managed to pass my eleven-plus I had opted out of the grammar school and chosen to return to the upper part of Cephas Secondary Modern because I knew I could leave there at the age of fifteen. I wanted to go out into the world to earn a living and be independent as soon as I possibly could and more than this I wanted a place of my own. Something I could afford. An unfurnished bedsit perhaps. Rooms could be furnished cheaply in those days with bargain second-hand furniture. Even for the working classes during this time of things being on the up, with the country more affluent, most could afford to replace their old things and redecorate their homes in the new contemporary style.

Everyone wanted the new look, including my parents. Fireplace walls were being decorated to stand out and papered with jazzy patterns, different to the other three walls in a room. Calligraphy in black, red, grey and white was the fashion, as was mass-produced, inexpensive furniture with spindly legs on everything. Newly weds wanted Formica, wall-to-wall carpet and spaceship chandeliers with white glass shades splashed with a bit of colour – red, black and gold. Even though I still had a few years to go before I could think of getting my own place, I already knew what I wanted: wooden furniture that I could paint whatever bright colour I fancied, with brilliant white walls everywhere.

With the desire to be independent, I knew that I was going to have to get myself a Saturday job, preferably in one of our local hairdressers, which were busier than ever with manageresses on the lookout for twelve- to fourteen-year-olds to sweep floors, tidy curlers and hairpins and make tea or coffee for staff and customers. I was hardly workshy since I had been earning pocket money, alongside Margaret, since I was six years old, but now it was time to pass on our tools of the trade to Albert and his friend John – our pushchair and our guy which we kept in the bike shed.

The girls in my class at the age of thirteen were talking of getting a first size bra and boys were flocking around the few who already had small proud breasts. It seemed to me that changes were going on everywhere – around the country and, more importantly, in my domain. Margaret's brother George was the first in her family to get married and move out of Stepney and soon after this her sisters flew from the nest. Helen married and lived in a flat nearby and Julie went to America. So the inevitable was bound to happen sooner or later. Just before my fourteenth birthday Mrs McGregor put in for an exchange and in the summer of 1959 they moved off our estate and Margaret was a good twenty minutes' walk away across the Mile End Road. With this drastic change in our lives I suppose we couldn't help but drift apart even more.

The build-up to them moving out was horrible, the

strangest time of my life, and then much worse once they had gone. My second family had left me behind. All good things come to an end of course, but us two? The three-year-olds who arrived on to Bancroft Estate and clung on to each other for a decade through thick and thin? We had our rows but were like blood sisters. On the day of their big move I didn't want to be there. I didn't want to see their possessions loaded on to a removal lorry and taken away so I went to see Aunt Polly. The day after was much worse than I thought it was going to be: Margaret was gone, Helen and Julie nowhere to be seen, her brother elsewhere and, worse still, a stranger was clipping Mr McGregor's prize roses.

No more would I see Mrs McGregor with her cigarette in the corner of her mouth, stuck to her lip as she talked, or suddenly roaring with laughter over something that Margaret or I had said or got up to. No more would I see her enjoying a little natter and a bit of gossip with her neighbour over the garden fence. It was over. It was quiet. My best friend had gone and taken Damby the dog with her. Our lovable big black unclipped crossbred poodle would no longer come bounding up to me in the grounds of our flats.

Albert was seven years old and Gary just two when Margaret moved away, so having them to fuss over helped. They were adorable and different characters and they loved me as much as I loved them. A new family immediately moved into Margaret's house and one of the sons was my age. I gradually got to know and like the family, especially the mother, a small-framed woman and another of those who lived for her children. Her youngest son Chris Murphy and I became good friends and chatted to each other for hours and sometimes into the night on the small wall in our grounds or on the brick wall of his garden. When the weather was sunny we sat on the green where I could keep an eye on my brothers while they played.

Our friendship grew and gradually turned into a young teenage romance and at thirteen we were boy and girl-friend, going on picnics to Redbridge by the river and for walks to the park and the Tower of London. He was my first boyfriend and the first to have kissed me. It was all very new and strange. Nothing and no one could replace my friend Margaret though.

While a summer romance was something to brag about at school I was too young for the love stuff. By then I was fourteen and going with one or two of my school friends to a youth club in Bethnal Green. Here we could either play shuttlecock or jive or simply sit at the milk bar watching other people. I opted for jiving most of the time because I was quite an expert, having privately practised to the sound of my older brothers' records since I was nine, using the door handle in my bedroom as a partner.

I loved to dance and I jived with my girl friends until the lads got bold enough to break us up. It was a time when boys formed themselves into gangs, all macho and tough and not to be messed with. Image was everything in the late fifties. Our local gang was called the Roman Road. They played on their sexy image, leather biker jackets and the James Dean look, deep eyes floating in melancholy and scorn on their lips, but they were soft as putty beneath the surface and were still in the process of changing from boy to man. The influence of American films had filtered through to even those of us in the East End with such movies as *The Wild One*, starring Marlon Brando. Our boys were no different from those fictional characters who were fry-cooks and grease monkeys all week, working at dreary jobs they hated, to break out at weekends to be somebody to be taken notice of. Guys who went to dance halls but hardly deigned to dance and sometimes broke up the decorum and the toilet fittings for the hell of it.

By the time I was out there, flick-knives, coshes, bicycle chains and razors were on the wane and out of date. Teds, motorbikes, black leather, brass-studded jackets were already old-fashioned. The Roman Road and Bethnal lads wore the latest gear and hard expressions, but when one of these cool guys walked one of us girls home on a starry night, the tough image melted away and the gentle romantic side of sons of neighbours, who were once little boys playing marbles in the streets, shone through.

I fell hopelessly in love with a boy called Stanley at that time and was drawn to him like a moth to the candle. Sadly, I was a few inches taller and I think this might have put him off. But it didn't matter for long because they were exciting times with the constant release of new songs, new singers and new idols. The United States influenced the so-called youth-quake and we came in at the tail end before the Mods arrived and a different fashion hit the streets.

Bless the tough guys who wandered around all macho eyeing us up because I loved it, even though I hadn't quite blossomed the way most girls of my age had. I was flat-chested, and not allowed to wear any make-up. Of course it didn't take long to find a way round that. At a friend's house I would share an older sister's make-up bag and pile on the mascara, panstick, eye shadow, pale apricot lipstick and then more mascara. I wasn't quite ready for a padded bra though.

Usually we girls played the part of coy wallflowers when romantic songs resounded through our youth club and the guys stood at the milk bar. Established young courting couples of course smooched on the darkened floor under the dim lights and when it was time to rock and roll, we girls really got kicking on that floor. A guy called Victor, tall and slim, was an incredible mover; he knew it and so did the rest of us. If he held out a hand with a silent invitation to dance, it was like being touched by a king. And yes, he did eventually hold out his hand to me, after months of my showing off my skills to the full when jiving with my friends. Victor was seventeen and I wasn't even close to approaching my fifteenth birthday and it was the biggest boost I could have wished for.

Most of the girls wanted to partner him and we were all hopeful when he walked slowly around the hall, cool and handsome, watching us rocking our souls to music. Once the pair of us got together on the floor I let him throw me everywhere – over his shoulder, between his legs, around his waist – all to the throbbing sound of Elvis Presley and 'Blue Suede Shoes'. After that, for a short while, until the next best girl swinger came along, we became the couple who cleared the floor, with the rest of them watching, clapping in time, or singing to whichever record was playing.

Little did they know how much this boosted my ego. I, Sally Lipka, was chosen to partner the master of steps! It changed the way I looked at myself in Mum's full-length mirror. Instead of seeing the worst of myself I saw the best. Apart from my flat chest, I thought I looked okay. My hair was still natural blonde and almost white, and rather than seeing a skinny sexless girl I saw one who was modestly up with the fashion. The hourglass figure, after all was said and done, was out of date.

Ready to cheat a little, I used my earnings from helping out in local hairdressers on Saturdays plus my babysitting money from my brother Billy to buy my first bra and a pair of falsies to go inside, from Woolworths. I borrowed my sister's clothes when she wasn't looking and happily accepted from my fashionable sister-in-law a full circle skirt and pumps that she had no more use for. From a cousin called Nelly, who was eight years older than myself, had come my first pair of stiletto-heeled pointed shoes which had given her blisters. Dressed in my finery, I looked into the wardrobe mirror in Mum and Dad's bedroom and couldn't wait for the following Friday night, the dance hall and Victor. I also wheedled make-up out of one of my brother Johnny's girlfriends, who gave me a spit and brush mascara, pale blue eye shadow and a half-used pale apricot lipstick, Corn Silk, as a present.

All this make-up, of course, was wiped off before I reached home using my handkerchief, a bit of spit, and the mirror in the red telephone kiosk on our estate to change from one image to the other. If Dad was going to continue to be dictatorial, which looked to be the case, what choice had I other than to quietly outsmart him?

The reputation of our youth club-cum-dance hall grew and guys a year or so older than us flocked in to play snooker on the top floor and wandered down for the last few slow dances in the semi-dark dance hall. From my class at school I persuaded other girls to come along on Friday nights. We gradually formed a friendly group, going off together to the club and back home again late at night, with perhaps one or two of us missing should one of the boys have deigned to walk one home under a star-studded navy blue sky.

There were fights between local gangs but mostly it was no more than territorial hogwash, although once I did witness someone I admired kick the shit out of another boy when a rival gang came into the snooker room of our youth club. It was deliberate baiting because rumour was spreading that the chaps were taking over territory that didn't belong to them. Stuff and nonsense though it was, one of the troublemakers who came in to stir things up was taken away in an ambulance, blood oozing from his head. I was shocked to see lads that I knew and liked turn into a small pack of wolves, snarling and out for blood. That night as I lay in my bed I decided it was time for me to move on. I didn't go back to the club again after that fight and strangely enough I didn't miss it. It had been terrific fun and a stepping stone from childhood into the grown-up world. A first taste of that thrill and excitement that comes when fledglings leave the nest to go where parents may not enter.

My girl friends, just like me, loved rock and roll, jiving and the twist. We danced to Bill Haley, Elvis Presley, Jerry Lee Lewis, Chuck Berry, Paul Anka, and the Crickets. We also moved around the floor to the sound of That'll Be the Day,' sung by the wonderful Buddy Holly who we mourned but still continued to listen or dance to his records as well as those by the Platters, Ink Spots and the Coasters. Everly Brothers favourites were 'Bye Bye Love' and 'All I Have to do is Dream'.

Towards the end of the fifties there were quite a few changes. The Vespa scooter was taking over from the motorbike and shorter skirts to the knee were creeping into the fashion magazines. Older chaps were saving up to buy a Mini motorcar and art arrived into our realm. Bohemians were packing into our Whitechapel Gallery to look studiously at the exhibition of collages and pictures of soup cans and Brillo boxes. Most families owned a television set at this point but were still being entertained by Phil Silvers as Sergeant Bilko, by Gracie Allen and George Burns and the schmaltzy Liberace, his piano, his candlesticks and his white suits. It was 1959 with the swinging sixties just around the corner.

During my last term at school I was still working every free hour and spent less and less time at home. Time was suddenly going as fast as I wanted it to and changing like a kaleidoscope. We girls loved to slouch across one or other of our beds and talk about boys, life, our hopes and dreams and yet I still felt the need to visit my aunts and uncles. The child and the adolescent at odds with one other.

I enjoyed popping into 24 Cleveland Way on a Saturday

afternoon to be part of the traditional family gathering. I even dropped in during the week to touch base with my round-faced, blue-eyed, lovely Uncle Harry, who had taken Grandfather's chair by the fire with Wheezy, old and arthritic, at his feet. He and his wife Mary with their son, my cousin Barry, had moved into Grandfather's house.

Quite a few family parties took place in that spacious parlour on the first floor in the months after Grandfather passed away, with one or other of the adults doing their star turn on the piano. The ladies believed they were as good as Vera Lynn and the men showed how well they could impersonate Frank Sinatra or Dean Martin after a few pints and a couple of whiskies. Uncle Harry and I had a party piece that we often performed. Our rendition of 'There's a Hole in my Bucket' became a bit of a family legend.

These were some of the happiest times of my life when living in that close-knit community, the old East End with its traditions, rules and regulations. I still missed Margaret and saw less and less of Josephine but I had got friendly and close to a girl who was in the same A-stream class in the fourth year of senior school, Ruth. My life was changing and bits of the old one were slowly falling away like dying leaves in the autumn. Whitehead Street, our house in the cobbled turning where I was born in the bedroom where Mum, Dad, Laura and I slept, had been razed to the ground to make way for new council houses, while at the same time tower blocks were appearing all around us. The strange thing is that I have no recollection of our old turning during the time it was being bulldozed and rebuilt. I can remember the new houses once they were finished with people living in them, though. I can also see the old door in the ivy-covered wall at the end of the turning but that's all. I can't recollect the beautiful old almshouses set around the green having been pulled down either but, alas, they were. I know there is a 1970s light brick council estate there now and I can't help wondering if those who live there would not prefer to be living in that wonderful historic and peaceful place. If so, where would they park their cars?

I spent quite a bit of time in my friend Ruth's home playing Monopoly with her sisters and brother and was almost accepted as one of the family – part and parcel of the furniture. Her mum, with a welcoming smile on her round face as she opened the door to me, always said the same thing, 'Hello, Sally love. Come on in.'

I had already got used to the fact that I was not allowed to have friends in our home after my many years' friendship with Margaret when I spent so much time at hers. Ruth was part of a bigger family than ours and was one of eight children, who, apart from her younger sister Lucy, were working adults. A few had flown the nest. The family-sized maisonette was a warm, open kind of a home with sisters and brothers coming and going. I knew what time they ate their evening meal and Sunday dinner so would visit accordingly so as not to intrude because the family, no different from others in that part of London, were living on a tight budget.

Spending time with that family made me think again about the ways in which my mother was different from some others living in the East End that I had got to know. Ruth's mother was content to wear clean but plain clothes whereas mine was glamorous and dressed in the height of fashion when Dad's back pocket was lined and, according to some members of his family, it often was lined, due to him being a fence. Dad was proud of her, and took her to the best local stores for a nice new coat, beautiful leather shoes, or a lovely gown. I can't remember ever seeing her wearing a wrap-over pinafore except for when we were in Kent during the hop picking season, whereas Ruth's mum wore one most of the time. Clean and patterned and clearly sending a message: I am a working mother and proud of it.

Ruth's mother's reward for her arduous years of bringing up her children was the modern appliances her working offspring collectively bought for her. The telephone in their home at that time in 1958 was a luxury for most of the working class living in the East End. The kitchen in Ruth's home was modern, streamlined and with plenty of cupboards above and below convenient working surfaces. Her mum, like so many other women, often spoke of her relief at seeing an end to living in dark, damp, Victorian properties. Her previous timeworn rented house was similar to others from what she told me, with dark, old-fashioned kitchen dressers taking up space and light. The age of oak and walnut and cracked willow-patterned plates was over for the older generation, but, ironically, it was slowly becoming fashionable with the young arty lot.

Even though I continued to enjoy a Friday night out with my girl friends and worked every Saturday I had become a keen student at school in the commerce class, which really was a turning point in my life and had been established by Mrs Kate Flenner, a special person as well as an excellent teacher. She fought tooth and nail for our right to a free school uniform and won, which may not sound much to ask for, but it made quite a difference to us girls, who had to try and find something clean and ironed to wear for school. Once Mrs Flenner had won her struggle, we were all entitled to two white blouses, one grey skirt and a green cardigan chosen from the small Marks and Spencer's store in Hackney with all bills being sent directly to our school.

Our strong-minded teacher didn't stop there but beavered away, writing to the powers that be, until she finally persuaded the authorities to provide typewriters and office desks to go with them for her newly founded commerce class. Kate had taken it upon herself to teach us typing and shorthand with only the basics of Pitman's under her belt. I wasn't interested in learning shorthand but wanted to learn to touch-type and as fast as I possibly could. While other girls of my age were happy to furtively write in their diaries I had been scribbling stories, which always seemed to find a way into my mind and made my head feel as if it would burst if I didn't get them out. As time went on the desire to write grew stronger and some-times in class, while lessons were quietly being taught, I was writing a story.

The attempt at a novel I wrote in an exercise book during what I considered to be a boring geography lesson turned from a couple of pages of wicked prose into a book I titled

The Men and their Lovers. The girls in my form couldn't wait to get their hands on the weekly instalment that was passed around on the underground which took our class from Bethnal Green to Fairlop every Friday for sports and cross-country running. I had many hiding places for that hot book: under my mattress, the back of my drawer, the top of our coat cupboard and the air vent in the bedroom. On one awful occasion I forgot where I had slipped it and had to maniacally search for it, in fear of my life, terrified that Dad might have found it. I had named every grown-up relative in our large extended family and their friends – my parents included – and had them all jumping in and out of bed with each other. When I did eventually discover it hidden under the rag rug in my bedroom I thanked the Almighty for saving me from a fate worse than death and went straight outside and threw it down the rubbish chute.

At fourteen, none of us girls knew that much about sex other than what we'd heard on the street but we did know about Lolita. Some of the girls in our school did brag now and then that the best-looking lad had given her a snog in the caretaker's shed and slipped his hand inside her knickers. And this really was the only lesson we had on the subject.

I discovered later on that Mrs Flenner knew that my so-called daydreaming was a little more than this and so used to leave me be when I was writing. The same applied when studying the dictionary, which she sometimes thought was the Bible. Both were big and black. I was almost caught out when looking up the rudest words I could find during a five-minute gap between teachers coming and going. The rest of my class were flicking ink pellets, arguing, or talking about sex quietly. Our teacher came into the room and I was too engrossed in looking up the words which the boys came out with to sense her presence. I was surprised to see that the forbidden 'C' referred to female genitals as well as an unpleasant or stupid person.

In the silence of the classroom while our teacher stood forbiddingly at her desk restoring order with her presence, I was dismayed to hear her talking about me. Telling the others that they should take a leaf out of my book during spare time between teacher changeovers. Telling them that there was a lot to learn from the Bible and that some of the stories were far more interesting than the comics kept hidden in desks and read secretly during lessons.

My heart began to thump with blood rushing to my cheeks as she walked slowly towards me, the telltale page of my timeworn black book still open at the C word. 'It's not the Bible, miss,' I said, 'it's the dictionary.' I then carefully closed it and hoped she wouldn't question me as to which word I was looking up. She drew breath and glanced at the others who were trapping laughter behind cupped hands. They knew exactly the sort of words I liked to shock them with when giving the correct meaning.

'One is as good as the other, Sally Lipka,' said the teacher, slowly nodding as she turned to the others. 'It would do all of you good to read the dictionary now and then.' More muffled laughter and some inaudible quips from the boys. I got away with it and not because Mrs Flenner didn't know what I had been up to. She never missed a trick and I don't think she cared which words I was checking so long as I was using my brain and doing so of my own accord. We couldn't have wished for a more sensitive, intelligent and caring woman at the helm. Had it not been for her, I would not have learned to touch-type with a speed of forty-five words per minute at school-leaving age. Fifteen. Instead of getting through my first interview as junior office girl with flying colours I might have been turned away.

I wasn't the only one whose destiny was altered by our teacher. She and her husband Ben did more for the poor children of the East End than anyone had done, with little or no government funding. They worked hard all through their lives and never expected praise or thanks. All they wanted in return was to see joy shining from the eyes of deprived children who without them would have had nowhere to go once school was over other than on the streets.

I did go back to visit my teacher in the East End later on in life once I was married and away. After a cup of tea and animated conversation going over old times, Ben, who had been responsible for the success of the local East End Jewish boys club, casually told me what had come in the post that day: an invitation to Buckingham Palace. He was to be awarded the OBE for his long service in helping deprived children. I could hardly believe it. Our Ben Flenner of the East End had been awarded the OBE in the same year that the Beatles had and he wasn't interested?

'What good is this?' he said, holding up his invitation from Buckingham Palace. 'It's funds that we've needed all these years. With funds we could have done so much more

for the poor little sods in this area.' I sat there open-
mouthed as he tossed his invitation to accept the award
into his waste-paper bin.

I said, 'You can't be serious, Ben? You're not going to
turn it down, are you?'

He looked at Kate, my personal heroine, and said, 'Do
you want us to go and accept it?'

'I'm not bothered one way or the other,' she said.

'And neither am I,' said her husband of nearly fifty years.
'Waste of bloody time,' Ben muttered.

And really, that summed up the spirit of many old East
Enders who needed money not medals in order to improve
the lives of the downtrodden.

13
Dreams of an Hour-Glass Figure

My eldest brother Billy and his family had settled nicely into their small self-contained flat on the top floor of a six-storey Victorian tenement block. He had by then been promoted to become a manager of one of a chain of small supermarkets in the style of Sainsbury's and he was the proud owner of a second-hand light blue Zodiac saloon with chrome so polished you could see your face in it. He cut a dash in our block of flats when he arrived to collect and take me back to his flat to babysit while he and his young wife, June, went out for the evening. He was as handsome as any Hollywood film star and I felt special in the soft leather seat next to him, being chauffeur-driven to his contemporary decorated flat. I was his trusted babysitter to my niece, earning half a crown to do little else other than watch television and eat the sweets that my brother left out for me.

Not too long after Billy married it was the turn of Johnny and his Scottish girlfriend Margo. They too were in the same boat as Billy and June had been and so their wedding was also a little on the rushed side and followed a similar pattern, except that the church wedding was in Essex and not the East End. I was almost fifteen by then with only a few months to go before I left school. When it came to having the hourglass-shaped bridesmaid's dress fitted I wanted to curl up and die. I had hardly grown breasts, was five feet six inches tall with a bone structure older girls said they would kill for. They were welcome to it.

The dressmaker did her best to raise my confidence when she said, 'No one feels sorry for those who feel sorry for themselves.' Fine.

Self-conscious in the close-fitted A-line bridesmaid's dress with Margo's shapely sister either side, I was given a special padded bra to wear to not only lift my spirits but to improve the look of the gown for the sake of the photographs. When I look at the wedding album now, I don't think I looked half as bad as I felt in that frock. One of Margo's sisters, a bleached blonde with a beehive hairstyle, was my age and looked like a model with her 38, 24, 38 figure. Next to her I felt like Olive Oyle with blonde hair.

Days after the wedding and still wondering how I could put on some weight and have a nice curvy figure, I bumped into one of my childhood school friends. It was a typical Saturday afternoon in the Whitechapel Waste which at that time was a bit like a catwalk with the girls showing off their new clothes. The guys too for that matter. Most of the young were looking for romance as they strolled along the Waste as far as Aldgate East to the coffee bar which was a casual meeting place where the boys could eye the girls going by or coming in to join them, cool and hopeful. Most of us would stop at the famous Paul's record stall to flip through his many boxes of new and old 45s, with some of us girls hanging around chatting before the hour of three o'clock when it was time to wander into the Italian milk and coffee bar for a hot drink and a cigarette.

I was wearing my new pleated skirt and blouse purchased on the weekly by Mum. The clothes were in preparation for the day I started work, not far off now, and I thought I was the bee's knees but suddenly next to my friend, who always looked stunning even in casual clothes, I felt like a schoolgirl. Her casuals were cashmere and silk, tasteful and expensive. She looked beautiful, with little make-up, a good cut to her soft, wavy, fair hair and a modest figure of 36, 24, 36. We went for a coffee and she told me what she was doing for a living and said that I could easily do the same and earn a lot more than five pounds a week copy-typing.

She was a hostess to rich clients at the age of sixteen, sipping cocktails in exclusive clubs with wealthy attractive men, who sometimes only wanted her company or a kiss and a cuddle. She made her work sound sociable, innocent and fun. She could turn them on or off with a slight change in conversation, steer them to bed or into a long mono-logue about themselves. It all depended whether she found them attractive or not. Whatever happened, they paid her and paid handsomely. My old school friend had embarked on her glittery lifestyle six months after she left school when as a favour to a friend she had been an escort to a handsome rich visitor from overseas and taken to a West End show and dinner. She hadn't looked back since. She was beautiful, chic and sophisticated in her expensive designer clothes and would have looked just as lovely in jeans and a sweatshirt. I was so envious it hurt.

We chatted for over an hour and I couldn't find a reason

to condemn what she was doing for a living. She was as natural as she had always been and not in the least bit what I expected from someone who had men pay for their pleasure. Not any old man, let me add. Carefully selected clients. She had become a worldly wise escort enjoying life to the full, with only a few select, rich and famous people on her list. When I casually said that I was still a virgin she told me it was time I did something about it, and then drew on her French cigarette through a small amber and gold holder as if she had told me to blow my nose.

Once we parted company with the usual firm promise of meeting up again, I felt as if I wanted to chase after her and say, 'Take me into the fold and show me what to do.' But of course being a good girl I wouldn't have been able to pull it off. What would Frederick Charrington, our local hero, have thought of me? He had launched vicious attacks on men who looked to women for paid sex on the cheap. But what of those who paid highly for their pleasures? Would that have been all right, I wonder? Had there been one law for the wealthy and one for those on the breadline?

Not feeling quite as cool in my new clothes as I had when I first put them on, I continued along the Waste heading for Paul's record stall because it was nearly my sister's birthday and I wanted to buy her a record from the top ten charts. She had been working in the accounts office of a factory in Aldgate called Brody Limited. Later on in life she married the handsome young Rodney Brody and her lifestyle certainly changed from rags to glitter. The company manufactured and fashioned the most beautiful sequinned fabric fit for a queen's gown and still do.

Passing the Whitechapel railway station I eased myself through a small group of older women who were giving out flyers for the Salvation Army band who were there as usual on a Saturday. Taking a leaflet from one of the ladies I caught the eye of the woman I had been so curious about when I was a child: Rose Lipka. It had been a few years since our paths had crossed.

Braver by then and no longer melodramatic, I smiled at her and then stepped closer to take the bull by the horns. I said, 'Excuse me, I hope you don't mind my asking but since we've got the same surname, is it possible that we could be related?'

Looking thoughtful for a moment, she smiled warmly at me and said, 'You're the little girl who sang a carol to my brother and me. I recognise those blue eyes and that white hair.'

'But we're not related? Is that what you're saying?'

'Why do you ask? It's not as if my name is that unusual. There are probably lots of us spread around London.'

'I realise that,' I said, 'but a long time ago outside Trinity Square a friend of yours told me to ask my grandfather about you. She said that he would know more than she did.'

'And did you ask him?' she said, a melancholic expression in her eyes.

I paused for a moment because I suddenly realised something. For years, the idea at the back of my mind had been that perhaps Rose had been married to my grandfather. That maybe she was my dad's real mum and my real gran. But in that second, as I finally was about to ask her, directly,

I knew that if she had been his first wife I had to be careful so as not to offend her. After all, no one in our family had ever wanted to think that there might have been a skeleton in the cupboard and Rose herself, it seemed, had not been one to rock a boat.

'I just thought you might be my grandfather's sister but had had a family row and so weren't on speaking terms. That's all.' It wasn't totally the truth but it seemed close. All my childhood wonderings seemed far-fetched at this point.

'I'm not the man's sister but we knew each other at one time. It's all water under the bridge and there's no point in raking it up. Best you leave it be.'

'But we might be family,' I said.

'And what if we are? I dare say that hundreds living in this area are related and don't know it. I have my few friends and my own life. You can have many relatives but only a handful, if that, of good friends.' She then smiled faintly and turned to the group of women who were by then clearing a space for the Salvation Army band and for the music to start up.

I dropped a threepenny bit into the collection box and turned away to walk back home. I had not solved the mystery but it no longer seemed important. Somehow Rose Lipka in her own way made it feel like an inconsequential part of life's bigger mysteries. I felt lighter, happier. The song that suddenly resounded and bounced off the building in Whitechapel made me smile: 'There Is a Green Hill Far Away'. I hoped so. I loved my life in the East End but I still missed the hop fields, rivers and sloping green hills of the Kent countryside.

I left school in the summer of 1960 and started work two weeks later just after my fifteenth birthday in August, with a recommendation from my teacher for my typing skills and little else other than being polite and studious and hard-working. I secured a position in the post room of E. Pollard & Co, a large shop-fitting company in St John's Street, Clerkenwell. I travelled on the underground from Bethnal Green to Farringdon Station and it felt strange buying a ticket every time and not slipping through the barrier on the sly as Margaret and I had done for most of our lives. But I was earning a living now which meant that I could afford the fare, just, and go out at weekends with my friends.

I hadn't been at Pollard's for too long when I was promoted into the secretary's office with the promise of a pay rise of ten shillings when assessment time came round in six months or so. I had my own desk, filing cabinet and shelves for my boxed files and in no time at all I was responsible for sorting small brown envelopes containing every member of staff's fortnightly salary, which was duly collected, once signed for. I was a very busy girl on a frugal salary for the times and for the responsibilities placed in my hands. But I loved the ambience and the friendly atmosphere between the ordinary staff.

That said, I saw this highly successful and profitable company as my first stepping stone into a bigger world. My heart's desire, though, was to work for a publishing company, newspapers and journals not books. I wanted to be a reporter and planned to stay for a year or so at Pollard's and then move on. I travelled to and fro on the train with a girl who I was to eventually become good friends with called Carol Smith. And it was she who, through her older sister, arranged for a group of us to go on an economy holiday for two weeks the following summer by train, boat and coach to the coast of sunny Spain.

I was asked if I fancied going and was in like a shot and so were another two new friends of mine, Pat Tranter and Irene Middleton. We four girls had just ten months to save up the money. The total cost of it all at a modest three-star hotel, full board, including all travelling expenses came to thirty-nine guineas. I calculated that with my salary and by working weekends at a tobacconist-cum-sweet shop in Islington, I could just afford to put enough by. Mum required five pounds a fortnight for my keep, which was half of my take-home pay and I had also to find my fares to work each day.

I knew that floating the idea of going abroad to Spain past my father would be a waste of time because he had created blue murder when my sister Laura had gone against his wishes and chugged off on a boat to Belgium with her best friend. He was far from pleased when she came home with love in her eyes having met her Belgian sweetheart, Eddie Van Wemmel. A foreigner! Dad did his level best to break that up and warned me not to think of following in her footsteps. So what choice had I other than to keep secret the fact that I was going to go to Spain come what may? I forged Dad's name on my passport form and since I had imagined myself perhaps living and working in a sunnier climate one day this to me was an opportunity to go and see how the land lay and to explore a little secret dream more fully.

I was so excited at the prospect of going to a place with beautiful golden beaches, but I knew that if I was to have my way I had to contain my excitement so I told no one at home what I was planning. The first step was to have a passport photo taken, so one day I went to a photographer in Islington during my lunch break from Pollard's, one which my colleagues at Pollard's had used before me and recommended. They were all for me spreading my wings.

A few days after I had collected my passport photo I received a phone call at work from the photographer. I had been at the switchboard when the call came. The young man had asked to speak to Sally Lipka and I told him that I was she. He wanted to know if I would go back to the studio and sit for him. Shocked by this, I immediately thought the worst of him and pulled out the plug and cut him off there and then. Turning to one of the girls who were removing her headphones to go to the lavatory, I said, 'Dirty bastard. What does he think I am? I don't look like one of them, do I, Marge?'

'One of what, lovey?' she said, amused as ever at what she saw as my forthright, no-nonsense manner.

'That dirty old sod, the photographer I went to wants to take nude pictures of me.' She burst out laughing so I repeated what I had told her and one of the other girls heard and also cracked up.

Once they stopped laughing they explained that they had sent me to a respectable photographer who wouldn't have wanted me to take off my clothes. 'You might be a long sexless thing, lovely,' said Marge, my senior, 'but you've got a terrific bone structure, sweetheart, and you're photogenic. Why don't you go?'

My answer was short and to the point. 'I'm not that fucking desperate for money!' I left the post room, affronted, believing they thought me to be an East Ender with no self-respect.

I hadn't been back in my office at my desk for five minutes when the phone rang. It was Marge. She said, 'Sally, the photographer's back on the phone. He thinks he was accidentally cut off when he first called. Why don't you just talk to him, lovey? And try not to swear this time, eh?'

I told her to ask him what he wanted. She repeated what he had said earlier. I told her to ask him if he wanted me to undress. She started to laugh again and told me to hang on. I waited a few seconds and then put the phone down and went to the ladies cloakroom to look at myself in the full-length mirror. The girls were right. I did have a long sexless body and I was too tall. I was quite pretty, yes, and I had nice blue eyes. I pushed my face forward and it didn't look too bad. I had an ordinary nose that only slightly tipped up at the end. My aunts and uncles had told me that I would be a stunner one day and even if I say so myself, as I studied my reflection, I felt that that day might be coming. I was still looking at myself when the door opened and my friend, another telephonist, June, popped her head around the door saying, 'If you miss this chance of a lifetime, Sally, you're a fool.'

The next time the photographer called he gave Marge a message, telling her that I could bring my mother with me if I wanted and that all he cared about was taking some shots of me, fully clothed. The girls tried their best to persuade me to go and I pretended I wasn't interested but deep down I was too scared to even consider it and I think I knew why. Because of the rude man in the lane in Kent, the grotesque fat man in the cinema, the disgusting man on the stairs in our flats, the man on the bike outside our flats, the man who I used to get my separate shilling from and last and by no means least, the driver of the lorry who wanted to take me and Margaret further than the tunnel. They had left a scar and I was a doubting Thomas where men were concerned.

When the final call came from the photographer, I took it and was polite as I listened to him, a touch more interested when he said that if I wouldn't sit for him, he would pass me on to a friend, a well-known photographer highly respected in the publishing world, fashion magazines being his forte. He would not mention this famous photographer's name unless I turned up to meet him at his studio. He assured me that top models waited in hopes of the call that he was making to me. Said that I was a natural. I talked it over with the girls and was tempted but still that little voice inside was definitely saying, 'No, Sally, this isn't for you.'

Apart from anything else, I was wearing a padded bra in those early days of my development and believed that as soon as this was discovered, I would be sent packing from the photographer's studio as an impostor. The photographer had mentioned Jean Shrimpton in passing and I knew that she had small breasts. It was all so far away from my own world that I couldn't take it in and in any case at that time I was so preoccupied with the incredible fact that I, Sally Lipka, the once ragged urchin, was going to go abroad to Spain and nothing compared to this. I didn't get back to the photographer.

14
Sun, Sea and Sangria

On the day of departure into the unknown, with Laura's small suitcase packed and hidden under the iron bed I still shared with her, I feigned a stomach bug, saying I was too ill to go to work. I waited until Mum went out shopping and left a note in the kitchen saying that I hadn't left home but just gone away to the seaside and to tell my treasured little brothers, Albert and Gary, that I would be back soon with a present each for them. I have to admit that they were the only thing keeping me at home and not searching for a flat somewhere in London to perhaps share with one of my friends.

Most of the clothes in my suitcase were on loan from Laura's wardrobe with a few things borrowed from the girls at work. My sister had been working for two years and had been to Belgium the previous summer so of course she had a bikini, shorts and a couple of sundresses. I'm sure she would have let me borrow them had I asked but I didn't want her to be caught up the lies nor in the trouble I was bound to be in once back home. I slunk out of our flat to meet my friend Carol Smith. She had told her parents about it but hadn't told them that I was sneaking off without getting permission from mine. We started our journey at Stepney Green underground station and we made our way to Victoria, excited as schoolchildren and incredibly happy. It was the summer of 1961 and we had already been having a whale of a time, partying every weekend.

Our destination – a small village resort in Spain called Blanes on the Costa Brava. The travel was hardly first class but we didn't know any different and were happy to go by train to Dover, on a boat to France, then through to the Spanish border on an overnight train. We slept in a compartment for two on bunk beds and it was all I expected it to be, absolutely fabulous and very exciting. After the long train journey, we boarded a coach that took us up into the mountains that separated France from Spain, high up into the sky around hairpin bends. We were in fear of our lives and loving every second of it. The Spanish driver wanted to give a thrill to the coachload of people and especially to us seven girls travelling without one male escort.

It was magical and worth the long hours of working five days a week at Pollard's and weekends in the sweet and tobacconist shop. Being driven along that route brought a lump to my throat, it was so beautiful. I had only ever seen pictures of long golden sands and clear blue sea. I was in heaven and already planning how I might stay and work in the vineyards picking grapes, and return to England in a year or so.

On arrival at the small Hotel Ruiz in Blanes we were given refreshments and then ushered into our rooms. Carol and I shared one which had two single beds with sparkling white sheets and clean fresh-smelling covers. But the best of it all was that we had a small gleaming bathroom with shower and shiny chrome taps for just the two of us! We could hardly believe our good fortune. Unaccustomed to the bidet and not knowing what it was for we used it to pee in when one or the other of us was have a wee on the loo.

From the first glimpse of the tiny resort from our seats in the coach we could see that it was alive and bustling, with French students of around our age. It was also full of handsome, romantic Spanish waiters and ordinary Spanish families wearing traditional clothes. It was wonderful. It was unhurried. It was a bit of old Spain coming into the twentieth century. That afternoon Carol and I browsed around the two tiny tourist shops, which were set in the midst of a bakery, a butcher and a grocery shop. We kept on glancing each other and smiling. We just couldn't believe that we were there.

In the evenings, once I had showered, set and back-combed my hair, put on my make-up and a favourite full circle skirt and matching top of Laura's, I was ready for the discotheques, ready to jive and twist the night away. The place was magical with songs and music blasting out from a jukebox, nearly all from the British hit parades. It was party time every night. The drinks cost the equivalent of fourpence in new money for a martini. The Cellar night-club was to be our haunt for the next twelve nights after bathing on soft clean sand and swimming in crystal turquoise sea under a sunny blue sky, with us girls coming and going to our hotel for meals throughout the day. Low cost though our holiday was, it included breakfast of crois-sants, fresh warm rolls, butter, jam and cheese. Lunch was a three-course meal as was dinner. And Dad would have stopped me from going there had I let him have his way? Crazy.

Carol fell madly in love with Peppito, our gorgeous, brown, fair-haired waiter, with warm hazel eyes who was small and lean and suited my friend down to the ground, while I was drawn to a tall, broad, handsome baker's assistant who gave me free cakes. He never came into the Cellar nightclub though because he was working. I danced the night away with gorgeous French guys under the special white lighting that made a slight tan look dark and illuminated anything white we wore. I did find a little time to romance with the baker though, who gave us girls delicious cakes mid-morning.

Heaven had opened its door to us with everything so perfect it now seems impossible to believe we didn't all do our level best to go back the next spring to get seasonal work in the hotels, bars or clubs in that part of Spain until the early autumn. It was a perfect place for it. I was deliriously happy there from the moment I woke in the morning until I slipped in between crisp white sheets long after midnight every night. We girls even flirted with the young local policemen at night on our way home from dancing and they were fun. I didn't want to come back to London and our English lads who suddenly seemed dull in comparison to those handsome Latin lovers. When our holiday came to an end we boarded our coach on a sad afternoon and waved goodbye to romance, sea, sand and eternal sunshine as we trundled off along the coastal road, weepy, but with a determination to return and pick up where we had left off. I couldn't help wondering, though, what Dad and the rest of the family had thought when they received my postcards, sent at the beginning of the holiday.

After our return journey of coach, train and boat we arrived back to a dull grey August day in London, Victoria. Being so fair-skinned I had only managed to get a slight tan but my glowing rosy cheeks and freckles gave me a healthy glow and my fair hair had been sun-bleached back to what it once was when a four-year-old – almost as white as snow. I had no worries and no cares and shrugged at the thought of Dad giving me a hiding for going off like that leaving only a note in the kitchen similar to the one I had left all those years ago when I had the romantic notion of running away from home.

But as it turned out my family, brothers, cousins, uncles and aunts thought that it was hilarious so I got away with it. Laura had been worried for me though and told me that night in bed that she couldn't believe I would have the guts to do something like it. Dad had found it amusing too, as it just so happened, but of course he had to say something fatherly such as, 'Don't you ever do a thing like that again.'

'No, Dad, of course I won't,' I said, only just keeping a straight face to match his own mood. I had every intention of going back the following year. Same place, same time, same bunch of girls, same fun. Nothing was going to stop me. Wild horses could try.

15
My Close Arrest

My first day back at work and I was longing to tell the girls all about the glorious time I had had. I rushed into the post room before I had even taken off Laura's summer jacket that I had borrowed. Marge was at the switchboard and I believed that the puzzled look she gave me was because I was in five minutes early instead of ten minutes late as usual. But not so. There were far more serious matters afoot. I had been a careless girl on the Friday before I left for my well-earned Spanish extravaganza. Marge didn't say much to me other than, 'Mrs Johnston wants to see you first thing, lovey.'

Ignoring this, I pushed my face in front of hers and grinned, saying, 'What do you think of my tan then?'

'You look a treat, sweetheart,' said Marge. 'I take it you had a nice time?'

Nice? It was brilliant. I expected her to realise this and couldn't think why she wasn't smiling at me. She answered a call on the switchboard, dealt with it and then looked up at me again and sighed. 'I should go and ring the bell on Mr Pollard's door now, Sally. Before the place gets too busy.'

'All right, Marge,' I grouched, disappointed that she didn't want to know about my holiday. 'I'll go in now and when I come out I'll tell Rita what a nice time I had. Or Wendy. Or June.' I left the post room to go and stand outside the mahogany door into the MD's room on which an ornate brass handle and name plate shone. Happiness was a million miles away across the sea and I was back in this archaic building with its out-of-date rules and regulations and stale smells. I had nothing to smile about.

When Mrs Johnston opened the door to me I saw by the expression on her face that all was definitely not well. I was invited into the plush room with a short, graceful wave of the hand and a murmur from the elegant lady that I couldn't quite catch. The king of this empire was sitting with his legs crossed in a velvet armchair and I suddenly felt closed in as the heavy door behind me clicked shut. The atmosphere was stilted and I was soon to find out why. It seemed that I was chief suspect of a single-handed robbery.

On the Friday before my departure to sun, sand and sea, so happy and excited, I hadn't been as attentive as I should have been while at my desk; only just sixteen, that could hardly have been a surprise considering that I was preparing myself for a different world from the one I was in. I had done as always on paydays and handed out departmental salaries from the desk in the secretary's office where I worked to those individuals who arrived to collect staff salaries for their department. At that time most people were still paid in cash and we were no exception.

When a certain quiet young man had stood by my desk on the Friday afternoon before I left for my vacation, it had been at the end of a very busy day and no doubt my attention was by then on my holiday. The trusted employee, a young man in smart suit and tie, signed for seven salaries but, unbeknown to me at the time, there had actually been eight pay packets in the bundle which was bound by an elastic band. I had passed this to him and once outside the building, thinking his ship had come in, he slipped the extra pay packet into his pocket.

Once the missing salary came to light, while I was sunning myself in Spain, the security officer on permanent staff at Pollard's apparently felt that I had deliberately planned to steal the pay packet and use it as spending money while in Spain. The police were called in and I was interrogated the next day for hours on end and over a few more days that week. I told no one at home what was going on because I didn't want Dad or my elder brothers or uncles to arrive at Pollard's in a fury, which I felt sure they would do had they known what I was going through at the time.

I naturally felt sure it would all come out in the wash and that the pay packet would turn up somewhere in my office because I didn't think for one minute that the respectable young man would be guilty of such a serious theft and of course none of us knew that even though he had signed for seven salaries he had taken eight pay packets.

The intense interrogation from the hard-nosed young detective inspector was awful. He behaved like a bully in a school playground. He questioned me in the intimidating wood-panelled boardroom for hours each day until I broke into tears. Sadly, all those at Pollard's who knew what was going on believed that I had taken that hefty pay packet to spend on a good time in Spain. My workmates, my office manager and the young detective inspector were all eyeing me with suspicion. Scared and feeling very much by myself at that time, I had been throwing up in the ladies lavatory at work without telling anyone about it. I had even begun to feel guilty of the crime when I knew I was innocent. I had nobody to talk to about it away from work because I couldn't let my family know what was going on. And I suppose deep down I knew that justice would out in the end.

There was one particularly bad interrogation from the detective inspector when he had gone on and on at me, saying I was from a background where thieves lived and that the young man who had collected the salaries was from an exceptionally good family, his uncle an officer with the Metropolitan Police. He grilled me so intensively, repeating over and over that I was from a criminal background, one of my uncles having been in prison at one time or another, that I almost screamed at him that I was fucking guilty just to get him off my back. But I didn't. I was down but not out and wasn't going to give up on myself.

After all that he had put me through, on the last occasion when he had grilled me in that boardroom, as I pulled open the heavy mahogany door to leave the tone of his cold voice telling me to ask the young man who had collected that pay packet to come in caused me to want to turn around and punch him in the face.

But I kept my mouth shut and gave the guy the instruction, feeling sick inside. He looked at me and instead of turning away, as was my wont, I looked into his eyes and I didn't think he was guilty and I felt sorry for what he was about to go though. We smiled weakly at each other. He would have been able to see that I had been crying and I could see that he too was close to tears. I wanted to say, 'In you go then. Just like me, the lamb to the slaughter.' But of course I didn't.

But once inside and questioned yet again he confessed. That simple. No doubt he had had a similar grilling to me. I have no idea, but while the news of his confession swept through to the girls in the post room and of course the managing director, I was once again throwing up in the ladies cloakroom. Ten minutes or so later, and still in there gripping one of the small white sparkling washbasins so as not to give in to the million stars which seemed to be shooting through my head, I was summoned to the managing director's room by one of my workmates, who had a tender look on her face and a gentle smile on her lips.

Once inside that oak-panelled room, standing on the thick, plush carpet, I felt that old anger that came to the fore so often when a child. The one that would get me into trouble with Dad. It was slowly rising from the pit of my stomach. I was told by the managing director's personal secretary, Mrs Johnston, that the man had confessed. I said nothing but simply nodded and then left after I had been told in a kind voice that she and the king of the empire, Mr Pollard, had never really thought that I had taken that pay packet.

I left the MD's suite and once outside my workmates, the girls, came at me with open arms and tears, laughing and crying at the same time. I was congratulated and hugged and left cold by it all. To me their joyous reaction meant only one thing: that they too believed that I had stolen the pay packet.

I didn't go into work the next day because I had been throwing up all night long. I think Mum was suspicious that I had got myself pregnant on holiday. Later on that day, clad in her mink coat with a hint of expensive perfume, Isabel Johnston arrived in our council estate in the depths of the East End in her chauffeur-driven Bentley. I couldn't believe it when from my bedroom I heard her voice. It was as if the queen had come into the slums, funny but at the same time annoying. She sat in the living room with Mum, talking, while I made a pot of tea and gave her a clean but chipped cup. I gave her this because that's what I wanted her to drink from: a cup with a chip on its shoulder. When she left after saying how sorry they all were at Pollard's, she placed a pair of stockings and two pound notes on our kitchen table. I wanted so badly to tear up the money but in our house at that time it would have been a foolish thing to do because money was hardly thick on the ground, even though we were not living in poverty.

I did return to Pollard's once I felt better physically and emotionally only to learn that had the young man not confessed, it was on the cards that I was going to be arrested and taken to the police station in Islington and charged. Holloway was not far away. Just up the road, in fact. The guilty young man was not charged or even sacked but simply transferred to another of Pollard's subsidiary companies. It might have been Hammond & Champness, Haskins and Company, Blunt & Way, Morris Singer or S

& M. I don't know because I was never told and didn't much care. I was obviously supposed to forget all about it; after all was said and done I had been compensated for all I had been put through: a pair of nylons from Harrods out of the Christmas present cupboard and two pound notes from Mr H.E. Pollard's back pocket.

My saving grace was that I had achieved a slight tan from my holiday in Spain and my blonde hair was almost white and suddenly I was attracting attention from the lads when out in the evening and partying. This boosted my ego and reminded me of where I had been. To Spain. It also alerted me to how easily life could change overnight. From good to bad and vice versa.

There were parties going on everywhere in those early sixties and my friends and I were also initiated into a set of people from the other side of the track: medical students attached to the London Hospital who frequented our Prospect of Whitby down by the river. In their own way of doing things they too were enjoying the swinging sixties. Even though I found them strangely attractive I had fallen madly in love with a guy of seventeen whose name was Michael Jackson. He was the handsomest, coolest boy I had ever set eyes on, up to the minute where fashion was concerned, with his Italian suit and pointed, Cuban-heeled shoes. He had a cracking smile and deep, dark blue eyes and I simply melted when dancing up close to him to love songs when lights were down low.

On one summer evening, after a proper date with this new love of my life and being kissed goodnight on the staircase in our block of flats I half opened my eyes to gaze into his, and saw the face of my authoritarian father, six feet tall and glaring down at me from the top of the staircase. The clock hadn't quite struck midnight. With a jerk of his thumb he gave me a silent, dictatorial order to get inside. He then said, 'What do you think you are, a pair of fucking stray cats?'

This time, whether he had had a bad day or not, he had gone too far. Even so, I dared not stand up to him in front of Michael who I expected to make a hasty exit. Any lad would have done if they were confronted with that fierce expression. But Michael just ignored him and behaved as if he hadn't realised he was there and quietly said to me, 'Will you be all right, Sally?' I said I would and urged him to go.

Of all nights for Dad to be in one of his ugly moods this was the worst he could have chosen. But that little scenario made me warm even more to the seventeen-year-old who had walked me home. I was in love. Properly in love this time and not just infatuated the way I had been when in Spain. We saw each other the following weekend at another party and brushed up against each other in the fashionable pubs but it wasn't very long before he met another girl while on a holiday in England with his friends and courted her. When I saw him arm in arm with her my heart sank, but I managed a feeble smile to show I couldn't possibly be hurting inside.

But, it being the early sixties, parties were going on all over the place, so I danced my way through it with young modern boys who outnumbered us girls. Most of the parties were spur of the moment after a whip-round for beer and a couple of bottles of spirits, soft drinks and some Babychams. It was brilliant. We girls drank quite a lot of vodka and lime, and rum and Coke. I did get to dance with Michael once he was back in the fold without the girl on his arm but I knew that for us it was over. Dad had killed off the romance.

The all-night parties in the sixties were brilliant. In a happy state, my girl friends and I, a little intoxicated, often walked through the back streets of Wapping and Stepney at dawn in a wonderful trance-like state, while the lads were drunk and out for the count, sleeping on armchairs, sofas and floors. I was allowed by Dad to stay at any of my friends' houses overnight, which of course I did, because their parents in the main were more relaxed about the time we got in. I still can't fathom his thinking behind it though. I had to be in before midnight but could stay out all night when he believed I was sleeping at a friend's house. I wasn't going to question it because it suited me down to the ground.

I met another cool guy and courted him briefly. His name was Billy May and he was polite, good-looking and very nice. We went out together for a short while and one evening when he had seen me home at a decent hour, around eleven at night, Dad was still up and watching television. When I went into the living room he asked who had put the glow in my cheeks and I told him I had a boyfriend. He asked what his name was and his friendly manner drew me in. He seemed to be in a good mood. I told him it was Billy May. 'Oh, is it now?' said Dad, slowly nodding, a wry smile on his face. 'Well, you tell Billy May that he'd better fucking well not.' And that was the total sum of my lesson on the birds and the bees from my parent.

I was too young for all that courting lark though. Far too young. I was only just beginning to spread my wings after all. So with my friends I went further afield to the pubs, clubs and parties in other parts of London, Hampstead, Highgate and Islington. Not too enamoured by the types we met there, we girls were soon back into the buzz of the East End at the Prospect of Whitby.

There I found it odd that female medical students drank pints of beer instead of a port and lemon, rum and blackcurrant or a Babycham. But it was good fun and loads of laughs. I lapped it up and sang with the best of them. We were invited to their parties which were held in spacious, high-ceilinged flats in plush parts of London. The guys in this other world that we found ourselves in were on the bohemian side and wore big chunky roll-neck sweaters, their hair curling around the collar and they didn't flock around us like bees to the honeypot as our East End lads tended to do.

This is what made them attractive. This was the lure. They were cool and they asked interesting questions about our area and our background. It was all great fun and in a sense it was also spiritual the way everyone joined in to sing a melody when quite drunk. We liked this new set of people we'd come to know and they liked us. Some were miffed because we didn't jump into bed with them the way they expected us to but that, after all was said and done, was part of the fun of the chase. The lads and the girls brought their own kind of music into the Prospect which was different to what we were used to but great. A solo performance from a flautist or someone playing a bit of classical music on a guitar made a nice change from the jukebox and gave our Prospect of Whitby an individual atmosphere of its own and I liked it.

I felt as if my world was slowly expanding to take in other cultures and breeds and that I could go wherever I wanted when I wanted. And I knew that I wanted to travel further afield than Spain and to work my way around as much of the world as possible. But as happens with many people, fate had a very cruel blow in store. I wasn't going to be able to spread my wings anywhere because out of the blue and with no warning Dad had a massive heart attack and would never work again. It was a shock for all of us – we found it hard to accept that such a thing could happen to a six foot tall, broad and seemingly healthy, docker. While he was in a special heart unit at Hammersmith hospital, my sister Laura and I became much closer and she told me her innermost secret. She had been keeping in touch with and even seeing the Belgian boyfriend she had met while on holiday the previous summer. And without any of us knowing, this boyfriend was coming to London to stay in a small hotel and they were going to be engaged. My sister planned to live and work in Belgium to be nearer to her fiancé, her first real sweetheart, who had swept her off her feet in his home town, Ostend. The reason she hadn't mentioned this to us before the diamond ring was placed on her finger was because Dad had always said that his girls would only ever be allowed to marry an English boy – and she had taken him at his word.

This was Laura's first experience of rebelling against his rules, which I had been taking liberties with for years, doing what I wanted when I wanted. So she deserved to spread her wings and fly away. This of course meant that I was going to be the only one at home earning a salary though, and there were five of us to feed: Mum, Dad, my little brothers Albert and Gary and myself. My elder brothers each had their own families to take care of, so money was thin on the ground.

Dad did pull through after a sixteen week stretch in hospital but he returned a different man. He was on strict instructions not to smoke, drink, or exert himself and going to work, even on a part time basis, was out of the question. It was during this period, when the fact of being in recovery made him a slower quieter person, that I spent more time with him and we got to understand each other and became good friends. We played cards and board games with my little brother Albert and the adorable youngest of the family, Gary, in our sitting room by the fire during winter and with the veranda doors wide open in summer time. Sadly, he only lived for another two years and passed away at the age of forty-eight in the middle of the night, in his bed with Mum and myself by his side. This was the darkest time in all of our lives and the sense of sudden loss was awful but we eventually pulled together as a family again and, when there were social gatherings in the flat, we were just as close as we had all been when Dad was alive.

I began a new career as copy typist at a publishers in Moorgate and never looked back. I was working with journalists and editors and loved it. I had found a new world where my imagination, overactive since childhood, was fired again and so in my spare time I tapped out short stories in my bedroom on a second hand typewriter. When one of the journalists at work gave me some tips on writing he suggested I went to a once-a-week creative writing evening class in Holborn. This idea both excited and scared me at the same time; but I needn't have worried because the tutor, Naomi Lewis, was impressed with what I had written and read out, during one of the sessions.

After a few weeks she took me aside and asked about my background and my schooling, which compared to others in the adult education class, was very basic. She told me that I was one of the few writers she had met with what she considered to be a 'virgin mind'. I had not read any of the classics or much else, come to that, since I was a child and in and out of the library. I told her about my school teacher in senior school, Kate Flenner, and how she had encouraged me to write. That summer evening, I walked away from the City Lit happy and inspired. I was going to do what I had always dreamed of. I was going to become a writer.

My very first short story to be accepted went out on BBC Radio 4 two years later. I felt as if I was on top of the world. At last I could put my imagination to good use and I wanted to tell someone about it, someone special. I telephoned Margaret, and after a few years of not seeing each other, we met up for a coffee and were immediately best friends again . . . and have been ever since.